Sixth Edition

KEEPING THE BOOKS

BOOKS
Basic Recordkeeping
and Accounting
for the Successful
Small Business

Linda Pinson

Dearborn™
Trade Publishing
A **Kaplan Professional** Company

Vice President and Publisher: Cynthia A. Zigmund
Acquisitions Editor: Jonathan Malysiak
Senior Managing Editor: Jack Kiburz
Interior Design: Eliot House Productions
Cover Design: Design Solutions
Typesetting: Eliot House Productions

Published by Dearborn Trade Publishing
A Kaplan Professional Company

Printed in the United States of America

05 06 10 9 8 7 6 5

Library of Congress Cataloging-in-Publication Data
Pinson, Linda.
    Keeping the books: basic recordkeeping and accounting for the successful small business/Linda Pinson.—6th ed.
        p.   cm.
    Includes index.
    ISBN 0-7931-7929-7 (paperback)
    1. Bookkeeping. 2. Small business—United States—Accounting. I. Title.
HF5635.P649 2004
657'.2—dc22   2003024192

DEDICATION

This book is dedicated to Virginia Haverty, a wonderful friend who is now gone, but not forgotten. Her gifts of encouragement and confidence live on in this book.

CONTENTS

ACKNOWLEDGMENTS

I would like to take this opportunity to thank two people who have generously given of their time to help improve the quality of this book. The first is Marilyn Bartlett, C.P.A., who contributed the indispensable chapter entitled, "Financial Statement Analysis." I would also like to recognize Judee Slack, Enrolled Agent, who spent a great deal of her time going through the entire book to check it for correctness of content and who wrote the section entitled, "Independent Contractors: Facts vs. Myths."

I would also like to thank all of my students and readers. My books are better because of the input I have received from classes and individual users.

Last, but not least, I thank my husband, Ray, who has put up with the many inconveniences caused by my single-mindedness while writing and revising books. With his encouragement, understanding, and patience, I have found it much easier to reach my goals.

CHAPTER 1

RECORDKEEPING BASICS

The keeping of accurate records is imperative if you are going to succeed at business. From time to time, I have had students in my small business classes who have wonderful ideas for products or services, but who do not want to be bothered with the details of recordkeeping. Their businesses are already doomed to failure. This book was written with the assumption that you are starting from scratch and know nothing about the recordkeeping process. I have tried to solve the puzzle for you. By the time you have finished applying the principles in the book, I hope that you will understand how all of the pieces fit together to develop a simple, but accurate set of books.

• • • • •

FUNCTIONS OF RECORDKEEPING

The first, and most important, function of recordkeeping is to provide you with information that will help you to see the trends that are taking place within your operation. You will see, as you study this book, that a complete and simple set of records will make it possible to tell at a glance what is happening with your business—which areas are productive and cost-effective and which will require the implementation of changes. The second function of recordkeeping is to provide you with income tax information that can be easily retrieved and verified.

Who Should Do Your Recordkeeping?

You, the business owner, should be personally involved rather than delegating this job to an outsider. Keeping your own books and records will make you doubly aware of what is going on in your business, and it will also save you money that can be used to benefit your business in other areas. For example, you may now be able to afford a piece of effective advertising that will generate more sales. Even if time will not allow you to keep your own records and you assign the task to someone else, it will be a major benefit to you to make every attempt to understand how your records are organized and to learn how to read and use them to make decisions in your business.

Do You Need an Accountant?

I do not advocate the elimination of an accounting professional. In fact, end-of-the-year tax accounting requires special expertise and will best be handled by an accountant who can maximize your tax benefits. You will have to decide whether to use a Certified Public Accountant (CPA), Enrolled Agent (tax accountant), or noncertified bookkeeper/tax preparer. The first two are empowered to represent you at an IRS audit. All accounting professionals are dependent on the financial information that you provide. To ensure the most profitable results for your business, you will need to set up and maintain general records as the source of financial data. You should also work with the accountant to establish a good line of communication and a smooth flow of that data.

Depending on the size and scope of your business, you will have to decide which of the recordkeeping chores you can handle and which ones should be delegated to an expert. For instance, you may be able to do all of your accounting except for payroll, which is very exacting and will probably be more effectively handled by your accountant. You may also decide that you would like to use an accountant at the end of the month to generate your financial statements. In fact, if the scope of your business becomes very large, it may become necessary to turn over your entire accounting operation to an expert. If so, it will still be imperative that you understand the process, so you will be able to use your financial information to make sound business decisions.

Accounting Software

One of the most frequently asked questions is about which accounting software programs will make the process easy. There are many programs on the market today that will adequately take care of your needs. However, if you do not understand the recordkeeping basics, you will not know how to tailor the program to your business or feed in the proper information. You may best be served by beginning with a manual system. You can always translate it into a computer application as the need arises. At that time, if you are working with an accountant, it will probably be best to use a software program that he or she suggests and one that will easily interface with what is currently being used in that office. Coordinating with your tax accountant may even enable you to work together via Internet transmissions.

Every Business Is Unique

The system you use must be tailored to your individual needs. Obviously a service-oriented industry will not use the same records as a retail business. Because no two businesses will have exactly the same concerns, it is imperative that you develop your own system. You will have to consider any information that will be used by your particular venture and set up your records according to those needs.

WHEN DOES RECORDKEEPING BEGIN?

Your business commences as soon as you begin to refine your idea. You do not have to wait until you have a license and are open for business to start with your recordkeeping. In fact, you will do yourself a great disservice if you are not keeping records at this very moment. Many of your initial expenses are deductible if you have begun to actively pursue your business. A good way to begin is as follows:

- *Deductible expenses.* The first thing you should do is familiarize yourself with the expenses that are commonly deductible for a business. When you are doing things that relate to your business, begin to think of the costs involved and record them for future use. (See Chapter 2, "Income and Expenses.")

- *Diary.* Buy yourself a hardbound journal at your local stationers. Keep a diary of your thoughts and actions related to your new business. Number the pages, write in pen, and initial any corrections you make. Your journal will serve to protect your idea as well as provide you with a record of your contacts and the information you gather for the future. You can also list any expenses incurred and file away your receipts. Be sure to date all entries.

- *Beginning journal.* I like to utilize the last few pages of the journal to keep a record of income and expenses during the planning stages of a business. It need not be complicated. You can set it up like the sample Beginning Journal provided on page 4.

Simplicity Is the Key

Simplicity is the key to small business accounting. Your records must be complete, but not so complicated that they cannot be read and interpreted. It will be the function of this book to not only introduce you to the terminology and forms necessary to set up a recordkeeping system for your business, but to enable you to actually set up records that will give you the information you need to satisfy tax requirements, examine trends, make decisions, and implement changes that will make your business venture more profitable and rewarding.

Beginning Journal for ABC Company

Date	1. Check # 2. Cash 3. C/Card	Paid To or Received From	Explanation of Income or Expense	Income		Expense	
1/07/04	Pers. Check 1476	Coastline Community College	Registration for "Small Business Start-Up"			65	00
1/09/04	Cash	Tam's Stationers	Office Supplies			25	63
1/17/04	Cash	Ace Hardware	Tools			71	80
2/03/04	VISA	A-1 Computer	Pentium Computer			1821	34
2/04/04	Pers. Check 1493	AT&T	January Telephone Business Calls			52	00

REMEMBER: All expenses relating to your new business endeavors should be recorded. A few examples are as follows:

1. Conference, seminar and workshop fees
2. Mileage to and from business pursuits
3. Meals related to business (see tax rulings)
4. Books, tapes, videos, etc. purchased for business
5. Office supplies (notebooks, journals, pens, etc.)
6. Telephone calls relating to business
7. Professional organizations (dues, fees, etc.)
8. Materials used for developing your product
9. Tools or equipment purchased for your business

There are many other business expenses, including those mentioned under the pages on "Common Deductible Expenses." A good rule of thumb is that when a purchase or activity seems to have any possible bearing on your business, journalize it, keep receipts, look up tax rulings, and then utilize the information accordingly.

CHAPTER 2

INCOME AND EXPENSES

Accounting for small businesses is based on one premise. Every transaction that takes place involves money that is earned, spent, infused into, or taken out of the business. All earnings and monies spent as a result of doing business fall under one of two classifications: income (or revenue) and expenses. Before you set up your records, it is necessary to understand some basic facts about the two terms.

• • • • •

INCOME (OR REVENUE)

Income is all the monies received by your business in any given period of time. It is made up of monies derived from retail sales, wholesale sales, sale of services, interest income, and any miscellaneous income.

You will want to be sure that you do not mix income with expenses. Under no circumstance do you use monies received to purchase goods and plan to deposit the remainder. A simple formula for tax accounting requires that your income equals your deposits. It is interesting to note that the IRS does not require you to keep copies of your receipt book if you follow this formula. The income equals deposit equation is supported by the 1986 Tax Reform.

EXPENSES

Expenses are all monies paid out by your business. They include those paid by check and those paid by cash. All require careful recording. Expenses fall into four distinct categories.

1. **Cost of goods sold (inventory)**
   - The cost of the merchandise or inventory sold during an accounting period.
   - Includes material and labor or the purchase price of manufactured goods.

2. **Variable (selling) expenses**
   - Those expenses directly related to the selling of your product or service.
   - Includes marketing costs, production salaries, shipping, research and development, packaging, sales commissions and salaries, vehicle expenses, machinery and equipment, and any other product or service overhead.

3. **Fixed (administrative) expenses**
   - These are costs not directly related to your production or rendering of services. They are the type of expenses that all businesses have in common.
   - These expenses include normal office overhead such as accounting and legal, bank charges, office salaries, payroll expenses, rents, licenses, office equipment, office supplies, telephone, utilities, insurance, etc. Administrative expenses are those that generally remain constant if your business suddenly ceases production or services for a period of time.

4. **Other expenses**
   - Interest expense.
   - Includes monies paid out for interest on purchases, loans, etc.

Note: Some categories of expense may be divided into both selling and administrative and selling expenses. Examples are:

- **Utilities.** Those used for production as differentiated from utilities consumed in the office, heating, restrooms, etc.

- **Telephone.** Telemarketing and advertising are selling expenses. Monthly charges and office telephone charges are administrative expenses.

- **Freight and postage.** Shipping of your product is a selling expense. Postage used as office overhead is an administrative expense.

The categories into which certain expenses should be placed can be confusing. The important thing to remember is that all expenses must be recorded somewhere. If you erroneously record a selling expense as an administrative expense, it will not carry any serious consequence. However, if you can properly classify expense information, you will have a good basis for analyzing your business and implementing changes.

WHAT ARE "DEDUCTIBLE" EXPENSES?

Deductible expenses are those expenses that are allowed by the IRS when you are computing the net profit (loss) or taxable income at the end of your business tax year. In order to pay the least amount of income tax and maximize your own profits, you need to become familiar with those expenses that you are allowed by law to deduct.

The next two pages contain information on common deductible expenses.

COMMON DEDUCTIBLE EXPENSES

The list on the next page will help you to identify many of those items that are normally deductible for income tax purposes. The new business owner should become familiar with those appropriate to the business. DO NOT wait until tax preparation time to look at this list. Knowing ahead of time which expenses are deductible will help you to better utilize them to your advantage while keeping proper records for income tax verification and business analysis. DO keep in mind that this is only a partial list. There may very well be additional deductible expenses relating to your business. Call or visit the IRS. They have free publications that will answer many of your questions. Another source of information is your accounting professional. Be sure to have documentation for all expenses so you can verify them if you are audited.

Fully Deductible or Depreciable?

Expenses fall into two major categories: (1) Those that are deductible in their entirety in the year in which they are incurred, and (2) those items that are depreciated and deducted over a fixed number of years.

1. **Fully deductible expenses.** All expenses incurred in the operation of your business are deductible in their entirety in the year in which they occur and reduce your net income by their amount unless they are major expenses that fall in the depreciable assets category. Expenses will have to be itemized for tax purposes and receipts should be easily retrievable for verification.

2. **Depreciable expenses.** If you buy business property that has an expected life in excess of one year and that is not intended for resale, it is considered depreciable property. The cost (generally in excess of $100) must be spread over more than one year and the depreciation deductions claimed over the useful life or recovery period of the property. They generally include such tangible assets as buildings, vehicles, machinery, and equipment, and also intangible properties such as copyrights or franchises. Depreciation is taken at a fixed rate. The portion allowed for the current year is deducted as an expense.

   Under Code Section 179, you can elect to treat all or part of the cost of certain qualifying property as an expense rather than as a depreciable asset. The total cost you can elect to deduct for a calendar tax year has been increased from $25,000 in 2002 to $100,000 for 2003–2005. This maximum applies to each taxpayer and not to each business operated by a taxpayer.

CAUTION: Be sure that you do not list the same costs of any purchase as both a deductible expense and a depreciable asset. For example, if you have purchased a computer for $3,000 and you are depreciating it, be sure that it is not also listed as a fully deductible expense under office equipment. It is wise to keep a separate list of all purchases that might be depreciable and let your tax accountant make the final determination as to whether each item should be expensed under Section 179 or depreciated.

Home office expenses. In order for your home to qualify as a business expense, that part of your home used for business must be used "exclusively and on a regular basis." There are also some additional requirements relating to where your income is earned, where you see your clients, etc. For further information on what is and is not allowed, send for free IRS Publication #587, *Business Use of Your Home*.

Common Deductible Expenses

Note: There may be other expenses that apply to your business. Those listed below are the most common.

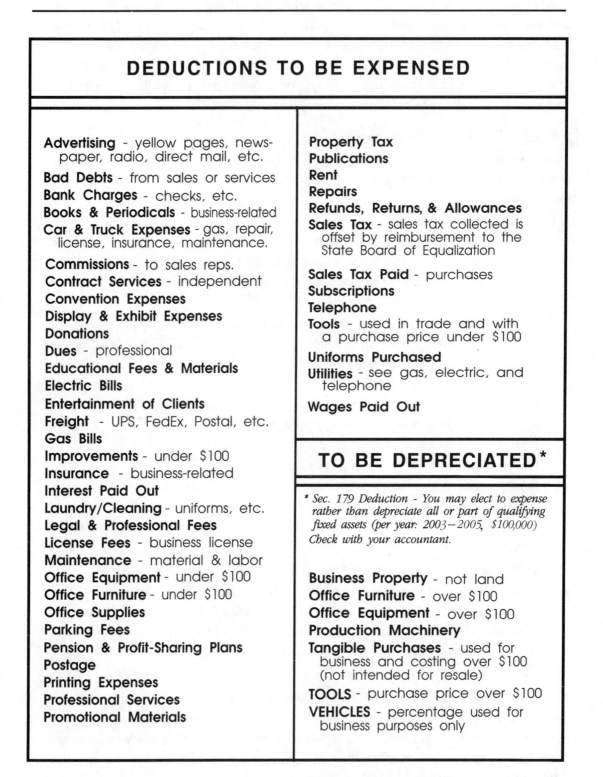

DEDUCTIONS TO BE EXPENSED

Advertising - yellow pages, newspaper, radio, direct mail, etc.

Bad Debts - from sales or services

Bank Charges - checks, etc.

Books & Periodicals - business-related

Car & Truck Expenses - gas, repair, license, insurance, maintenance.

Commissions - to sales reps.

Contract Services - independent

Convention Expenses

Display & Exhibit Expenses

Donations

Dues - professional

Educational Fees & Materials

Electric Bills

Entertainment of Clients

Freight - UPS, FedEx, Postal, etc.

Gas Bills

Improvements - under $100

Insurance - business-related

Interest Paid Out

Laundry/Cleaning - uniforms, etc.

Legal & Professional Fees

License Fees - business license

Maintenance - material & labor

Office Equipment - under $100

Office Furniture - under $100

Office Supplies

Parking Fees

Pension & Profit-Sharing Plans

Postage

Printing Expenses

Professional Services

Promotional Materials

Property Tax

Publications

Rent

Repairs

Refunds, Returns, & Allowances

Sales Tax - sales tax collected is offset by reimbursement to the State Board of Equalization

Sales Tax Paid - purchases

Subscriptions

Telephone

Tools - used in trade and with a purchase price under $100

Uniforms Purchased

Utilities - see gas, electric, and telephone

Wages Paid Out

TO BE DEPRECIATED*

* Sec. 179 Deduction - You may elect to expense rather than depreciate all or part of qualifying fixed assets (per year: 2003−2005, $100,000) Check with your accountant.

Business Property - not land

Office Furniture - over $100

Office Equipment - over $100

Production Machinery

Tangible Purchases - used for business and costing over $100 (not intended for resale)

TOOLS - purchase price over $100

VEHICLES - percentage used for business purposes only

CASH ACCOUNTING VERSUS ACCRUAL ACCOUNTING

There are two different recordkeeping methods based on the timing of the recording and reporting of the income and expenses you learned about in the last chapter. Selecting the method to be used by your company is an important decision that must be made very early in the life of your business. Once it has been established, it is difficult to change due to IRS legalities.

The two methods are (1) cash accounting and (2) accrual accounting. In the following pages, I will explain the difference between the two methods, show you how and when income or expenses would be recorded using each method, and give you some of the pros and cons associated with each method.

· · · · ·

"CASH" AND "ACCRUAL" ACCOUNTING DEFINED

Cash accounting. The reporting of your revenues and expenses at the time they are actually received or paid. A company that uses the cash accounting method is considered to have made a transaction when the cash is physically received or paid out for services or products.

Accrual accounting. The recognition of revenues and expenses at the time they are earned or incurred, regardless of when the cash for the transaction is received or paid out.

Two Examples Illustrating the Difference

1. **Sales/revenue transaction**.

   On January 16th, ABC Company billed XYZ Company $500 for consulting services. XYZ Company paid the invoice on February 5th.

   Accounting method used:

   - **Cash basis.** On January 16th, no recordkeeping entry is required because there has been no cash exchanged between the two companies. ABC Company will not record the sale until it receives payment in February. It will then be recorded and will be considered as a February sale.

   - **Accrual basis.** On January 16th, the sale is recorded by ABC Company even though no cash has been exchanged. ABC Company is considered to have earned the income on January 16th (the invoice date), even though it will not receive the cash until February 5th. In other words, it is a January sale.

2. **Purchase transaction.**

   On January 25th, ABC Company purchased $125.32 of office supplies from Office Super Store. Office Super Store bills ABC Company at the end of the month. ABC Company pays the invoice on February 10th.

   Accounting method used:

   - **Cash basis.** On January 25th, no recordkeeping entry is made by ABC Company because it did not exchange cash with Office Super Store. ABC Company will not record the expense until it makes payment on February 10th. The transaction will be reflected as a February expense.

   - **Accrual basis.** On January 25th, the expense is recorded by ABC Company even though it did not exchange cash with Office Super Store. ABC Company is considered to have incurred the expense on January 25th when it purchased the office supplies, even though it will not pay for them until February 10th. The transaction will be reflected as a January expense.

WHICH METHOD WILL YOU BE REQUIRED TO USE?

The most popular method used by businesses is the cash basis because it is the most simple and direct to deal with. However, the IRS requires that certain types of business use the accrual basis of accounting.

According to the IRS, "Taxpayers that are required to use inventories must use the accrual method to account for purchases and sales." Simply said, if your business revenues are generated from the sale of inventory (retail stores, wholesalers, manufacturers, etc.), on your tax return you will be required to report revenues and expenses by the accrual method.

There are other circumstances under which accrual accounting is generally used. Also by IRS specifications, C Corporations and businesses that have gross receipts of over $5 million generally use the accrual method as their overall method of accounting for tax purposes.

In addition, there are a few specific circumstances under which a company may be required to use or exempted from using this method.

Check with Your Tax Accounting Professional

I will give you some of the pros and cons of both methods. However, to make the most intelligent determination as to whether your business should use the accrual basis or the cash basis for your recordkeeping and reporting method, it would be wise to check with your tax accounting professional who can clarify the requirements and help you make your decision.

PROS AND CONS OF THE TWO METHODS

Pros

1. **Cash basis.**
   - Easier of the two methods
   - Allows for use of single entry accounting
   - Taxes paid only on cash actually received

2. **Accrual basis.**
   - Provides a better analytical tool because it closely matches revenues and expenses to the actual period in which the transactions occurred

Cons

1. **Cash basis.**
   - Does not closely match revenues and expenses to the actual period in which the transactions occurred

2. **Accrual basis.**
   - Requires a more complex double entry system of accounting
   - Income tax is paid on revenues invoiced out, but not yet received

CAN YOU CHANGE METHODS FROM YEAR TO YEAR?

For IRS purposes, you must choose a method and stay with it. Again, my advice would be to consult with your tax professional before setting up your records and select the method that will do the best job for you and satisfy the IRS when you file your tax returns.

Summary

At this point you have taken only the first step in learning about recordkeeping for your business. The introduction of the accrual and cash accounting methods may very well seem confusing to you at this point. However, because the selection of the appropriate method is an early decision that you will have to make in regard to the timing of the recording and reporting of your revenues and expenses, I felt that this was a good time to familiarize you with the concept.

Once you have selected either the accrual or cash basis for your recordkeeping, you will be ready to go on to the next section where you will learn about the general records that you will maintain for your company.

CHAPTER 4

ESSENTIAL GENERAL RECORDS FOR SMALL BUSINESS

In this chapter you will learn about the general records that are used to track the daily transactions of your business. You will also be introduced to single entry and double entry accounting, and you will learn how to develop a chart of accounts that is customized to your business. Also in this chapter you will learn about some of the advantages to be gained by using accounting software.

• • • • •

The most common general records are as follows:

- **Cash in Bank***
- **Revenue & Expense Journal***
- **Invoices & Sales Receipts**
- **Petty Cash Record**
- **Inventory Records**
- **Fixed Assets Log**
- **Accounts Receivable**
- **Accounts Payable**

- **Independent Contractor Record**
- **Payroll Records**
- **Mileage Log**
- **Travel & Entertainment Logs**
- **Customer Records**
- **Business Checkbook****
- **Filing System**

* *Cash in Bank is the accounting software equivalent for the Revenue & Expense Journal used in manual bookkeeping.*

** *A physical business checkbook will be used for manual bookkeeping. Most accounting software provides for checks to be written and printed directly from within the software. However, if a business prefers, it may use a physical checkbook in preference to, or in addition to, utilizing the check-printing feature.*

Again, I would like to emphasize the need to keep your records as simple as possible. You will need to think about all the things that will pertain to your business and then determine the simplest way to have the information at your fingertips. All of the above records will be discussed, and you will learn how they can be used to help you with your business. You will also be shown a filled-in example of each of the forms. In Appendix II, you will find blank forms that you can use as general records for your own business. You may have to customize some of the records to serve your particular industry. You should also eliminate any records that are unnecessary. For instance, if you are a repair business and your customers pay you when you perform your service, you will not need an Accounts Receivable record. You may also wish to develop new records that will help you to keep track of information that will make your business more effective.

Keep to Standard Formats

All of your records will be utilized in the development of your financial statements. For this reason, it will be important to use forms that have been developed using an accepted format. The forms discussed in this section will provide you with records that are easy to use and interpret, both by you and by anyone else who has occasion to retrieve information pertaining to your business.

SINGLE AND DOUBLE ENTRY SYSTEMS

There are two basic bookkeeping methods: (1) single entry and (2) double entry. In the past, only double entry accounting was thought to be proper for businesses. However, it is now generally recognized that a single entry system will adequately serve many smaller (micro) businesses. As the business grows and becomes more complex, it will become necessary to move into double entry accounting (best accomplished through the use of software) in which each transaction is posted as a debit to one account and a credit to another. In the past this was done manually through the use of ledger and journal entries utilizing debits and credits. Manual double entry systems have now been replaced by accounting software.

Single Entry

This is a term referring to a manual bookkeeping system that uses only income and expense accounts. Its main requirement is a Revenue & Expense Journal that you maintain on a daily basis for recording receipts and expenditures. You will also need to keep General Records in which you record petty cash, fixed assets, accounts payable and receivable, inventory, mileage, travel and entertainment, and customer information. (Note: Payroll will be discussed later and should be handled by your accountant.) Single entry bookkeeping is the easier of the two systems to understand and maintain manually and can be extremely effective and 100% verifiable.

Double Entry

This is a bookkeeping and accounting method by which every transaction is recorded as debits and credits. This is based on the premise that every transaction has two sides. A sale, for example, could be both a delivery of goods and a receipt of payment. On your Balance Sheet, the delivery of goods to your customer decreases your inventory and would be recorded as a credit (reduction of assets), while the payment to you for the goods purchased from you would increase cash and would be recorded as a debit (increase of assets). You should note that the words *debit* and *credit* do not have the usual nonaccounting connotation in this application.

The two halves of the double entry always have to be equal. Through the utilization of software, the process has been simplified for the user, because the transaction is easily entered and matched to its primary account. The software then automatically debits or credits the proper corresponding account.

Although accounting software streamlines the small business accounting process, it still adheres to the adage, *"Garbage In, Garbage Out."* A smart business owner should learn the basics of bookkeeping before attempting to set up and utilize accounting software. Even then, it would probably be wise to have an accountant help you with the initial setup.

· · · · ·

** BE SURE TO READ THIS **

In the next nine pages, you will be introduced to some basic information on double entry accounting and the utilization of accounting software. If your business is small and very simple, you may choose manual single entry accounting. Talk to your accountant if you are in doubt.

Micro Businesses Planning to Use Manual Single Entry Systems
Skip to Manual/Single Entry Bookkeeping on page 25

Note: Even though you will not immediately utilize software for your business, it would be a wise move to familiarize yourself with the accounting principles presented on the following pages before skipping ahead to the Revenue & Expense Journal, where you will begin setting up your own bookkeeping system as described in the rest of the chapter.

More Complex Businesses Planning to Use Software/Double Entry Accounting

If you are a larger, more complex business and plan to use software, the next few pages will give you a basic understanding of the underlying principles of accounting. Armed with this knowledge, you will be ready to work with your accountant to tailor the software setup for your business.

Note: Before you attempt to set up and use accounting software, you will find it worthwhile to read and understand the general records that are discussed on pages 26 through 60. It is important to understand what these general records are and what information is required by the IRS for each type of deduction. If you take the time to study them, you will find it easier to understand and utilize your accounting software.

FLOW OF ACCOUNTING DATA

After a transaction is completed, the initial record of that transaction, or of a group of similar transactions, is evidenced by a business document such as a sales ticket, a check stub, or a cash register tape. On the basis of the evidence provided by that document, transactions are then entered in chronological order in the accounting software. The amounts of the debits and credits are automatically transferred to the proper accounts within the software. The flow of data from transaction to individual accounts may be diagrammed as follows:

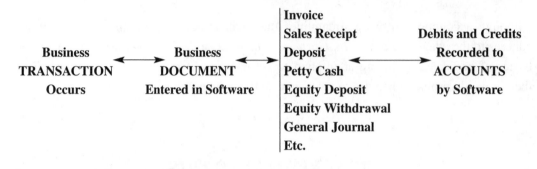

CHART OF ACCOUNTS

Double entry/software accounting requires that you set up a chart of accounts. These accounts are used when recording transactions in the software in order that they will be properly posted to the correct accounts. In the next chapter of this book, we will be discussing Financial Statements. Two of these statements, the Balance Sheet and Income Statement (Profit & Loss), can be automatically generated by your software. The nice thing is that some accounting software will allow you to do so on any day and for any time period you choose. The information utilized to generate a Balance Sheet and Income Statement is derived from the chart of accounts you set up in your software.

Major Divisions of a Chart of Accounts

All accounts in the bookkeeping are divided into the following major divisions:

- **Assets**
- **Liabilities**
- **Capital (Net Worth/Equity)**
- **Revenues (Income)**
- **Cost of Goods Sold**
- **Expenses**

Each division contains its own individual accounts. Each of these accounts may also be further divided down into subaccounts.

Setting Up a Chart of Accounts

On the following page, I have developed a sample chart of accounts for a fictitious business. Your own accounts will match your operation. Also, as your business progresses, new accounts may be necessary in order to better reflect your company's transactions. Software has the advantage of permitting the later insertion of these new accounts in their proper sequence without disturbing the original setup.

Chart of Accounts for a Fictitious Business

Balance Sheet Accounts	Income Statement Accounts

ASSETS
    Cash in Bank
    Petty Cash
    Accounts Receivable
    Inventory
    Prepaid Expenses
    Fixed Assets
        Land
        Buildings
        Equipment
        Furniture
        Vehicles
    Accumulated Depreciation
 	
LIABILITIES
    Notes Payable
    Accounts Payable
    Taxes Payable
 	
CAPITAL (Equity/Net Worth)
    John Jones, Capital
    John Jones, Drawing
    Year-to-Date Net Income
	REVENUES (INCOME)
	    Product Sales, Taxable
	    Product Sales, Nontaxable
	    Services Income
	
	COST OF GOODS SOLD
	    Material & Labor (Manufacturer)
	    -or-
	    Products Purchased for Resale
	
	EXPENSES
	    Accounting, Legal, Licenses
	    Commissions on Sales
	    Depreciation Expense
	    Insurance
	    Interest Expense
	    Marketing/Advertising
	    Payroll Taxes
	    Salaries/Wages
	    Rent
	    Repair & Maintenance
	    Taxes
	    Travel & Entertainment
	    Utilities
	    Vehicle Expenses

Your Chart of Accounts Must Match Your Business

If you have been in business for a period of time, it will be fairly easy to set up your chart of accounts. It will be the categories of assets, liabilities, capital, revenues, cost of goods sold, and expenses that you have been keeping track of in the past. If you are a new business, deciding on your initial chart of accounts will take some thought. I suggest that you look at each category and determine what things you will be dealing with in your business. Assets, liabilities, and capital will be fairly standard and match those you will use in a balance sheet. Revenues, cost of goods, and expenses will be according to the kind of business you are operating. Your revenue accounts would be the major types of products and/or services you offer. Cost of goods would match the types of revenue products. Expenses would be the categories of selling and administrative expenses that your company would have. Your accountant can help you with the chart of accounts setup.

DEBITS AND CREDITS

All double entry accounting—and all accounting software—is based on the premise that every transaction affects at least two accounts. For every entry you make, one account will be debited and the other will be credited. And the debits *must* equal the credits.

Computer software will automatically take care of both sides of this entry. When you enter the transaction as a check or into a check register, the software will credit (decrease) your bank account (asset) and you will record the account to which the expense applies, office supplies. Office supplies (expense) will then be debited (increased).

What are debits and credits? When you are recording transactions in an accounting application, you will be asked to choose the account (from your chart of accounts) to which the transaction applies. Your choice will trigger the software to debit and credit the proper accounts. For this reason, it is not imperative that you have a clear understanding of the terms *debit* and *credit*. However, taking time to learn how debits and credits work will help you to better understand what is happening in the accounting process.

There is a well-known accounting equation that must always remain true in your business bookkeeping. The equation is as follows:

$$\text{Assets} - \text{Liabilities} = \text{Net Worth (Equity/Capital)}$$

The accounting equation is kept in balance through the double entry system. In the sample Chart of Accounts we set up six categories. Increases and decreases in each of these accounts are represented by debits or credits (generally) as follows:

	Increase	Decrease
Assets	Debit	Credit
Liabilities	Credit	Debit
Net Worth (Equity/Capital)	Credit	Debit
Revenues (Income)	Credit	Debit
Cost of Goods Sold	Debit	Credit
Expenses	Debit	Credit

Example 1. When you buy office supplies with a check, you must credit (decrease) your bank account (an asset) and you will debit (increase) your office expense account (expense). One is debited and the other is credited in an equal amount.

Example 2. Another example of the accuracy of double entry accounting would be the purchase of an asset with borrowed funds. You purchase $10,000 of office furniture and equipment, you make a down payment of $1,000, and take a loan for the $9,000 balance. The correct (double entry) entry for this transaction would be:

	Debit	Credit
Office furniture (Increase – Asset)	$10,000	
Loan (Increase – Liability)		$9,000
Cash in bank (Decrease – Asset)		$1,000

Note: The debits and the credits balance ($10,000), but the "increases" and the "decreases" do not have to balance. This can be confusing to many small business owners.

The next step in this transaction would be the loan payment. If your payment is $300 per month, this payment consists of two parts, principal payment (decrease liability) and interest (increase expense). If this entry is correctly reported each month, your balance sheet will correctly reflect the balance due on your loan.

Note: Thanks to Peter Hupalo, author of *Thinking Like an Entrepreneur* (HMC Publications), I have learned a simple rule that makes the understanding of debits and credits much easier. It is this: The one giving in the transaction is the credit(or), and the one receiving in the transaction is the debit(or). For example, if you sell one hour of your service, service revenue is the giver (so it's credited) and cash in bank is the receiver (so cash is debited) and increased. Why didn't I think of that?

– A PEEK INTO SOFTWARE ACCOUNTING –

The next few pages offer a glimpse into how to use software/double entry accounting to streamline the flow of information from transaction to financial reporting. Although I have not targeted the use of software to micro businesses, it is equally appropriate for the smallest of companies. The choice between manual and computer accounting is strictly by choice.

I have chosen QuickBooks Pro® by Intuit as the application I will use to illustrate some of the tasks that can be accomplished by using accounting software. This is not to be construed as an endorsement of QuickBooks Pro in preference to other accounting software applications. I do use it in my own business and have found it to be effective for my company. It is my understanding that most popular accounting software packages will perform the same basic functions.

If you do not use a computer and intend to set up a manual bookkeeping system, feel free to skip this section. Move ahead to "Revenue & Expense Journal" and start there with the setting up of your accounting records.

AN OVERVIEW OF FOUR ACCOUNTING TASKS
USING QUICKBOOKS PRO®

1. Invoicing

Invoicing is the process of billing a customer for sales or services that are provided, *but not due to be paid until a future time*. If you use the accrual method of accounting, these invoices are your Accounts Receivable.

The invoice is entered in your accounting software on a screen that will look similar to the one below:

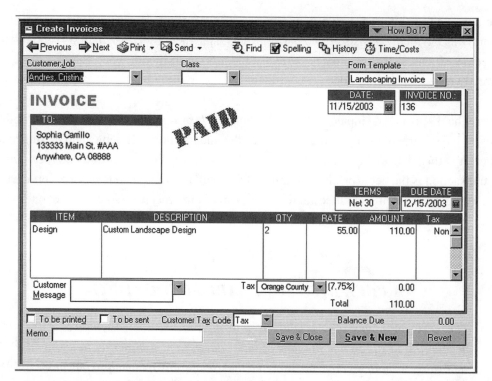

In this case, Sophia Carrillo, the customer, purchased $110 in custom landscape design services, to be paid Net 30. When the invoice information is entered and saved (11/15/2003), accounts receivable will automatically be debited (increased) for $110 (the amount of the invoice). The software will credit the matching revenue account (custom landscape design) in an equal amount.

When the invoice is paid (12/15/2003) and the funds are entered either as an undeposited check or a deposit to cash in bank, the invoice will automatically be marked as paid. At that time, the software will credit (decrease) accounts receivable in the amount of $110 and debit (increase) undeposited checks or cash in bank.

By the time the sale has been invoiced, recorded as paid, and subsequently deposited, the information will also automatically have been factored into the company's profit & loss (income) statement and balance sheet—perfectly completing the accounting process.

2. Entering a Sales Receipt

Sales receipts are entered for sales or service transactions that are *paid for with cash, checks, or credit cards at the time of purchase*. After entering the information, a sales receipt can be printed as an original and copy for you and your customer or you can enter the information after the fact strictly as an accounting task.

The sales receipt screen in your accounting software might look similar to the one below:

In this case, the customer, John Smith, purchased $100 in tree removal service and paid with a check.

When the sales receipt information is input and the transaction saved, undeposited funds will automatically be debited (increased) for $100 (the amount of the sales receipt). At the same time the software will credit the matching account (tree removal service) in an equal amount.

When the check is later deposited to cash in bank, the software will debit (decrease) undeposited funds in the amount of $100 and debit (increase) cash in bank for an equal amount.

Again, the information will also automatically have been factored into the company's profit & loss (income) statement and balance sheet, completing the accounting process.

3. Writing a Check

Your company's checks can be written, printed, and the amount recorded (debited and credited) to the proper accounts in a single operation.

The check writing window in your accounting software might look similar to this QuickBooks screen:

In this case, Computer Services by DJ charged the company $243.57 for installing a new version of Windows and for reinstalling and setting up the company's other software applications.

A check was written to pay for the service. During input, Repairs: Computer Repairs was selected as the account related to the expense. The software then debited that account (increased computer repair expense account). At the same time, the software credited (decreased) the matching account, cash in bank, also in the amount of $243.57.

The check was also printed out, complete with address to insert in a windowed envelope, ready to stamp and mail to Computer Services by DJ.

As before, the information will also automatically have been factored into the company's profit & loss (income) statement and balance sheet to complete the accounting process.

4. Cash in Bank (Your Software Check Register)

When you deposit or transfer funds, write checks, earn interest, record bank charges during reconciliation, or record any other transaction that either adds or removes money from your bank account, it will automatically be reflected in your cash in bank account.

This account serves the same purpose as your check register in a bound checkbook. At any time, you can review the checks you have written and deposits or withdrawals that have been made to your account.

The cash in bank window may look similar to the one below:

To show the flow of information from the preceding three transactions described through to cash in bank, I have marked them 1, 2, and 3 to correspond with each of the transactions.

Note: In reality, the company would have grouped any undeposited funds together and made one deposit. For purposes of this example, each of the transactions has been entered and deposited separately so that you would be able to follow them more easily.

SUMMARY: ACCOUNTING SOFTWARE

The information on the preceding pages is meant to serve as an introduction to accounting software. The days of manually posting transactions to journals and ledgers are gone. Computer technology has ushered accounting into a new generation. The benefit for business owners is the opportunity to participate at a higher level in the financial administration of their businesses.

Invoicing, sales receipts, check writing, and the subsequent flow of information into a cash in bank register are among the important basic features found in most accounting software applications. However, these processes represent only a small portion of the accounting procedures that can now be done electronically. It has already been mentioned that various accounting software applications enable you to generate an income (profit & loss) statement and balance sheet at any time and for any chosen period. Some other advantages include such things as:

- Accounts receivable tracking
- Accounts payable tracking
- Petty cash accounting
- Bank statement reconciliation
- Customer reports
- Generation of 1099 information
- Inventory tracking

Choosing the Right Software for Your Business

There are many different accounting software packages on the market. Some are designed as general accounting applications, and some are designed for specific industries. Some have basic packages as well as more advanced ones with modules added to accomplish certain tasks.

It is up to you to select the software that is most appropriate for your business. However, I would suggest that you work with your accountant to find the accounting package that will best accommodate both of you. Your accountant can then help you with the setup, work with problem solving throughout the year, and easily transfer your end-of-year information at tax reporting time. The end result will be the maximizing of profits for your business.

What's Next?

If you are planning to use accounting software, you can skip pages 25–29. However, on pages 30–60, you will learn about the various general records that a business is required to keep. Don't skip this section. There is a lot to learn that will be of value as you use the software of your choice.

This Is the Beginning

of

** MANUAL/SINGLE ENTRY BOOKKEEPING **

This is where you will begin if you are going to maintain your records by the single entry method. At this point you will begin to set up your General Records as presented in the remainder of the chapter, beginning with the Revenue & Expense Journal.

Flow of Accounting Data

If you read the information on double entry/software accounting, you learned that a business transaction occurs and is recorded within the software debiting and crediting related accounts selected from your Chart of Accounts. Remember that there are six major types of accounts (Assets, Liabilities, Capital/Equity, Revenues/Income, Cost of Goods Sold, and Expenses). These same accounts will be used in your manual bookkeeping system. You will develop a better understanding of these divisions as you progress through the General Records. They should become even more clear by the time you complete the financial statement chapter (Chapter 5) of this book.

The advantage of single entry bookkeeping for micro business owners is that the recording of transactions is accomplished by simply entering revenues and expenses on a single form and requires no formal accounting education. You are still required to keep those general records pertinent to your business (such as Petty Cash, Accounts Receivable and Payable, Fixed Assets, Travel and Entertainment, Inventory, etc.), but in a very simple, logical way that can still provide for perfect retrieval of needed tax and business analysis information.

With this method, the flow of accounting data will be as follows:

		Entry
Business	**Business**	**Recorded in**
TRANSACTION ◄─►	**DOCUMENT** ◄─►	**REVENUE & EXPENSE JOURNAL**

Now you are ready to set up your bookkeeping system. I will take you a step at a time through the entire process. Turn to the next page and begin with the Revenue & Expense Journal.

REVENUE & EXPENSE JOURNAL

A Revenue & Expense Journal is used to record the transactions of a business. They are recorded as revenues (income) and expenses.

1. **Revenues (income)** are the transactions for which monies are received. Equity deposits and loan funds are not revenues.

2. **Expenses** are all transactions for which monies are paid out. Owner draws and principal payments on loans are not included.

To make your accounting more effective, you will need to have enough columns in the Revenue & Expense Journal to cover major categories of income and expenses (or create two separate forms, one for revenues and one for expenses. If you have done your homework and figured out the areas of direct and indirect expenses, these divisions will serve as headings in your journal. Usually, a 12-column journal will suffice for most small businesses, but feel free to use more or less, as long as your report is clear and easy to interpret.

Avoiding Errors

The Revenue & Expense Journal is an important part of your bookkeeping. On this form, **each entry is recorded twice** to help with checks and balances at the end of each month. If you look on the sample form, the first two columns are headed Revenue and Expense. Every transaction is entered in one of these two columns. The next groups of three and five columns are breakdowns of revenues and expenses. The entry is first recorded as a revenue or expense and then entered in its corresponding breakdown column. For example, an advertising expense of $100 would be entered under the heading Expense and also under the expense breakdown heading Advertising. When the columns are totaled, the amount under Expense will equal the sum of all expense breakdown columns. The Revenue total will equal the sum of all revenue breakdown columns. This serves as a check for accuracy and will save hours of searching your records for errors when attempting to balance your books.

Headings in the Revenue & Expense Journal

The column headings in the Revenue & Expense Journal for any business will follow the same format. The first five column headings are:

1. Check No.
2. Date
3. Transaction
4. Revenue
5. Expense

Remaining columns are used for individual categories of revenue and expense for which you most frequently write checks or receive income.

1. **Revenue breakdown columns** will be divided by source (e.g., as a publisher and teacher, I have Book Sales, Software Sales, Sales Tax, and Seminar Fees).

2. **Expense breakdown columns** reflect the categories for which you most frequently write a check (e.g., Inventory Purchases, Freight, Advertising, Office Supplies, Vehicle Expenses, etc.).

The headings for the individual revenue and expense columns will vary from business to business. Every business is different, and it may take some time to determine the categories that will best reflect the transactions of your particular venture. If you are coordinating your bookkeeping with a tax accountant, you might ask that person to help you develop your headings. The best rule of thumb is to devote a column to each type of expense for which you frequently write a check.

Miscellaneous Column

The last column in any Revenue & Expense Journal should be Miscellaneous. This column serves as a catchall for any expense that does not fall under a main heading. For example, insurance may be paid only once a year and, therefore, a heading under that title would not be justified. Record that transaction first under Expense and secondly under Miscellaneous, with an explanation either under the Transaction column or in parenthesis next to the amount in the Miscellaneous column (e.g., you write only one check every six months in the amount of $500 for insurance, so you put "$500 (insurance)"). The explanation is a must. This will allow you to group infrequent expenses under one column and still be able to allocate them to the proper expense categories at the end of the month when you do a Profit & Loss (or Income) Statement.

Totals

Each column should be totaled at the bottom of each journal page. (Remember to check accuracy. The sum of all revenue breakdown columns = the sum of the column headed Revenue, and the sum of all expense breakdown columns = the sum of the column headed Expense.) All totals are then transferred to the top of the next page and added in until you have completed a month. At the end of the month, the last page is totaled and checked. The breakdown revenue and expense totals are transferred to your Profit & Loss Statement and a new month begins with a clean page and all zero balances.

Sample Revenue & Expense Journal

In order for you to better understand how to develop and make entries in your own Revenue & Expense Journal, we will: (1) create headings for a fictitious company, (2) enter six transactions, and (3) total the page.

1. **The headings are determined:**

   - The first five and the last column are standard: Check No., Date, Transaction, Revenue, Expense, and Miscellaneous.

   - The individual revenue headings are determined. (Our company sells and services computers. We want to know how much of our revenue comes from sales and how much comes from service. We also want to know how much sales tax is collected. The column headings are: Sales, Sales Tax, and Service.)

   - The individual expense columns are determined. (Checks are most frequently written to purchase inventory, advertise, ship orders, and purchase office supplies. The column headings are: Inventory Purchases, Advertising, Freight, and Office Supplies.)

2. **The transactions are as follows:**

   - This is the second journal page used for the month of July. The totals from the first page are brought forward and entered on the line entitled "Balance forward."

   - The new transactions to be entered are as follows:

     — Check 234 dated July 13th was written to J. J. Advertising to pay for an advertising promotion ($450.00).

     — Check 235 dated July 13th was written to T & E Products to buy a computer to resell to a customer ($380.00).

     — Check 236 dated July 16th was written to Regal Stationers for office supplies ($92.50).

     — $1,232.00 was deposited in the bank. ($400.00 + $32.00 sales tax came from taxable sales, $165.00 in sales were sold to an out-of-state customer, $370.00 was for a sale to another reseller, and $265.00 was received for repairing a customer's computer.)

     — The bank statement was reconciled on July 19th. (The bank charged $23.40 for new checks.)

     — Check 237 dated July 19th was written to Petty Cash. ($100.00 was deposited to the Petty Cash Account.)

3. **The journal page is full (total and check columns):**

   - Add individual revenue columns and check to see that the sum of their totals equals the total of the Revenue column ($3,058.00).

   - Add individual expense columns and check to see that the sum of their totals equals the total of the Expense column ($1,880.90).

Revenue & Expense Journal for ABC Company

July 2004, page 2

CHECK NO.	DATE	TRANSACTION	REVENUE	EXPENSE	SALES	SALES TAX	SERV-ICES	INV. PURCH	ADVERT	FREIGHT	OFF SUPP	MISC
		Balance forward----	1,826 00	835 00	1,218 00	98 00	510 00	295 00	245 00	150 00	83 50	61 50
234	7/13	J. J. Advertising		450 00					450 00			
235	7/13	T & E Products		380 00				380 00				
236	7/16	Regal Stationers		92 50							92 50	
***	7/17	Deposit:	1,232 00									
		1. Sales (Taxable)			400 00	32 00						
		2. Sales (O.S.)			165 00	O.S.						
		3. Sales (Resale)			370 00	Resale						
		4. Services					265 00					
O.K. BANK	7/19	Bank Charges		23 40								(bank chg) 23 40
237	7/19	Petty Cash Deposit		100 00								(p/cash) 100 00
		TOTALS	3,058 00	1,880 90	2,153 00	130 00	775 00	675 00	695 00	150 00	176 00	184 90

PETTY CASH RECORD

Petty cash refers to all the small business purchases made with cash or personal funds instead of with a business check. These purchases may account for several thousand dollars by the end of the year. Failure to account for them can result in a false picture of your business and additional cost in income taxes. It is imperative that you keep an accurate record of all petty cash expenditures, that you have receipts on file, and that you record them in a manner that will enable you to categorize these expenses at the end of an accounting period.

Where Do Petty Cash Funds Come From?

In order to transfer cash into the Petty Cash Fund, you must first draw a check and expense it to Petty Cash in the Revenue & Expense Journal (see entry in Revenue & Expense Journal). That same amount is entered in the Petty Cash Record as a deposit. When cash purchases are made, they are entered in the Petty Cash Record as expenses. When the balance gets low, another check is drawn to rebuild the fund. At the end of the tax year, you can let the balance run as a negative, write a final check in that amount, and deposit it to petty cash to zero out the fund. The end result will be that you will have deposited an amount that is exactly equal to your petty cash expenditures for the year.

Format

The two purposes of petty cash accounting are: (1) to account for personal expenditures relating to business and (2) to provide information that will classify those expenses for income tax retrieval and for business analysis. Any accountant will warn you that a large miscellaneous deduction will be suspect and may very well single out your return for an IRS audit. Dividing your Petty Cash Record into the following categories will provide for individual purchases to be summarized, combined with expenses on the Revenue & Expense Journal, and entered on the Profit & Loss Statement.

- **Date of transaction**
- **Paid to whom**
- **Expense account debited**
- **Deposit**
- **Amount of expense**
- **Balance**

Sample petty cash record. On the next page you will see how deposits and expenses are recorded. If a cash expense also needs to be entered in another record (Inventory, Fixed Assets, etc.), do so at the same time to keep the record current and eliminate omissions.

Petty Cash Record
for ABC Company

PETTY CASH - 2004					Page 6	
DATE	PAID TO WHOM	EXPENSE ACCOUNT DEBITED	DEPOSIT	AMOUNT OF EXPENSE	BALANCE	
	BALANCE FORWARD				10	00
Jul. 19	✳ ✳ Deposit (Ck. 237)		100 00		110	00
20	ACE Hardware	Maintenance		12 36	97	64
23	Regal Stationers	Office Supplies		20 00	77	64
23	U.S. Postmaster	Postage		19 80	57	84
31	The Steak House	Meals		63 75	(5	91)
Aug 1	✳ ✳ Deposit (Ck.267)		100 00		94	09

Toward the end of the year, you can let the Petty Cash account run a minus balance. On December 31st, a check is written for the balance and the account is zeroed out.

The amount of cash spent during the year will be exactly equal to the amount deposited into the Petty Cash Account from your checking account.

NOTE:
1. Save all receipts for cash purchases.
2. Exchange receipt for cash from petty cash drawer.
3. Use receipts to record expenses on petty cash form.
4. File receipts. You may need them for verification.
5. Be sure to record petty cash deposits.

INVENTORY RECORD

The term *inventory* is used to designate: (1) merchandise held for sale in the normal course of business and (2) materials in the process of production or held for such use. The recording of inventories is used both as an internal control and as a means of retrieval of information required for the computation of income tax.

The Great Inventory Myth

Before proceeding with the mechanics of keeping your inventory, I would like to clear up a misconception about the pros and cons of the relationship of inventory size and income tax due. Any business that has had to deal with inventory will almost certainly have heard the statement: "Put your cash into inventory. The larger it is, the fewer taxes you will have to pay." Conversely, you may also hear that if your inventory is reduced, your taxes will also be reduced. Both are nonsense statements, and I will prove it to you mathematically. The fact is that your net profit remains the same regardless of the amount reinvested in inventory. Ten thousand dollars is $10,000 in your checking account or on the shelves as saleable goods. This can be proved as follows:

Companies A & B:
1. Both had beginning inventories of $25,000.
2. Both had gross sales of $30,000.
3. Both sold their product at 100% markup and reduced their beginning inventory by $15,000.

Company A: Reinvested $20,000 in inventory and deposited $10,000. This gave it an ending inventory of $30,000.

Company B: Reinvested $5,000 in inventory and deposited $25,000. The result was an ending inventory of $15,000.

Net profit is arrived at by subtracting deductible expenses from your gross profit. The following computation will prove that Companies A and B will in fact have the same gross profit (and will not have their net profit affected by the amount of reinvestment in inventory):

	Company A	Company B
1. Beginning inventory	$25,000	$25,000
2. Purchases	$20,000	$ 5,000
3. Add lines 1 & 2	$45,000	$30,000
4. Less ending inventory	$30,000	$15,000
5. Cost of goods sold (line 4 minus 3)	$15,000	$15,000
6. Gross receipts or sales	$30,000	$30,000
7. Less cost of goods sold (line 5)	$15,000	$15,000
8. GROSS PROFIT (line 6 minus 7)	**$15,000**	**$15,000**

The Gross Profits Are Exactly the Same!

It is very important that you understand the above concept. Inventory only affects your net profit as a vehicle to greater sales potential. How much or how little you stock at tax time will neither increase nor decrease your taxes. Companies A & B will both have a gross profit of $15,000 and will be taxed the same. Some states, however, may have inventory taxes and this could enter in as a factor.

Inventory Control

Keeping records for the IRS is actually the lesser reason for keeping track of inventory. I personally know of two companies that nearly failed due to a lack of inventory control. One was a restaurant whose employees were carrying groceries out the back door at closing time. Although the restaurant enjoyed a good clientele and followed sound business practices for the food industry, their year-end profit did not justify their existence. A careful examination of their records showed a failure to properly inventory their stock. By instituting strict inventory control, pilferage was ended and the next year's increase in profit saved the business. Inventory control in a retail business can help you to see such things as turnover time, high and low selling periods, and changes in buying trends. Periodic examinations of your inventory and its general flow may be the meat of your existence.

Format

Basic inventory records must contain the following information in order to be effective:

- **Date purchased**
- **Item purchased** (include stock no.)
- **Purchase price** (cost)
- **Date sold** (This information is especially helpful for determining shelf life and trends in market value of your product.)
- **Sale price** (This information is also especially helpful for determining shelf life and trends in market value of your product.)

If your inventory is at all sizable, you will want some sort of Point-of-Sale (POS) inventory system. However, it is possible to keep it in handwritten form based on two premises: (1) you begin immediately and (2) you keep it current and do it regularly. My husband owns a clock shop with approximately 2,000 items for sale. On any given day, he knows how long he has had each item, which items are selling repeatedly, and what time periods require the stocking of more inventory. Keep in mind that all businesses differ.

Compile your inventory according to your specific needs. Be sure that it is divided in such a way as to provide quick reference. I sort mine out by using separate pages for each company from which I make my purchases. Another method might be to separate pages by type of item. The important thing is to make your inventory work for you.

Common Kinds of Inventory

- Merchandise or stock in trade

- Raw materials

- Work in process

- Finished products

- Supplies (that become a part of a product intended for sale)

To arrive at a dollar amount for your inventory, you will need a method for identifying and a basis for valuing the items in your inventory. Inventory valuation must clearly show income and, for that reason, you must use this same inventory practice from year to year.

Cost Identification Methods

There are three methods that can be used identify items in inventory. They are as follows:

1. **Specific identification method.** In some businesses, it is possible to keep track of inventory and to identify the cost of each inventoried item by matching the item with its cost of acquisition. In other words, there is specific identification of merchandise and you can determine the exact cost of what is sold. There is no question as to which items remain in the inventory. Merchants who deal with items having a large unit cost or with one-of-a-kind items may choose to keep track of inventory by this method.

For those businesses dealing with a large quantity of like items, there must be a method for deciding which items were sold and which remain in inventory.

2. **FIFO (first-in-first-out).** This system assumes that the items you purchased or produced first are the first sold. This method most closely parallels the actual flow of inventory. Most merchants will attempt to sell their oldest inventory items first and hopefully will have the last items bought in current inventory.

3. **LIFO (last-in-first-out).** This method assumes that the items of inventory that you purchased or produced last are sold first. You must check tax rules to qualify before electing this method.

The FIFO and LIFO methods produce different results in income depending on the trend of price levels of inventory items. In a period of rising prices, valuing your inventory by the LIFO method will result in a higher reported cost of goods sold and a lower reported net income. This is because it is assumed that you sold goods purchased at the higher price.

Conversely, in a period of falling prices, the LIFO method would result in a lower reported cost of goods sold and a higher reported net income than the FIFO method.

Valuing Inventory

The two common ways to value your inventory if you use the FIFO method are the specific cost identification method and the lower of cost or market method. If at the end of your tax year the market price of items in your inventory decline, you may elect to use the following method of evaluation:

- **Cost or market, whichever is lower.** At inventory time, if your merchandise cannot be sold through usual trade channels for a price that is above its original cost, the current market price is determined and compared to your accepted costing method (FIFO, LIFO, or Specific Identification). The lower figure, "cost" or "market," is selected. This is especially useful for outdated inventory. If you use this method, you must value each item in the inventory.

- **You must be consistent.** As a new business using FIFO, you may use either the cost method or the lower of cost or market method to value your inventory. However, you must use the same method consistently and, again, you must use it to value your entire inventory. You *may not* change to another method without permission of the IRS.

Physical Inventories

You must take physical inventories at reasonable intervals and the book figure for inventory must be adjusted to agree with the actual inventory. The IRS requires a beginning and ending inventory for your tax year.

Sample inventory records. The sample inventory record on the next page is for the Specific Identification Method of taking inventory. Remember, it is for inventory of those products that differ from each other and can be individually accounted for as to purchase date, description, and cost.

The sample inventory record two pages ahead is for Non-Identifiable Inventory. An example would be the purchase or production of 2,000 units of a like item—the first thousand being produced at a unit cost of $5 and the second at a unit cost of $6. It would be impossible to determine which remain in inventory. They must be identified by the FIFO or LIFO method and valued accordingly to figure taxable income.

For further information on inventory rules, please read "Cost of Goods" in IRS Publication 334, *Tax Guide for Small Business.*

Inventory Record—Identifiable Stock
for ABC Company

WHOLESALER: _All Time Clock Company_							Page _1_

PURCH DATE	INVENTORY PURCHASED		PURCH. PRICE		DATE SOLD	SALE PRICE		NAME OF BUYER (Optional)
	Stock #	Description						
9/23/03	25-72-D	Oak Gallery (25")	352	00				
11/19/03	24-37-A	Desk Alarm (1)	18	00	12/08/03	28	50	N/A
		(2)	18	00				
		(3)	18	00				
2/21/04	26-18-C	"The Shelby" GF	1,420	00	4/20/04	1,865	00	J. Kirkland
3/19/04	25-67-D	Mahog. Regulator	247	00				
5/04/04	26-18-C	"The Shelby" GF	1,420	00				

NOTE:

1. Use this record for keeping track of identifiable goods purchased for resale. If your inventory is very large, it may be necessary to use some sort of **Point-of-Sale** inventory system.

2. Each page should deal with either (1) purchases in one category or (2) goods purchased from one wholesaler.

3. Use the name of the wholesaler or the category of the purchase as the heading.

Inventory Record—Non-Identifiable Stock
for ABC Company

DEPARTMENT/CATEGORY: _Ski Hats / Headwear_

PRODUCTION OR PURCHASE DATE	INVENTORY PURCHASED OR MANUFACTURED		NUMBER OF UNITS	UNIT COST		VALUE ON DATE OF INVENTORY (Unit Cost X Units on Hand)	
	Stock #	Description				Value	Date
2/05/02	07-43	Knitted Headbands	5,000	2	50	0	1/04
3/25/02	19-12	Face Masks	3,000	5	12	450.80	1/04
9/14/02	19-10	Hat/Mask Combo	1,200	7	00	3,514.00	1/04
4/18/03	19-09	Hats, Multi-Colored	10,500	4	00	5,440.00	1/04
8/31/03	19-07	Gortex (w/bill)	10,000	8	41	50,460.00	1/04
BEGIN 2004							
2/01/04	19-12	Face Masks	2,500	4	80		
2/28/04	19-09	Hats, Multi-Colored	10,300	4	00		

NOTE: 1. This record is used for inventory of like items that are purchased or manufactured in bulk. It is a good idea to divide your records by department, category, or by manufacturer.

2. Inventory these items by a physical count or by computer records. A physical inventory is required at the close of your tax year.

3. Inventory is valued according to rules that apply for **FIFO** or **LIFO.** Read the information in your tax guide carefully before determining inventory value. The selected method must be used consistently.

FIXED ASSETS LOG

At the end of each tax year you will have to provide your accountant with a list of all assets for which depreciation is allowed. Many different kinds of property can be depreciated, such as machinery, buildings, vehicles, furniture, equipment, and proprietary rights such as copyrights and patents. These are items purchased for use in your business usually at a cost in excess of $100.

What Can Be Depreciated?

In general, property is depreciable if it meets these requirements:

- It must be used in business or held for the production of income.

- It must have a determinable life and that life must be longer than one year.

- It must be something that wears out, decays, gets used up, becomes obsolete, or loses value from natural causes.

You can never depreciate land, rented property, or the cost of repairs that do not increase the value of your property. You cannot depreciate your inventory or any item that you intend for resale.

Section 179 Deduction

You can elect to treat all or part of the cost of certain depreciable property as an expense rather than as a capital expenditure. The total cost you can elect to deduct for a calendar tax year has been increased to $100,000 for 2003–2005. In lay terms, instead of depreciating assets placed in service during the current year, you may be allowed to directly expense them up to a $100,000 limit. There are some restrictions that apply and you will need the help of your accountant to make the final decision for tax purposes.

Keeping Track of Fixed Assets

You will need to keep an inventory of depreciable purchases made during the current tax year. You will also have to be able to tell your accountant if any of these purchases were entered in your Revenue & Expense Journal to avoid double-expensing. Be aware that you are also accountable for disposition of these items. If you have depreciated an automobile down to $2,000 and then sell it for $3,500, you will have to report a profit of $1,500. Depreciation can be very tricky and the laws change. Your job is to be able to provide your accountant with basic information. Your accountant must then apply the law to maximize your benefits.

Sample fixed assets log. The form that follows will help you to do your part and have a general overview of what assets you have that fall in this category.

Fixed Assets Log for ABC Company

COMPANY NAME: _ABC Company_

ASSET PURCHASED	DATE PLACED IN SERVICE	COST OF ASSET	% USED FOR BUSINESS	RECOVERY PERIOD	METHOD OF DEPRECIATION	DEPRECIATION PREVIOUSLY ALLOWED	DATE SOLD	SALE PRICE
1999 Dodge Van	1/08/00	18,700 00	80%	5 yr.	5 yr. Auto	15,469 00	9/12/04	8,500 00
IBM Computer	7/15/01	6,450 00	100%	5 yr.	MACRS	3,625 00		
Canon Copier	12/29/01	3,000 00	100%	5 yr.	MACRS	1,469 00		
Fence	6/17/01	4,500 00	100%	15 yr.	MACRS	—		
2005 Dodge Van	8/05/04	21,000 00	80%	5 yr.	5 yr. Auto	—		
Desk (Office)	8/15/04	1,500 00	100%	7 yr.	MACRS	—		

NOTE: See IRS Publication 334, _Tax Guide for Small Business_, for more detailed information on depreciation. Also see Publications 534, 544, and 551.

ACCOUNTS RECEIVABLE

An accounts receivable record is used to keep track of money owed to your business as a result of extending credit to a customer who purchases your products or services. Some businesses deal in cash transactions only. In other words, the product or service is paid for at the time of the sale. If this is the case in your business, you will not need accounts receivable records. However, if you do extend credit, the amount owed to you by your credit customers will have to be collected in a timely manner to provide you with the cash needed for day-to-day operations. It will be essential to have detailed information about your transactions and to always know the balance owed to you for each invoice. This can be accomplished by setting up a separate accounts receivable record for each customer.

Format

In order to ensure that you have all the information needed to verify that customers are paying balances on time and that they are within credit limits, the form used will need to include these categories:

- **Invoice date.** This will tell you the date the transaction took place and enable you to age the invoice.

- **Invoice number.** Invoices are numbered and can be filed in order. If you need to refer to the invoice, the number makes it easy to retrieve.

- **Invoice amount.** Tells how much the customer owes for each invoice.

- **Terms.** Tells the time period allowed until invoice is due and also if a discount applies (e.g., "Net 30/2% Net 10" means the invoice is due in 30 days, but a 2% discount will be allowed if payment is made in 10 days).

- **Date paid.** Shows when the invoice was paid.

- **Amount paid.** Shows whether the customer made a partial payment or paid the invoice in full.

- **Invoice balance.** Tells what portion of the invoice is not paid.

- **Header information.** The customer's name, address, and phone number will tell you where to send statements and how to make contact.

At the end of a predetermined billing period, each open account will be sent a statement showing its invoice number and amounts, balance due, and preferably age of balances (over 30, 60, and 90 days). The statement should also include terms of payment. When the payment is received, it is recorded on the accounts receivable record. The total of all the outstanding balances in Accounts Receivable is transferred to Current Assets when preparing a Balance Sheet for your business.

Sample accounts receivable record. The form on the next page contains a sample form to show you how it should be filled out. There is a blank form in Appendix II for you to copy and use.

Accounts Receivable
for ABC Company

CUSTOMER: *T-Quarter Circle Transfer*

ADDRESS: *222 T-Quarter Circle Road*
Winnemucca, NV 89445

TEL. NO: *(775) 843-2222*　　　　　ACCOUNT NO. *1016*

INVOICE DATE	INVOICE NO.	INVOICE AMOUNT		TERMS	DATE PAID	AMOUNT PAID		INVOICE BALANCE	
6/09/04	3528	247	00	Net 30	7/02/04	247	00	0	00
7/14/04	4126	340	00	Net 30	8/15/04	340	00	0	00
9/26/04	5476	192	00	N30/2%10	10/02/04	188	16	0	00
10/03/04	5783	211	00	N30/2%10	11/01/04	109	00	102	00
10/12/04	6074	386	00	N30/2%10				386	00

ACCOUNTS PAYABLE

Accounts payable are those debts owed by your company to your creditors for goods purchased or services rendered. Having open account credit will allow your company to conduct more extensive operations and use your financial resources more effectively. If you are going to have a good credit record, the payment of these invoices must be timely, and you will need an efficient system for keeping track of what you owe and when it should be paid. When your accounts payable are not numerous and you do not accumulate unpaid invoices by partial payments, you may wish to eliminate accounts payable records and use an accordion file divided into the days of the month. Invoices Payable may be directly filed under the date on which they should be paid, taking into account discounts available for early payment.

Format

If your Accounts Payable are stretched over a longer period, you will need to keep separate records for the creditors with whom you do business. The form used will need to include these categories:

- **Invoice date.** This will tell you when the transaction took place.

- **Invoice number.** If you need to refer to the actual invoice, the number makes it easy to retrieve. File unpaid invoices behind the record.

- **Invoice amount.** Tells the amount of the transaction.

- **Terms.** Tells the time period allowed until invoice is due and also if a discount applies (e.g., net 30/2% net 10 means the invoice is due in 30 days, but a 2% discount will be allowed if payment is made in 10 days).

- **Date paid.** Shows when you paid the invoice.

- **Amount paid.** Shows whether you made a partial payment or paid the invoice in full.

- **Invoice balance.** Tells what portion of the invoice is not paid.

- **Header information.** The creditor's name, address, and phone number will tell you where to send payments and how to make contact.

You will be billed regularly for the balance of your account, but the individual records will help you to know at a glance where you stand at any given time. They should be reviewed monthly and an attempt should be made to satisfy all your creditors. After the invoice is paid in full and the payment is recorded, mark the invoice paid and file with the rest of your receipts. At the end of your accounting period, the total for Accounts Payable should be transferred to the Current Liabilities portion of the Balance Sheet.

Sample accounts payable record. The next page contains a sample form showing how it should be filled out. A blank form is located in Appendix II for you to copy and use.

Accounts Payable
for ABC Company

CREDITOR:: _Charles Mfg._

ADDRESS: _1111 E. Trenton Road_
Tarington, NH 03928

TEL. NO: _(603) 827-5001_   ACCOUNT NO. _2072_

INVOICE DATE	INVOICE NO.	INVOICE AMOUNT		TERMS	DATE PAID	AMOUNT PAID		INVOICE BALANCE	
2/16/04	10562	1,500	00	Net 15	2/24/04	1,500	00	0	00
2/25/04	11473	870	00	Net 30	2/18/04	870	00	0	00
3/17/04	12231	3,200	00	N30/2%10	3/25/04	3,136	00	0	00
7/02/04	18420	2,400	00	N30/2%10	8/01/04	1,800	00	600	00
8/15/04	19534	2,600	00	N30/2%10				2,600	00

PAYROLL RECORDS

The decision to add employees should not be taken lightly. In addition to having a responsibility to the employees you hire, you also acquire the responsibility to withhold, report, and pay taxes to the federal, state, and sometimes your local government. The next four pages will be devoted to taking you through the necessary steps of putting employees on your payroll, paying them, making payroll tax deposits, completing quarterly payroll tax returns, and making year-end reports.

At the end of this section, I will make a suggestion as to how you might work with an accounting professional to make sure that everything is done according to requirements.

FEIN, W-4, Form I-9, Official Notice

If you decide to hire employees, you will have to do the following:

- **FEIN.** When you decide you will hire employees, you must file for a Federal Employer Identification Number (FEIN). This is done by completing Form SS-4 and sending it to the Internal Revenue Service. You will receive a packet that includes Circular E, *Employer's Tax Guide.* This publication contains the charts you will use to determine the amount of federal income tax to be withheld from your employees' paychecks. (In addition to registering as an employer with IRS, you will need to determine your state and local government requirements.)

- **W-4s.** Your new employees MUST complete a Form W-4, furnishing their full names, addresses, Social Security numbers, marital status, and number of withholding allowances to be claimed, all of which you must have to compute your employees' first and succeeding paychecks.

- **Forms I-9.** Employers are required to verify employment eligibility for all of their employees. This is accomplished by completing Form I-9, *Employment Eligibility Verification.* When you register as an employer, the *Handbook for Employers* (containing complete instructions) will be sent to you.

- **Official notice.** As an employer, you will be required to adhere to regulations regarding minimum wage, hours, and working conditions. Again, as part of your "registration," you will receive the Official Notice describing these regulations. The notice must be posted for all employees to read. Now is the time for you to familiarize yourself with these regulations.

Paying Your Employees

You can determine how often you want to pay your employees: weekly, biweekly, semimonthly, or monthly. Your employees can be paid by the hour, job, or commission.

- **Determine gross wage.** Because taxes to be withheld will be based on the employee's gross wage, your first step is to determine that amount. For example, if your employee is hired to work 40 hours and the agreed upon hourly rate is $10, that employee's gross wage is $400.

- **FICA (Social Security).** FICA is calculated as a percent of the employee's gross wages. The percentage (7.65% in 2003) is a combination of old age, survivors, and disability insurance (OASDI at 6.2%) and hospital insurance (Medicare at 1.45%). This tax is also imposed in an equal amount on the employer and applies to the wage base of $87,000 in 2003 and $87,900 in 2004 for OASDI and no limit for Medicare tax.

- **Federal income tax.** Based upon the employee's marital status and the number of withholding allowances claimed on Form W-4, federal income tax must be withheld from each employee's paycheck. Publication 15, *Circular E, Employer's Tax Guide,* contains the charts used to calculate the amount of withholding. Separate charts are used according to frequency of payment (weekly, biweekly, semimonthly, or monthly) and marital status of the employee. **Note: State and local taxes may also apply.** It is your responsibility to determine these requirements.

Payroll Tax Deposits

The taxes that are withheld from employees' paychecks must be turned over to the IRS. In fact, you are liable for the payment of these taxes to the federal government whether or not you collect them from your employees.

- **Open a separate account.** To avoid "accidentally" spending these funds, you should open a *separate* bank account for withheld taxes. When you write your employees' paychecks, calculate your tax liability (FICA and Federal Income Tax withheld and the employer's matching share of FICA) and immediately deposit that amount into that account.

- **When tax liability is $2,500 or more.** If, at the end of any quarter, your total tax liability will exceed $2,500, you must make monthly deposits of the income tax withheld and the FICA taxes with an authorized commercial bank depository in a Federal Reserve bank. To do this you will have to complete a Federal Tax Deposit Coupon (Form 8109), write a check payable to your bank for your tax liability, and take it to the bank. Because the check is payable to the bank, it is important to get a receipt for your payment in case the IRS questions the amount of your deposits. TAXLINK, an electronic funds transfer system (EFT), allows tax deposits without coupons, paper checks, or visits to the depository. For information, call 800-555-4477 or 800-945-8400 or visit the Web site http://www. eftps.gov. If your total tax liability for any quarter is less than $2,500, you can pay the amount when you file your Form 941 instead of making deposits. If you're not sure if your total tax liability for the quarter will be less than $2,500, deposit using the monthly rules so you won't be subject to failure to deposit penalties.

Quarterly Payroll Tax Returns

At the end of each quarter (March, June, September, and December), you must send quarterly payroll tax returns to the IRS.

- **Social Security and the withholding of income taxes.** You will have to report to the IRS the total amount of wages you paid throughout the quarter, as well as the amount of taxes you withheld from your employees. This reporting is done on Form 941. Any monthly deposits you made will be reported on this form and will be applied to your tax liability. Any balance due (less than $2,500) must be paid with your return.

- **FUTA (unemployment tax) deposits.** If, at the end of any calendar quarter, you owe but have not yet deposited, more than $100 in Federal Unemployment Tax (FUTA) for the year, you must make a deposit by the end of the next month. Beginning in 2004, small businesses whose FICA/Federal Income Tax liability (Form 941) is less than $2,500 may pay their FUTA deposits with their annually-filed Form 940. Most states have reporting requirements that are similar to the IRS and that also include unemployment insurance payments. Contrary to popular belief, unemployment insurance is not deducted from your employees' paychecks. It is an expense of the employer.

Year-End Reports

The end of the year is a busy time for payroll reporting. Because it is also the end of a quarter, all of the quarterly tax returns described above are also due at the same time.

- **Annual FUTA return.** Form 940, *Employer's Annual Federal Unemployment (FUTA) Tax Return*, must be completed. This return reports each employee's wages that are subject to unemployment tax. Any quarterly deposits will be applied to the total tax liability.

- **Form W-2.** This form must be prepared for each employee. Form W-2 reports the total wages paid for the year and itemizes the total of each type of tax withheld from his or her paychecks. Multiple copies of these forms must be prepared. A packet of three to four are sent to the employee to be attached to his or her personal returns. You must send a copy to the Social Security Administration and additional copies to your state and local government agencies.

Accuracy in Reporting

It is vitally important that information reported on the Form W-2s, Form 941, *Employer's Quarterly Federal Tax Return*, and Form 940, *Employer's Annual Federal Unemployment (FUTA) Tax Return*, agrees. The Internal Revenue Service and Social Security Administration regularly compare information and will send notices to employers that have submitted conflicting information.

Can You Take the Responsibility?

The IRS, Social Security, and state and local agencies require that all of your reporting be exact. This can be a very heavy burden. The amount of paperwork alone requires many hours of work. The fact that you cannot afford to make a mistake makes it even more frightening.

Many small business owners buy a computer program, which supposedly makes the job easy. However, I have spoken with several of them that still find themselves not knowing what they are doing. Some hire an in-house employee to do the job. This too can be costly. My suggestion is this:

Hire a Professional!

You can have your payroll done by your accountant or by a payroll service for a very nominal fee. You will pay your employees and report wages paid to your payroll service. They will work with you, take the responsibility for collecting the proper information from you on wages paid, and see that all of the required reports are prepared and filed in a timely manner.

For Your Information

The tax section of this book (Chapter 7) will give you more information on tax reporting requirements for employees. There are also examples of forms W-2, W-3, W-4, FUTA, and FICA returns. Read over the information and familiarize yourself with the requirements. Then you can make a decision as to whether you wish to do your own or hire a professional.

For more detailed information, see IRS Publication 334, *Tax Guide for Small Business,* and Publication 15, *Employer's Tax Guide* (Circular E).

INDEPENDENT CONTRACTORS

One of the major problems that you, as a small business owner, must deal with is that of determining the status of people and/or companies that you hire to provide specific services for your company. Are they *independent contractors* (nonemployees) or are they, in fact, *employees* of your company?

- **If the service providers are independent contractors**, they are not eligible for unemployment, disability, or workers' compensation benefits. Also, you as the hiring firm do not have to pay employee-employer taxes or provide workers' compensation insurance, and you are usually not liable for the contractor's actions.

- **If the service provider is, in fact, an employee of your company,** rather than an independent contractor, the opposite is true. They are eligible for unemployment, disability, and workers' compensation benefits and you, as the hiring firm, must pay employee-employer taxes, provide workers' compensation insurance, and be liable for the contractor's actions.

Who Determines the Proper Classification of Service Providers?

The IRS and the laws of individual states determine whether a worker is an independent contractor or an employee. A contract between the hiring firm and the service provider is not proof of an independent contractor relationship. Workers are employees unless the hiring firm can prove otherwise.

The government looks negatively at the misclassification of bona-fide employees as independent contractors for two reasons: (1) Independent contractors are responsible for withholding their own taxes and Social Security. Many do not report their earnings and thus rob the system and other taxpayers of tax dollars. (2) The government wants to protect workers. They do not want businesses to circumvent the Social Security, disability, and unemployment insurance programs (and their costs) simply by calling their workers independent contractors.

Penalties for Misclassification

If your firm misclassifies an employee as an independent contractor, you will be assessed 1.5% of the gross wages (federal withholding, 20% of the amount that would have been the employee's share of FICA taxes, and the appropriate employer's share of FICA). This is providing that information returns (Form 1099-MISC) were filed and the failure to deduct was not intentional disregard of the requirement. If you fail to file information returns or fail to provide W-2s to employees, the penalty is doubled.

20 Common Law Factors

The IRS has a "List of the 20 Common Law Factors" that are used to evaluate the status of the provider. Independent contractors do not have to satisfy all 20 factors. The courts have given different weights for each factor according to the industry and jobs. If you are planning to use independent contractors, it would pay you to familiarize yourself with the 20 factors and avoid misclassification and costly penalties.

Recordkeeping and Reporting

If you have hired independent contractors, you will need to keep accurate records as to how much you paid each of them for the services performed for your company.

- Keep a record of each independent contractor and record the dates, check numbers, and amounts paid for each service performed.

- Keep a record of the independent contractor's name, company, address, telephone number, and Social Security/EIN number.

- Before January 31st of the new year, send each independent contractor a Form 1099-MISC. (See Chapter 7, "Taxes & Bookkeeping" for more information.)

- By February 28th, send in your forms 1099-MISC and transmittal form 1096 to the government. (See Chapter 7, "Taxes & Bookkeeping," for more information.)

Independent Contractors

Facts versus Myths

Appendix I of *Keeping the Books* will provide you with more comprehensive information regarding independent contractors. This section, entitled "Independent Contractors: Facts versus Myths," includes:

- The list of 20 common law factors

- Basic rules regarding independent contractor status

- Benefits and risks of hiring independent contractors

- Benefits and risks to the independent contractor

TRAVEL, TRANSPORTATION, AND ENTERTAINMENT EXPENSES

You will have to prove your deductions for travel, transportation, and entertainment business expenses by adequate records or by sufficient evidence that will support your claim. Records required should be kept in an account book, diary, statement of expense, or similar record. In the following paragraphs, I will discuss general information pertaining to transportation expenses, meal and entertainment expenses, and travel expenses. It is important that these expenses be recorded as they occur. It is difficult to remember them accurately after the fact.

Transportation Expenses

These are the ordinary and necessary expenses of getting from one workplace to another in the course of your business (when you are not traveling away from home). They *do* include the cost of transportation by air, rail, bus, taxi, etc., and the cost of driving and maintaining your car. They *do not* include transportation expenses between your home and your main or regular place of work, parking fees at your place of business, or expenses for personal use of your car.

Car expenses. If you use your car for business purposes, you may be able to deduct car expenses. You generally can use one of these two methods to figure these expenses:

1. **Actual expense.** Gas, oil, tolls, parking, lease or rental fees, depreciation, repairs, licenses, insurance, etc.

2. **Standard mileage rate.** Instead of figuring actual expenses, you may choose to use the standard mileage rate, which means that you will receive a deduction of a specific amount of money per mile (36.0 cents in 2003; projected at 37.5 cents for 2004) of business use of your car. Standard mileage rate is allowed if you own or lease the car or if you operate only one car at a time for business. Standard mileage rate is not allowed if you use the car for hire, operate two or more cars at the same time, or claimed depreciation in previous years using ACRS or MACRS depreciation, or a Section 179 deduction.

Mileage log. You are required to record business miles traveled during the year. A form is provided on the next page, and a blank one is available in Appendix II for your use. The first year, it may be helpful to compare the results of both methods before making your decision about how to report transportation costs. Also, be aware that if the use of the car is for both business and personal use, you must divide your expenses and deduct only the percentage used in business pursuit. For more detailed information get IRS Publication 463, *Travel, Entertainment, Gift, and Car Expenses,* and IRS Publication 334, *Tax Guide for Small Business.*

Mileage Log
for ABC Company

NAME: _ABC Company (John Morgan)_

DATED: From _November 1_ **To** _November 30, 2004_

DATE	CITY OF DESTINATION	NAME OR OTHER DESIGNATION	BUSINESS PURPOSE	NO. OF MILES
11-01	Orange, CA	ExCal, Inc.	Present proposal	67 mi.
11-03	Cypress, CA	The Print Co.	p/u brochures	23 mi.
11-04	Long Beach, CA	Wm. Long	Consultation	53 mi.
11-07	Fullerton, CA	Bank of America	Loan Meeting	17 mi.
11-23	Los Angeles, CA	Moore Corp.	Consultation	143 mi.
11-30	Los Angeles, CA	Moore Corp.	Consultation	140 mi.
			TOTAL MILES THIS SHEET	443

NOTE: 1. A mileage record is required by the IRS to claim a mileage deduction. It is also used to determine the percentage of business use of a car.

2. Keep your mileage log in your vehicle and record your mileage as it occurs. It is very difficult to recall after the fact.

Meals and Entertainment Expenses

You may be able to deduct business-related entertainment expenses you have to entertain a client, customer, or employee. The expense must be ordinary (common and accepted in your field of business) and necessary (helpful and appropriate for your business, but not necessarily indispensable). In addition, you must be able to show that they are (1) directly related to the active conduct of your trade or business, or (2) associated with the active conduct of your trade or business.

- **Entertainment includes.** Any activity generally considered to provide entertainment, amusement, or recreation (e.g., entertaining business associates at night clubs, social, athletic and sporting clubs, theaters, sporting events, on yachts, on hunting, fishing, vacation, and similar trips). Entertainment also may include satisfying personal, living, or family needs of individuals, such as providing food, a hotel suite, or a car to business customers or their families.

- **Entertainment does not include.** Supper money you give your employees, a hotel room you keep for your employees while on business travel, or a car used in your business. However, if you provide the use of a hotel suite or a car to your employee who is on vacation, this is entertainment of the employee.

- **Meals as entertainment.** Entertainment includes the cost of a meal you provide to a customer or client. It does not matter whether the meal is a part of other entertainment. Generally, to deduct an entertainment-related meal, you or your employee must be present when the food or beverages are provided.

- **50% limit.** You may deduct only 50% of business-related meals and entertainment expenses. You must record these expenses with date, place of entertainment, business purpose, the name of the person entertained, and the amount spent.

Sample entertainment expense record. The form provided on the next page will help you to record all information required to justify entertainment expenses. Be sure to fill in all categories. Keep all receipts for verification and file for easy retrieval. For more information, see IRS Publication 463, *Travel, Entertainment, Gift, and Car Expenses,* and Publication 334, *Tax Guide for Small Business.*

Entertainment Expense Record
for ABC Company

NAME: _John Higgins_

DATED: From _11-01-04_ To _11-30-04_

DATE	PLACE OF ENTERTAINMENT	BUSINESS PURPOSE	NAME OF PERSON ENTERTAINED	AMOUNT SPENT	
11-04	The 410 Club	Consulting	Wm Long	27	32
11-23	Seafood Chef	Consulting	Thomas Moore	23	50
11-27	The Cannon Club	Staff Dinner	Company Employees	384	00

NOTE: For more information on Meals and Entertainment, please refer to IRS Publication 463, *Travel, Entertainment*, Gift, and Car *Expenses*.

Travel Expenses

Deductible travel expenses include those ordinary and necessary expenses you incur while traveling away from your tax home on business. The lists that follow provide general guidelines.

Expenses that can be deducted

- **Transportation fares.** The cost of traveling between home and business destination.
- **Taxi, commuter bus, and limousine fares.** The fare between the airport and your hotel or temporary work site.
- **Baggage and shipping.** Actual costs between regular and temporary work locations.
- **Car expenses.** Includes leasing expenses, actual expenses, or the standard mileage rate (36.0 cents in 2003; projected to 37.5 cents for 2004).
- **Lodging.** If the trip is overnight or long enough to require rest to properly perform duties.
- **Meals.** Actual or standard meal allowance if business trip qualifies for lodging.
- **Cleaning and laundry expenses.** Cost of cleaning your business clothes while away from home overnight.
- **Telephone expenses.** Telephone usage, including fax and other communication devices.
- **Tips.** Related to any of the above services.
- **Other business-related expenses.** Any expenses connected with your travel (e.g., computer rental).

Expenses you cannot deduct

- That portion of travel, meals, and lodging for your spouse—unless a real business purpose exists for your spouse's presence.
- Investment travel (such as investment seminars or stockholders' meetings).
- Amounts you spend for travel to conduct a general search for, or preliminary investigation of, a new business.

Special rulings. You will need to study special rulings. For instance, when your trip is not entirely for business purposes, you will have to properly allocate the expenses. Treatment of expenses depends on how much of your trip was business-related and what portion occurred within the United States. Also, if you are not traveling for the entire 24-hour day, you must prorate the standard meal allowance and claim only one-fourth of the allowance for each 6-hour quarter of the day during any part of which you are traveling away from home.

Travel Record. When you travel away from home on business, you need to keep records of all the expenses you incur. The Travel Record on the next page shows the information that you will be required to keep. A blank form is located in Appendix II. You will also need to keep documentation such as receipts, canceled checks, or bills to verify your expense. For more information, see IRS Publication 463, *Travel, Entertainment, Gift, and Car Expenses.*

Travel Record for ABC Company

TRIP TO: _Dallas, Texas_

Dated From: _6-15-04_ To: _6-18-04_

Business Purpose: _Technology Expo (show exhibitor)_

No. Days Spent on Business _5_

DATE	LOCATION	EXPENSE PAID TO	MEALS				HOTEL	TAXIS, ETC.	AUTOMOBILE			MISC EXP
			Breakfast	Lunch	Dinner	Misc.			Gas	Parking	Tolls	
6-15	Phoenix, AZ	Mobil Gas				6 40			21 00			
6-15	Phoenix, AZ	Greentree Inn		12 50								
6-15	Chola, NM	Exxon							23 50			
6-15	Las Cruces, NM	Holiday Inn			27 00		49 00					
6-16	Las Cruces, NM	Exxon							19 00			
6-16	Taft, TX	Molly's Cafe		16 25								
6-16	Dallas, TX	Holiday Inn			18 75		54 00					
6-17	Dallas, TX	Expo Center								8 00		
6-17	Dallas, TX	Harvey's Eatery		21 00								
6-17	Dallas, TX	Holiday Inn			24 50		54 00					
6-18	Dallas, TX	Holiday Inn	9 50									
6-18	Dallas, TX	Expo Center		14 00						8 00		(Fax) 9 00
6-18	Dallas, TX	Holiday Inn			16 20		54 00					
6-19	Pokie, TX	Texaco							21 00			
6-19	Pokie, TX	Denny's		19 50								
6-19	Chola, NM	Holiday Inn			27 00		48 00					
6-20	Chola, NM	Holiday Inn	12 75									
6-20	Flagstaff, AZ	Texaco							22 00			
TOTALS ➛			22 25	83 25	113 45	6 40	259 00		106 50	16 00		9 00

Attach all receipts for Meals, Hotel, Fares, Auto, Entertainment, etc. Details of your expenses can be noted on the receipts. File your travel record and your receipts in the same envelope. Label the envelope as to trip made. File all travel records together. When expenses are allocated, be sure not to double expense anything. (Ex: Gas cannot be used if you elect to use mileage as the basis for deducting your car expenses.)

CUSTOMER INFORMATION RECORDS

To help a business deal more effectively with its customers, it can be very beneficial to develop a system to keep track of customer information. Without technology to enable them to reach out through databases and information services, many businesses have no way to keep specialized information on customers due to volume or change in clientele. Small businesses in the service industry and in specialty retail sales are finding that if they can incorporate specialized customer records into their operations, they have a better chance of retaining customers. Service businesses strive for repeat and referral business, plus new customers who come to them through commercial advertising. Specialty retail sales shops also look for repeats and referrals as their primary source of business.

By keeping a database that can selectively draw out information, the customer can be better served. For those without the electronic advantage, a file of 3 x 5 index cards—one for each customer—provides the business owner with ready information at his fingertips. In my husband's clock shop, he has effectively used a manual system of this type to service a customer list of approximately 10,000. The types of things that can be recorded and some uses of that information are as follows:

Service Industry

Includes. Name, address, telephone numbers (work and home), service performed, charges, special advice to customer, guarantees given, and any other information that you feel may be helpful.

Some uses of information. Protection of the business from customers' claims that services were performed that were not recorded, information as proof of dates of warranty service (benefiting both customer and business owner), information to help business owners remember customers and give them specialized attention.

Specialty Retail Sales Business

Includes. Name, address, telephone numbers (work and home), sales information, and special interests of customer.

Some uses of information. Use as a mailing list for special sales; when customer calls, use card to jog your memory as to his or her interests, what he or she has already purchased, and what he or she might like. These customers like to be remembered and have personalized information.

Sample customer files. See the next page for examples of customer files for (1) the service industry and (2) specialty retail sales.

Sample Customer Data Files

Service Industry

Jones, John W.   (H) (714) 555-2489
123 W. 1st Street   (W) (714) 555-1234
Anywhere, CA 97134

1. *Ridgeway G/F Clock (IHS) a. Repaired pendulum, rep.*
   $55.00 8/19/01   susp. sprg., serviced.

2. *S/Thomas O.G. a. Cleaned, bushed movement, balanced.*
   $155.00 6/07/02 Guarantee: 1 year

3. *Waltham L/WW (antique) a. Stem, clean, repair hspg.*
   $45.00 7/11/04

Specialty Retail Sales

Smith, Henry L. (D.D.S)   (W) (201) 555-1304
76 Main Street, Suite X
Somewhere, CA 96072
                                  Birthday: May 3rd
*Buys for wife's (Ann) collection: Anniversary: Oct. 21st

1. *08 CM M/Box w/"Lara's Theme" 1/18 (Rosewood burl)*
   $55.00 + Tax   4/28/02

2. *789 BMP 3/72 w/"Phantom of the Opera"*
   $675.00 + Tax 10/17/02

3. *Novelty M/B - Bear w/Heart $32.00 + Tax 2/13/04*

BUSINESS CHECKBOOK

Your business checkbook is not just a package of preprinted forms that represent your business bankroll. It is also the initial accounting record showing when, where, and in what amount money was dispersed and when, from what sources, and how much money was received by your company. This information is all kept on the recording space provided in your checkbook.

What Type of Checkbook Is Most Effective?

Don't get a pocket-size checkbook. This type of checkbook does not provide enough space for entry of information (and it is also easily misplaced). Some points to consider when selecting your business checkbook are:

- **Size.** A business-size checkbook is best. There is a personal desk type with three standard size checks on each righthand page and a register (recording) page of equal size on the left. Instead of one line of check register for each transaction, you will have room to record such things as invoice numbers and descriptions of purchases. You can divide amounts paid with one check into separate expenses. For instance, the payment of an invoice to an office supply store may involve $15 for office supplies and $45 for exhibit materials. Deposits can be divided into types of revenues received. These and other notations will be invaluable when you do your weekly bookkeeping, because you will not have to look for paperwork to supply missing information.

- **Duplicate feature.** Many business owners number among the ranks of those people who do not automatically record information when they write checks. To eliminate the frustration created by this unfortunate habit, banks can provide checkbooks made with carbonless copies underneath each check. If you fail to record a check at the time you write it, a copy will remain in your checkbook. I don't use one, but lots of people swear by them.

- **Preprinting and numbering of checks.** Your checks should be preprinted with your business name, address, and telephone number. They should also be numbered. Some businesses will not even deal with you if you try to use personal checks or ones without preprinted information. Some vendors with which you wish to do business perceive them as a possible danger signal and indicator of a lack of your credibility.

- **Deposit record.** There is one last feature that I like when it comes to my banking supplies. Instead of deposit slips that can get lost, I like to use a Deposit Record Book. It is a bound book of deposit slips arranged in sets of two. The original goes to the bank and the duplicate stays in your book and is dated stamped and initialed by the teller. The book can be kept in your bank bag and is ready to use for the next deposit. It ensures that you have a permanent record of all of your deposits.

Balancing Your Checkbook Manually

Once a month your bank will send you a statement of your account, showing a summary of your activity since the last statement date. It will list all deposits, check withdrawals, ATM activity, bank charges, and interest earned. You will need to reconcile it with your checkbook on a timely basis. This is one of those chores that is frequently ignored. "I will catch it up later when I have more time." This kind of attitude results in undiscovered errors and over-drawn accounts. It is not difficult to balance your checkbook if you follow these steps:

1. **Update your checkbook**

   Add:
   - Interest earned
   - Deposits not recorded
   - Automatic credits unrecorded

   Subtract:
   - Service charges
   - Checks not recorded
   - Automatic debits unrecorded
   - Payments not recorded

   Mark off:
   - Amount of all checks paid against statement
   - Amount of all deposits shown
   - All ATM and electronic transactions that are recorded

2. **List and total**
   - All deposits made and other credits not shown on the statement
   - All outstanding checks not shown on current or previous statements

3. **Balance**
   - Enter statement balance as indicated
   - Add the total of all deposits and other credits not shown on current or previous statements
   - Subtract items outstanding

Total should agree with checkbook balance.

BALANCE FORM

Statement Balance			
Add Deposits made and not shown on this statement			
Total	$		
Subtract Outstanding items			
Total Should agree with your checkbook balance	$		

Outstanding Items

Check No. or Date	Amount		Check No. or Date	Amount	
Total	$		**Total**	$	

If you are not in balance. Recheck your addition and subtraction in your checkbook. Check amounts in checkbook against those in your statement. Look for uncashed checks from previous statements and be sure they are not still outstanding. Check amount you are off and see if it matches amount on any of your checks. Be sure that you did not add a check when you should have subtracted. Be sure that you recorded and subtracted all ATM withdrawals in your checkbook.

Recording Bank Statement Information

When you are doing your regular bookkeeping, *you must remember* that you will have to record all bank charges (service charges, check orders, returned check charges, returned checks, etc.) in your Revenue & Expense Journal. If you do not, your expenses will be understated and you will pay more taxes. Also be sure to record interest earnings.

RECEIPT FILES

It is required by the IRS that you be able to verify deductions. For that reason alone, you must have a filing system that ensures that your receipts are easy to retrieve. This is also very important for your own benefit. There will be many times that you will need to find information on a transaction for any one of innumerable reasons. If your filing system is a mess, you are lost.

Where Do You Keep Receipts?

For most businesses, an accordion file divided into alphabet pockets will be the most efficient way of filing your receipts. These files also come with pockets divided into months, but I think it becomes cumbersome for retrieval. Picking out all of your utility bills, for example, would require that you pick from 12 different pockets. With the alphabet file, it would require only one. You will probably also need one or more two-drawer file cabinets for systematic filing of other paperwork.

One of the most frequent questions I get asked is, "How do I determine what letter of the alphabet to file the receipt under?" The easiest way is to use the first letter entered in a record. If you record a meal in Petty Cash as paid to cash because you don't know the name of a seller, file the receipt under "C." I do keep all the meal receipts in one envelope marked "Meals" and file it under "M," because that is an item frequently audited and I can pull all of the receipts quickly. I also keep all the records for a trip in a single envelope and mark it with the occasion and date. Then I file all travel records under "T" for the same reason. You may wish to keep a separate file for Petty Cash Receipts. I use the same one for those paid by check and by cash.

At the End of the Year

When the tax year is closed, you can add your bank statements, Revenue & Expense Journal, a copy of your tax return, and any other pertinent information for that year. All are put away in the one accordion file and labeled with the year. If, at a later date, you need information for a tax audit or for another purpose, everything is in one place.

* THIS ENDS THE GENERAL RECORDS SECTION *

You have now completed the General Records Section of the book and your day-to-day bookkeeping records should be set up and ready to go. In the next section of this book, you will learn about Financial Statements and how they are developed from the records with which we have just been concerned.

CHAPTER 5

FINANCIAL STATEMENTS

In the four previous chapters of this book, I have introduced you to the functions and types of record-keeping and some simple accounting terminology. I have discussed double and single entry accounting and worked through the process of setting up essential general records for your business.

Now it is time to see how financial statements are developed from your general records and how the use of those financial statements can help you to see the financial condition of your business and to identify its relative strengths and weaknesses. Business owners who take the time to understand and evaluate operations through financial statements over the life of the business will be far ahead of entrepreneurs who concern themselves only with the products or services.

• • • • •

WHAT ARE FINANCIAL STATEMENTS?

Financial statements show past and projected finances. These statements are both the source of your tax information (discussed in Chapter 7) and the means by which you analyze your business (discussed in Chapter 6). They are developed from your General Records and fall into two main categories: Actual Performance Statements and Pro Forma Statements. Before you proceed further, it is best to understand what financial statements are and which ones you will use for your business.

Actual Performance Statements

These are the historical financial statements reflecting the past performance of your business. If you are planning a new business, you have no history. However, as soon as you have been in business for even one accounting period, you will begin to generate these two financial statements, both of which will prove to be invaluable to you in making decisions about your business. They are:

1. **Balance sheet**
2. **Profit & loss statement (income statement)**

I will also introduce you to a Business Financial History, which is a composite of the Balance Sheet, Profit & Loss Statements, and legal structure information. It is used frequently as a loan application.

Pro Forma Statements

The word pro forma in accounting means projected. These are the financial statements that are used for you to predict the future profitability of your business. Your projections will be based on realistic research and reasonable assumptions, trying not to overstate your revenues or understate your expenses. The pro forma statements are:

- Pro Forma Cash Flow Statement (or Budget)
- Quarterly Budget Analysis (means of measuring projections against actual performance within budget)
- Three-Year Projection (Pro Forma Income Statement)
- Breakeven Analysis

How to Proceed

Each of the above financial documents will be discussed as to:

- definition and use.
- how to develop the statement.
- sources of needed information.

Every business owner will need to understand and generate Profit & Loss (Income) Statements, Balance Sheets, and Pro Forma Cash Flow Statements. Information from these three statements will then be utilized to perform a Quarterly Budget Analysis on a regular basis. Some additional financial statements will be required for a business plan and will serve as useful financial planning tools. The following are four guidelines for preparing financial statements in different situations:

1. **If you are a new business and you are going to seek a lender or investor**. You will be required to write a business plan. You will need to create all Pro Forma Statements included in this chapter. You will have no financial history and cannot include Actual Performance Statements.

2. **If you are a new business and you are not going to seek a lender or investor.** You should still think about writing a business plan. You will include all Pro Forma Statements. Even if you decide not to write one, it is especially important to plan your cash flow (budget).

3. **If you are an existing business and you are going to seek a lender or investor.** You will be required to write a business plan. You will include all financial documents discussed in this chapter, plus other elements. (See my book, *Anatomy of a Business Plan*, Dearborn Trade.)

4. **If you are an existing business and you are not seeking a lender or investor.** All financial statements are beneficial. The Profit & Loss, Balance Sheet, and Pro Forma Cash Flow Statements are a must.

NOW YOU ARE READY TO LEARN TO DEVELOP ACTUAL PERFORMANCE STATEMENTS

BALANCE SHEET

What Is a Balance Sheet?

The Balance Sheet is a financial statement that shows the financial position of the business as of a fixed date. It is usually done at the close of an accounting period. The Balance Sheet can be compared to a still photograph. It is a picture of what your business owns and owes at a given moment and will show you whether your financial position is strong or weak. By regularly preparing this statement, you will be able to identify and analyze trends in the financial strength of your business and thus implement timely modifications. A sample Balance Sheet is shown on page 65.

Format

The Balance Sheet must follow an accepted format and contain the following three categories so anyone reading it can readily interpret it. The three categories are related in that, at any given time, a business's assets equal the total contributions by its creditors and owners.

> **Assets** = Anything your business owns that has monetary value.

> **Liabilities** = Debts owed by the business to any of its creditors.

> **Net Worth (Capital)** = An amount equal to the owner's equity.

The relationship among these three terms is simply illustrated in a mathematical formula. It reads as follows:

$$\text{Assets} - \text{Liabilities} = \text{Net Worth}$$

Examined as such, it becomes apparent that if a business possesses more assets than it owes to creditors, its net worth will be a positive. Conversely, if the business owes more money to creditors than it possesses in assets, the net worth will be a negative.

Sources of Information

If you (or your accountant) use accounting software for your business, it should generate a Balance Sheet on command. If you do your accounting manually, the figures come from your general records. Look for the sources given at the end of the category explanations on the next page.

EXPLANATION OF CATEGORIES
BALANCE SHEET

Assets. Everything owned by or owed to your business that has cash value.

- **Current assets.** Assets that can be converted into cash within one year of the date on the Balance Sheet.
  - **Cash.** Money you have on hand. Include monies not yet deposited.
  - **Petty cash.** Money deposited to Petty Cash and not yet expended.
  - **Accounts receivable.** Money owed to you for sale of goods and/or services.
  - **Inventory.** Raw materials, work-in-process, and goods manufactured or purchased for resale.
  - **Short-term investments.** (Assets expected to be converted to cash within one year.) Stocks, bonds, CDs. List at whichever cost or market value is less.
  - **Prepaid expenses.** Goods or services purchased or rented prior to use (i.e., rent, insurance, prepaid inventory purchases, etc.).

- **Long-term investments.** Stocks, bonds, and special savings accounts to be kept for at least one year.

- **Fixed assets.** Resources a business owns and does not intend for resale.
  - **Land.** List at original purchase price. Land is not depreciated.
  - **Buildings.** List at cost, less any depreciation previously taken.
  - **Equipment, furniture, autos/vehicles.** List at cost less depreciation. Kelley Blue Book can be used to determine value of vehicles.

Liabilities. What your business owes; claims by creditors on your assets.

- **Current liabilities.** Those obligations payable within one operating cycle.
  - **Accounts payable.** Obligations payable within one operating cycle.
  - **Notes payable.** Short-term notes; list the balance of principal due. Separately list the current portion of long-term debts.
  - **Interest payable.** Interest accrued on loans and credit.
  - **Taxes payable.** Amounts estimated to have been incurred during the accounting period.
  - **Payroll accrual.** Current liabilities on salaries and wages.

- **Long-term liabilities.** Outstanding balance less the current portion due (i.e., mortgage, vehicle).

Net worth (also called "capital" or "owner equity"). The claims of the owner or owners on the assets of the business (document according to the legal structure of your business).

- **Proprietorship or partnership.** Each owner's original investment, plus earnings after withdrawals.

- **Corporation.** The sum of contributions by owners or stockholders, plus earnings retained after paying dividends.

Balance Sheet

Business Name:	**ABC Company**	**Date: September 30, 2004**

ASSETS

Current assets

Cash	$	8,742
Petty cash	$	167
Accounts receivable	$	5,400
Inventory	$	101,800
Short-term investments	$	0
Prepaid expenses	$	1,967

Long-term investments

	$	0

Fixed assets

Land (valued at cost)		$	185,000
Buildings		$	143,000
1. Cost	171,600		
2. Less acc. depr.	28,600		
Improvements		$	0
1. Cost			
2. Less acc. depr.			
Equipment		$	5,760
1. Cost	7,200		
2. Less acc. depr.	1,440		
Furniture		$	2,150
1. Cost	2,150		
2. Less acc. depr.	0		
Autos/vehicles		$	16,432
1. Cost	19,700		
2. Less acc. depr.	3,268		

Other assets

1.	$	
2.	$	

TOTAL ASSETS	**$**	**470,418**

LIABILITIES

Current liabilities

Accounts payable	$	2,893
Notes payable	$	0
Interest payable	$	1,842
Taxes payable		
Federal income tax	$	5,200
Self-employment tax	$	1,025
State income tax	$	800
Sales tax accrual	$	2,130
Property tax	$	0
Payroll accrual	$	4,700

Long-term liabilities

Notes payable	$	196,700

TOTAL LIABILITIES	**$**	**215,290**

NET WORTH (EQUITY)

Proprietorship	$	
or		
Partnership		
John Smith, 60% equity	$	153,077
Mary Blake, 40% equity	$	102,051
or		
Corporation		
Capital stock	$	
Surplus paid in	$	
Retained earnings	$	

TOTAL NET WORTH	**$**	**255,128**

Assets – Liabilities = Net Worth
and
Liabilities + Equity = Total Assets

PROFIT & LOSS STATEMENT
OR INCOME STATEMENT
What Is a Profit & Loss (Income) Statement?

This statement shows your business financial activity over a period of time, usually your tax year. In contrast to the Balance Sheet, which shows a picture of your business at a given moment, the Profit & Loss Statement (P&L) can be likened to a moving picture—showing what has happened in your business over a period of time. It is an excellent tool for assessing your business. You will be able to pick out weaknesses in your operation and plan ways to run your business more effectively, thereby increasing your profits. For example, you may find that some heavy advertising that you did in March did not effectively increase your sales. In following years, you may decide to utilize your advertising funds more effectively by using them at a time when there is increased customer spending taking place. In the same way, you might examine your Profit & Loss Statement to see what months have the heaviest sales volume and plan your inventory accordingly. Comparison of your P&Ls from several years will give you an even better picture of the trends in your business. Do not underestimate the value of this particular tool when planning your tactics.

How to Develop a Profit & Loss Statement

The Profit & Loss Statement (Income Statement) is compiled from actual business transactions, in contrast to Pro Forma Statements, which are projections for future business periods. The P&L shows where your money has come from and where it was spent over a specific period of time. It should be prepared not only at the end of the tax year, but at the close of each business month. It is one of the two principal financial statements prepared from the ledgers and the records of a business. Income and expense account balances are used in the P&L Statement. The remaining asset, liability, and capital information provides the figures for the Balance Sheet covered in the last three pages.

In double entry accounting, balances from your revenue, cost of goods, and expense accounts are transferred to your P&L Statement. If you utilize accounting software, you can generate a profit and loss statement for a period of choice (current month, this fiscal year, last fiscal year, specified dates, etc.) whenever you choose to do so. If an accountant does your bookkeeping, he or she should provide you with a P&L Statement at the end of every month as well as at the end of your tax year. If you set up a manual bookkeeping system (single entry) with General Records discussed in Chapter 4, the P&L Statement is generated by a simple transfer of the end-of-month totals from your Revenue & Expense Journal.

Format and Sources of Information

The P&L (or Income) Statement must also follow an accepted accounting format and contain certain categories. The following is the correct format and a brief explanation of the items to be included or computations to be made in each category in order to arrive at "the bottom line," or owner's share of the profit for the period.

Income

1. **Net sales/revenues (gross sales less returns and allowances).** What were your cash receipts for the period? If your accounting is on an accrual basis, what amount did you invoice out during the period?

2. **Cost of goods sold.** See the form on page 69 for computation.

3. **Gross profit.** Subtract Cost of Goods from Net Sales.

Expenses

1. **Variable expenses (selling).** What amounts did you actually spend on items directly related to your product or service? (Marketing, commissions, freight, packaging, travel, etc.)

2. **Fixed expenses (administrative).** What amounts were spent during the period on office overhead? (Rent, insurance, accounting, office salaries, telephone, utilities, etc.)

Net income from operations. Gross profit minus fixed and variable expenses.

Other income. Interest received during the period.

Other expense. Interest paid out during the period.

Net profit (loss) before income taxes. The Net income from Operations plus Interest received minus Interest paid out.

Income taxes. List income taxes paid out during the period (federal, self-employment, state, local).

Net profit (loss) after income taxes. Subtract all income taxes paid out from the Net Profit (or Loss) Before Income Taxes. This is what is known as "the bottom line."

Sample forms. The next two pages contain two Profit & Loss forms. The first is divided into 12 months. If filled in monthly, this form will provide an accurate picture of the year's financial activity at the end of the year. There is a blank form in Appendix II for your use. The form on page 69 (sample) is to be used for either a monthly or an annual P&L Statement.

Profit & Loss (Income) Statement for ABC Company

For the Year: 2004

	Jan	Feb	Mar	Apr	May	Jun	6-MONTH TOTALS	Jul	Aug	Sep	Oct	Nov	Dec	12-MONTH TOTALS
INCOME														
1. Net sales (Gr - R&A)	14,400	10,140	10,060	15,658	18,622	12,620	81,500	11,500	9,850	10,150	16,600	29,250	51,000	209,850
2. Cost of goods to be sold	2,800	2,900	4,200	7,700	7,350	2,750	27,700	2,959	2,580	2,740	6,250	13,400	23,290	78,919
a. Beginning inventory	27,000	31,000	48,500	48,600	42,000	35,600	27,000	33,800	40,800	40,900	51,700	53,300	54,700	27,000
b. Purchases	6,800	20,400	4,300	1,100	950	950	34,500	9,959	2,680	13,540	7,850	14,800	12,890	96,219
c. C.O.G. available for sale	33,800	51,400	52,800	49,700	42,950	36,550	61,500	43,759	43,480	54,440	59,550	68,100	67,590	123,219
d. Less ending inventory	31,000	48,500	48,600	42,000	35,600	33,800	33,800	40,800	40,900	51,700	53,300	54,700	44,300	44,300
3. Gross profit	11,600	7,240	5,860	7,958	11,272	9,870	53,800	8,541	7,270	7,410	10,350	15,850	27,710	130,931
EXPENSES														
1. Variable (selling) expenses														
a. Advertising	900	300	900	250	300	300	2,950	350	300	640	1,300	1,200	1,400	8,140
b. Freight	75	75	75	75	180	70	550	75	75	90	180	300	560	1,830
c. Fulfillment of orders	300	300	300	400	350	300	1,950	300	280	325	450	600	975	4,880
d. Packaging costs	2,100	0	0	0	600	0	2,700	0	200	230	0	0	0	3,130
e. Sales salaries/wages/commissions	1,400	900	1,300	1,400	1,100	900	7,000	1,400	1,400	1,400	1,400	1,400	1,400	15,400
f. Travel	0	500	700	0	0	400	1,600	0	540	25	80	0	0	2,245
g. Misc. variable expense	50	47	73	40	28	62	300	90	73	46	39	74	87	709
h. Depreciation	0	0	0	0	0	0	0	0	0	0	0	0	2,660	2,660
Total variable expenses	4,825	2,122	3,348	2,165	2,558	2,032	17,050	2,215	2,868	2,756	3,449	3,574	7,082	38,994
2. Fixed (admin) expenses														
a. Financial administration	75	75	75	475	75	75	850	75	75	75	75	75	75	1,300
b. Insurance	1,564	0	0	0	0	0	1,564	1,563	0	0	0	0	0	3,127
c. Licenses/permits	240	0	0	0	0	0	240	0	0	0	0	0	125	365
d. Office salaries	1,400	1,400	1,400	1,400	1,400	1,400	8,400	1,400	1,400	1,400	1,400	1,400	1,400	16,800
e. Rent expenses	700	700	700	700	700	700	4,200	700	700	700	700	700	700	8,400
f. Utilities	200	200	140	120	80	80	820	75	75	75	90	120	155	1,410
g. Misc. fixed expense	54	38	42	57	28	64	283	60	72	31	48	45	89	628
h. Depreciation	0	0	0	0	0	2,660	2,660	0	0	0	0	0	2,660	5,320
Total fixed expenses	4,233	2,413	2,357	2,752	2,283	4,979	19,017	3,873	2,322	2,281	2,313	2,340	5,204	37,350
Total operating expense	9,058	4,535	5,705	4,917	4,841	7,011	36,067	6,088	5,190	5,037	5,762	5,914	12,286	76,344
Net Income from Operations	2,542	2,705	155	3,041	6,431	2,859	17,733	2,453	2,080	2,373	4,588	9,936	15,424	54,587
Other Income (interest)	234	240	260	158	172	195	1,259	213	303	300	417	406	413	3,311
Other Expense (interest)	0	0	0	234	233	232	699	231	230	225	223	222	220	2,050
Net Profit (Loss) before Taxes	2,776	2,945	415	2,965	6,370	2,822	18,293	2,435	2,153	2,448	4,782	10,120	15,617	55,848
Taxes: a. Federal	1,950	0	0	1,950	0	1,950	5,850	0	0	1,950	0	0	0	7,800
b. State	350	0	0	350	0	350	1,050	0	0	350	0	0	0	1,400
c. Local	0	0	0	0	0	0	0	0	0	0	0	0	0	0
NET PROFIT (LOSS) AFTER TAXES	476	2,945	415	665	6,370	522	11,393	2,435	2,153	148	4,782	10,120	15,617	46,648

Profit & Loss (Income) Statement
for ABC Company

Beginning: January 1, 2004   **Ending: December 31, 2004**

INCOME		
1. Sales revenues		$ 500,000
2. Cost of goods sold (c – d)		312,000
a. Beginning inventory (1/01)	$ 147,000	
b. Purchases	320,000	
c. C.O.G. avail. sale (a + b)	467,000	
d. Less ending inventory (12/31)	$ 155,000	
3. Gross profit on sales (1 – 2)		$ 188,000
EXPENSES		
1. Variable (selling) (a thru h)		67,390
a. Advertising/marketing	$ 22,000	
b. Freight	9,000	
c. Fulfillment of orders	2,000	
d. Packaging costs	3,000	
e. Salaries/wages/commissions	25,000	
f. Travel	1,000	
g. Misc. variable (selling) expense	390	
h. Depreciation (prod/serv assets)	$ 5,000	
2. Fixed (administrative) (a thru h)		51,610
a. Financial administration	$ 1,000	
b. Insurance	3,800	
c. Licenses and permits	2,710	
d. Office salaries	14,000	
e. Rent expense	22,500	
f. Utilities	3,000	
g. Misc. fixed (administrative) expense	0	
h. Depreciation (office equipment)	$ 4,600	
Total operating expenses (1 + 2)		119,000
Net income from operations (GP – Exp)		$ 69,000
Other income (interest income)		5,000
Other expense (interest expense)		7,000
Net profit (loss) before taxes		$ 67,000
Taxes		
a. Federal	21,000	
b. State	4,500	26,000
c. Local	500	
NET PROFIT (LOSS) AFTER TAXES		$ 41,000

BUSINESS FINANCIAL HISTORY

Your financial history is a financial statement that would be required if you are writing a business plan to go to a lender or investor. It is a summary of financial information about your company from its start to the present. The form will generally be provided by the lender.

If You Are a New Business

You will have only projections for your business. If you are applying for a loan, the lender will require a Personal Financial History. This will be of benefit in that it will show him or her the manner in which you have conducted your personal business, an indicator of the probability of your succeeding in your business.

If You Are an Established Business

The loan application and your Business Financial History are the same. When you indicate that you are interested in obtaining a business loan, the institution considering the loan will supply you with an application. Formats may vary slightly among lenders. When you receive your loan application, be sure to review it and think about how you are going to answer each item. Answer all questions, and by all means be certain that your information is accurate and that it can be easily verified.

Information Needed and Sources

As you fill out your Business Financial History (loan application), it should become immediately apparent why this is the last financial document to be completed. All of the information needed will have been compiled previously in earlier parts of your plan. To help you with your financial history, the following is a list of information usually included about your business and the source you will refer to for that information:

- **Assets, liabilities, net worth.** You should recognize these three as Balance Sheet terms. You have already completed a Balance Sheet for your company and need only to go back to that record and bring the dollar amounts forward.

- **Contingent liabilities.** These are debts you may come to owe in the future (i.e., default on a cosigned note or settlement of a pending lawsuit).

- **Inventory details.** Information is derived from your Inventory Record. Also, in the Organizational section of your plan you should already have a summary of your current inventory policies and methods of evaluation.

- **Profit & Loss statement.** This is revenue and expense information. You will transfer the information from your Annual Profit & Loss (last statement completed), or from a compilation of several if required by the lender.

- **Real estate holdings, stocks, and bonds.** Refer back to the business portion of your plan. You may also have to go through your investment records for more comprehensive information.

- **Sole proprietorship, partnership, or corporation information.** There are generally three separate schedules on the financial history, one for each form of legal structure. You will be required to fill out the one that is appropriate to your business. In the Organizational section of your plan, you will have covered two areas that will serve as the source of this information—Legal Structure and Management. Supporting Documents may also contain some of the information that you will need.

- **Audit information.** Refer back to the Organizational section under Record-keeping. You may also be asked questions about other prospective lenders, whether you are seeking credit, who audits your books, and when they were last audited.

- **Insurance coverage.** You will be asked to provide detailed information on the amounts of different types of coverage (i.e., merchandise, equipment, public liability, earthquake, auto, etc.). The Organizational section contains information on coverage that can be brought forth to the financial history.

Sample Forms

Business Financial Statement form. On the following pages you will find an example of a Business Financial Statement that might be required by a potential lender or investor.

Personal Financial Statement form. Following the sample business financial statement, you will find a sample of a personal financial statement form. If you are a new business and need a personal financial statement for your business plan, you can get one from a lender, stationery store, or other supplier of office forms.

Business Financial Statement

Business Financial Statement
INDIVIDUAL, PARTNERSHIP, OR CORPORATION

FINANCIAL STATEMENT OF_____ Received At_____Branch

Name_____ Business_____

Address_____ At Close of Business_____20____

To

The undersigned, for the purpose of procuring and establishing credit from time to time with you and to induce you to permit the undersigned to become indebted to you on notes, endorsements, guarantees, overdrafts or otherwise, furnishes the following (or in lieu thereof the attached, which is the most recent statement prepared by or for the undersigned) as being a full, true and correct statement of the financial condition of the undersigned on the date indicated, and agrees to notify you immediately of the extent and character of any material changes in said financial condition, and also agrees that if the undersigned or any endorser or guarantor of any of the obligations of the undersigned, at any time fails in business or becomes insolvent, or commits an act of bankruptcy, or if any deposit account of the undersigned with you, or any other property of the undersigned held by you, be attempted to be obtained or held by writ of execution, garnishment, attachment or other legal process, or if any of the representations made below prove to be untrue, or if the undersigned fails to notify you of any material change, as above agreed, or if the business, or any interest therein of the undersigned is sold, then and in such case, at your option, all of the obligations of the undersigned to you, or held by you, shall immediately become due and payable, without demand or notice. This statement shall be construed by you to be a continuing statement of the condition of the undersigned, and a new and original statement of all assets and liabilities upon each and every transaction in and by which the undersigned hereafter becomes indebted to you, until the undersigned advises in writing to the contrary.

ASSETS	DOLLARS	CENTS	LIABILITIES	DOLLARS	CENTS
Cash In_____			Notes Payable to Banks_____		
(Name of Bank)					
Cash on Hand_____			Notes Payable and Trade Acceptances for Merchandise_____		
Notes Receivable and					
Trade Acceptance (Includes $_____Past Due)			Notes Payable to Others_____		
Accounts Receivable--$_____Less Reserves $_____			Accounts Payable (Includes $_____Past Due)____		
			Due to Partners, Employees		
Customer's . . . (Includes $_____Past Due)			Relatives, Officers, Stockholders or Allied Companies___		
			Chattel Mortgages and Contracts Payable (Describe		
Merchandise—Finished—How Valued_____			Monthly Payments) . . . . . $_____		
Merchandise—Unfinished—How Valued_____			Federal and State Income Tax_____		
Merchandise—Raw Material—How Valued_____			Accrued Liabilities (Interest, Wages, Taxes, Etc.)_____		
Supplies on Hand_____			Portion of Long Term Debt Due Within One Year_____		
Stocks and Bonds—Listed (See Schedule B)_____					
TOTAL CURRENT ASSETS			**TOTAL CURRENT LIABILITIES**		
Real Estate—Less Depreciation of: $_____Net			Liens on Real Estate (See Schedule A) $_____		
(See Schedule A)					
			Less Current Portion Included Avove $_____Net		
Machinery and Fixtures—					
Less Depreciation of: $_____Net					
Automobiles and Trucks—					
Less Depreciation of: $_____Net			Capital Stock—Preferred_____		
Stocks and Bonds—Unlisted (See Schedule B)_____			Capital Stock—Common_____		
Due from Partners, Employees,					
Relatives, Officers, Stockholders or Allied Companies____			Surplus—Paid In_____		
Cash Value Life Insurance_____			Surplus—Earned and Undivided Profit_____		
Other Assets (Describe_____			Net Worth (If Not Incorporated)_____		
TOTAL			TOTAL		

**PROFIT AND LOSS STATEMENT
FOR THE PERIOD FROM_____TO_____**

CONTINGENT LIABILITIES (Not Included Above)

Net Sales (After Returned Sales and Allowances)_____			As Guarantor or Endorser_____		
Cost of Sales:			Accounts, Notes, or Trade		
			Acceptance Discounted or Pledged_____		
Beginning Inventory			Surety On Bonds or Other Continent Liability_____		
Purchases (or cost of goods mfd.)			Letters of Credit_____		
TOTAL			Judgments Unsatisfied or Suits Pending_____		
Less: Closing Inventory			Merchandise Commitments and Unfinished Contracts_____		
Gross Profit on Sales			Merchandise Held On Consignment From Others_____		
			Unsatisfied Tax Liens or Notices From the Federal or		
			State Governments of Intention to Assess Such Liens___		
Operating Expenses:			**RECONCILEMENT OF NET WORTH OR EARNED SURPLUS**		
Salaries—Officers or Partners			Net Worth or Earned Surplus at Beginning of Period_____		
Salaries and Wages—Other			Add Net Profit or Deduct Net Loss_____		
Rent					
Depreciation			Total_____		
Bad Debts			Other Additions (Describe)_____		
Advertising			Total_____		
Interest			Less: Withdrawals or Dividends		
Taxes—Other Than Income			Other Deductions (Explain)_____		
Insurance			Total Deductions_____		
Other Expenses			Net Worth or Capital Funds on This Financial Statement___		
Net Profit from Operations			**DETAIL OF INVENTORY**		
Other Income					
Less Other Expenses			Is Inventory Figure Actual or Estimated?_____		
Net Profit Before Income Tax			By whom Taken or Estimated_____When?_____		
Federal and State Income Tax			Buy Principally From_____		
Net Profit or Loss			Average Terms of Purchase_____Sale_____		
(To Net Worth or Earned Surplus)			Time of Year Inventory Maximum_____Minimum_____		

Business Financial Statement

Business Financial Statement

INDIVIDUAL, PARTNERSHIP, OR CORPORATION – Page 2

SCHEDULE A   LIST OF REAL ESTATE AND IMPROVEMENTS WITH ENCUMBRANCES THEREON

Description, Street Number, Location	Title in Names of	BOOK VALUE		MORTGAGES OR LIENS		Terms of Payment	Holder of Lien
		LAND	IMPROVEMENTS	MATURITY	AMOUNT		
		$	$		$	$	
TOTALS		$	$		$	$	

SCHEDULE B   STOCKS & BONDS: Describe Fully. Use Supplemental Sheet if Necessary. Indicate if Stocks Are Common or Preferred. Give Interest Rate and Maturity of Bonds.

NO. OF SHARES AMT. OF BONDS	NAME AND ISSUE (DESCRIBE FULLY)	BOOK VALUE		MARKET VALUE	
		LISTED	UNLISTED	PRICE	VALUE
		$	$		$
	TOTALS	$	$		$

SCHEDULE C   Complete if Statement is for an Individual or Sole Proprietorship

Age _____ Number of Years in Present Business _____   Date of Filing Fictitious Trade Style _____

What Property Listed in This Statement is in Joint Tenancy? _____   Name of Other Party _____

What Property Listed in This Statement is Community Property? _____   Name of Other Party _____

With What Other Businesses Are You Connected? _____   Have You Filed Homestead? _____

Do You Deal With or Carry Accounts With Stockbrokers? _____ Amount $ _____   Name of Firm _____

SCHEDULE D   Complete if Statement is of a Partnership

NAME OF PARTNERS (indicate special partners)	Age	Amount Contributed	Outside Net Worth	Other Business Connections
		$	$	

Date of Organization _____   Limited or General? _____   Terminates _____

If Operating Under Fictitious Trade Style, Give Date of Filing _____

SCHEDULE E   Complete if Statement is of a Corporation

	AUTHORIZED	Par Value	OUTSTANDING			ISSUED FOR
			SHARES	AMOUNT	CASH	
Common Stock _____	$	$		$	$	
Preferred Stock _____	$	$		$	$	
Bonds—Total Issue _____	$	$		$	$	
Date Incorporated _____			Under Laws of State of _____			

Officers	Age	Shares Owned		Directors and Principal Stockholders	Shares Owned	
		COMMON	PREFERRED		COMMON	PREFERRED
President _____				Director _____		
Vice President _____				Director _____		
Secretary _____				Director _____		
Treasurer _____						

SCHEDULE F   Complete in ALL Cases   INSURANCE

Are Your Books Audited by Outside Accountants? _____ None _____

Date of Last Audit _____   To What Date Has the U.S. Internal Revenue Department Examined Your Books? _____

Are You Borrowing From Any Other Branch of This Bank? _____ Which? _____

Are You Applying for Credit At Any Other Source? _____ Where? _____

Have You Ever Failed In Business? _____ If So, attach a Complete Explanation and State Basis of Settlement With Creditors _____

Lease Has _____ Years to Run With Monthly Rental of $ _____

Merchandise _____ $ _____

Machinery & Fixtures _____ $ _____

Buildings _____ $ _____

Earthquake _____ $ _____

Is Extended Coverage Endorsement Included? _____

Do You Carry Workmen's Compensation Insurance? _____

Automobiles and Trucks:

Public Liability $ _____ M/$ _____ M

Collision _____ $ _____

Property Damage _____ $ _____

Life Insurance _____ $ _____

Name of Beneficiary _____

STATEMENT OF BANK OFFICER:
   Insofar as our records reveal, this Financial Statement is accurate and true. The foregoing Statement is (a copy of) the original signed by the maker, in the credit files as of of this Bank.

_____ Assistant Cashier-Manager

The undersigned solemnly declares and certifies that the above statement (or in lieu thereof, the attached statement, as the case may be) and supporting schedules, both printed and written, give a full, true, and correct statement of the financial condition of the under-Signed as of the date indicated.

Signature _____

By _____

(Title, If Corporation)

Personal Financial Statement

Personal Financial Statement

(DO NOT USE FOR BUSINESS FINANCIAL STATEMENT)

As of _____ 20_____

FINANCIAL STATEMENT OF

Name_____

Address_____

Received At_____Branch

Employed by_____

Position_____Age_____Spouse_____
Name of

If Employed Less Than
1 year, Previous Employer_____

The undersigned, for the purpose of procuring and establishing credit from time to time with you and to induce you to permit the undersigned to become indebted to you on notes, endorsements, guarantees, overdrafts or otherwise, furnishes the following (or in lieu thereof the attached, which is the most recent statement prepared by or for the undersigned) as being a full, true and correct statement of the financial condition of the undersigned on the date indicated, and agrees to notify you immediately of the extent and character of any material changes in said financial condition, and also agrees that if the undersigned or any endorser or guarantor of any of the obligations of the undersigned, at any time fails in business or becomes insolvent, or commits an act of bankruptcy, or dies, or if a writ of attachment, garnishment, execution or other legal process be issued against property of the undersigned or if any assessment for taxes against the undersigned, other than taxes on real property, is made by the federal or state government or any department thereof, or if any of the representations made below prove to be untrue, or if the undersigned fails to notify you of any material change as above agreed, or if such change occurs, or if the business, or any interest therein, of the undersigned is sold, then and in such case, all of the obligations of the undersigned to you or held by you shall immediately be due and payable, without demand or notice. This statement shall be construed by you to be a continuing statement of the condition of the undersigned, and a new and original statement of all assets and liabilities upon each and every transaction in and by which the undersigned hereafter becomes indebted to you, until the undersigned advises in writing to the contrary.

ASSETS	DOLLARS	CENTS	LIABILITIES	DOLLARS	CENTS
Cash In B of_____ (Branch)			Notes Payable B of_____ (Branch)		
Cash on Hand_____ (Other – give name)			Notes Payable_____ (Other)		
Accounts Receivable-Good_____			Accounts Payable_____		
Stocks and Bonds (Schedule B) _____			Taxes Payable_____		
Notes Receivable-Good_____			Contracts Payable_____ (To Whom)		
Cash Surrender Value Life Insurance_____			Contracts Payable_____ (To Whom)		
Autos_____ (Year-Make) (Year-Make)			Real Estate indebtedness (Schedule A)_____		
Real Estate (Schedule A)_____			Other Liabilities (describe)_____		
Other Assets (describe)			1._____		
1._____			2._____		
2._____			3._____		
3._____			4._____		
4._____			TOTAL LIABILITIES		
5._____			NET WORTH		
TOTAL ASSETS			TOTAL		

ANNUAL INCOME			and	ANNUAL EXPENDITURES (Excluding Ordinary living expenses)		
Salary_____				Real Estate payment (s) _____		
Salary (wife or husband) _____				Rent_____		
Securities Income_____				Income Taxes _____		
Rentals _____				Insurance Premiums _____		
Other (describe)				Property Taxes _____		
1._____				Other (describe-include installment payments other than real estate)		
2._____				1._____		
3._____				2._____		
4._____				3._____		
5._____						
TOTAL INCOME				TOTAL EXPENDITURES		

LESS TOTAL EXPENDITURES		
NET CASH INCOME (exclusive of ordinary expenses) _____		

Personal Financial Statement

Personal Financial Statement

Page 2

What assets in this statement are in joint tenancy? _____   Name of other Party_____

Have you filed homestead? _____

Are you a guarantor on anyone's debt? _____   If so, give details _____

Are any encumbered assets or debts secured except as indicated? _____   If so, please itemize by debt and security _____

_____

Do you have any other business connections? _____   If so, give details _____

Are there any suits or judgments against you? _____

Have you gone through bankruptcy or compromised a debt? _____

Have you made a will? _____   Number of dependents _____

SCHEDULE A — REAL ESTATE

Location and type of Improvement	Title in Name of	Estimated Value	Amount Owing	To Whom Payable
		$	$	

SCHEDULE B — STOCKS AND BONDS

Number of Shares Amount of Bonds	Description	Current Market on Listed	Estimated Value on Unlisted
		$	$

If additional space is needed for Schedule A and/or Schedule B, list on separate sheet and attach.

INSURANCE

Life Insurance $_____   Name of Company _____   Beneficiary_____

Automobile Insurance:

Public Liability →   yes ☐   no ☐   Property Damage → yes ☐   no ☐

Comprehensive personal Liability →   yes ☐   no ☐

STATEMENT OF BANK OFFICER:
Insofar as our records reveal, this Financial Statement is accurate and true. The foregoing Statement is (a copy of) the original signed by the maker, in the credit files of this Bank.

_____Assistant Cashier-Manager

The undersigned solemnly declares and certifies that the above statement (or in lieu thereof, the attached statement, as the case may be) and supporting schedules, both printed and written, give a full, true, and correct statement of the financial condition of the undersigned as of the date indicated.

_____   _____
Date signed   Signature

THIS IS THE BEGINNING OF THE SECTION ON PRO FORMA FINANCIAL STATEMENTS

PRO FORMA CASH FLOW STATEMENT OR BUDGET

What Is a Cash Flow Statement?

A third or more of today's businesses fail due to a lack of cash flow. You can avoid this trap with careful planning of cash expenditures. The cash flow statement (or budget) projects what your business needs in terms of dollars for a specific period of time. It is a pro forma (or projected) statement used for internal planning and estimates how much money will flow into and out of a business during a designated period of time, usually the coming tax year. Your profit at the end of the year will depend on the proper balance between cash inflow and outflow.

The cash flow statement identifies when cash is expected to be received and when it must be spent to pay bills and debts. It also allows the manager to identify where the necessary cash will come from. This statement deals only with actual cash transactions and not with depreciation and amortization of goodwill or other noncash expense items. Expenses are paid from cash on hand, sale of assets, revenues from sales and services, interest earned on investments, money borrowed from a lender, and influx of capital in exchange for equity in the company. If your business will require $100,000 to pay its expenses and $50,000 to support the owners, you will need at least an equal amount of money flowing into the business just to remain at a status quo. Anything less will eventually lead to an inability to pay your creditors or yourself.

The availability or nonavailability of cash when it is needed for expenditures gets to the heart of the matter. By careful planning, you must try to project not only how much cash will have to flow into and out of your business, but also when it will need to flow in and out. A business may be able to plan for gross receipts that will cover its needs. However, if those sales do not take place in time to pay the expenses, a business will soon be history unless you plan ahead for other sources of cash to tide the business over until the revenues are realized.

Time period. The cash flow statement should be prepared on a monthly basis for the next tax year. To be effective, it must be analyzed and revised quarterly to reflect your actual performance.

PREPARING YOUR CASH FLOW STATEMENT

Before preparing your budget, it might be useful to compile individual projections and budgets. They might be as follows:

- Revenue projections (product and service)

- Inventory purchases

- Variable (selling) expense budget (with marketing budget)

- Fixed (administrative) expense budget

Preplanning Worksheets

Because the cash flow statement deals with cash inflow and cash outflow, the first step in planning can be best accomplished by preparing two worksheets.

1. **Cash to Be Paid Out worksheet.** Cash flowing out of your business; identifies categories of expenses and obligations and the projected amount of cash needed in each category. Use the information from your individual budgets (inventory purchases, variable expenses, fixed expenses, owner draws, etc.). These expenditures are not always easy to estimate. If you are a new business, it will be necessary for you to research your market. If you are an existing business, you will be able to combine information from your past financial statements (such as your P&L) with trends in your particular industry.

2. **Sources of Cash worksheet.** Cash flowing into your business; used to estimate how much cash will be available from what sources. To complete this worksheet, you will have to look at cash on hand, projected revenues, assets that can be liquidated, possible lenders or investors, and owner equity to be contributed. This worksheet will force you to take a look at any existing possibilities for increasing available cash.

Sample worksheets. On the next few pages, you will find examples of the two worksheets (filled in for the fictitious company, ABC Company) with explanatory material to help you better understand how they are developed. (Blank forms for your use are located in Appendix II.) Note that the Cash to Be Paid Out worksheet shows a need for $131,000. It is necessary in projecting Sources of Cash to account for $131,000 without the projected sales, because payment is not expected to be received until November or December (too late for cash needs January through October). Next year, those revenues will be reflected in cash on hand or other salable assets.

Note: Be sure to figure all estimates on both of your worksheets for the same period of time (annually, quarterly, or monthly).

EXPLANATION OF CATEGORIES
CASH TO BE PAID OUT WORKSHEET

1. **Start-up costs**

   These are the costs incurred by you to get your business underway. They are generally one-time expenses and are capitalized for tax purposes.

2. **Inventory purchases**

   Cash to be spent during the period on items intended for resale. If you purchase manufactured products, this includes the cash outlay for those purchases. If you are the manufacturer, include labor and materials on units to be produced.

3. **Variable expenses (selling expenses)**

   These are the costs of all expenses that will relate directly to your product or service (other than manufacturing costs or purchase price of inventory).

4. **Fixed expenses (administrative expenses)**

   Include all expected costs of office overhead. If certain bills must be paid ahead, include total cash outlay even if covered period extends into the next year.

5. **Assets (long-term purchases)**

   These are the capital assets that will be depreciated over a period of years (land, buildings, vehicles, equipment). Determine how you intend to pay for them and include all cash to be paid out in the current period.

6. **Liabilities**

   What are the payments you expect to have to make to retire any debts or loans? Do you have any Accounts Payable as you begin the new year? You will need to determine the amount of cash outlay that needs to be paid in the current year. If you have a car loan for $20,000 and you pay $500 per month for 12 months, you will have a cash outlay of $6,000 for the coming year.

7. **Owner equity**

   This item is frequently overlooked in planning cash flow. If you, as the business owner, will need a draw of $2,000 per month to live on, you must plan for $24,000 cash flowing out of your business. Failure to plan for it will result in a cash flow shortage and may cause your business to fail.

   Note: Be sure to use the same time period throughout your worksheet.

Cash to Be Paid Out Worksheet

Business Name: ABC Company   Time Period Covered: Jan 1–Dec 31, 2005

1. START-UP COSTS		1,450
Business license	30	
Corporation filing	500	
Legal fees	920	
Other start-up costs:		
a.		
b.		
c.		
d.		
2. INVENTORY PURCHASES		
Cash out for goods intended for resale		32,000
3. VARIABLE EXPENSES (SELLING)		
Advertising/marketing	8,000	
Freight	2,500	
Fulfillment of orders	800	
Packaging costs	0	
Sales salaries/wages/commissions	14,000	
Travel	1,550	
Miscellaneous	300	
TOTAL SELLING EXPENSES		27,150
4. FIXED EXPENSES (ADMINISTRATION)		
Financial administration	1,800	
Insurance	900	
Licenses and permits	100	
Office salaries	16,300	
Rent expense	8,600	
Utilities	2,400	
Miscellaneous	400	
TOTAL ADMINISTRATIVE EXPENSE		30,500
5. ASSETS (LONG-TERM PURCHASES)		6,000
Cash to be paid out in current period		
6. LIABILITIES		
Cash outlay for retiring debts, loans,		9,900
and/or accounts payable		
7. OWNER EQUITY		
Cash to be withdrawn by owner		24,000
TOTAL CASH TO BE PAID OUT		**$131,000**

EXPLANATION OF CATEGORIES
SOURCES OF CASH WORKSHEET

1. **Cash on hand**

   Money that you have on hand. Be sure to include petty cash and monies not yet deposited.

2. **Sales (revenues)**

   This includes projected revenues from the sale of your product and/or service. If payment is not expected during the time period covered by this worksheet, do not include that portion of your sales. Think about the projected timing of sales. If receipts will be delayed beyond the time when a large amount of cash is needed, make a notation to that effect and take it into consideration when determining the need for temporary financing. Include deposits you require on expected sales or services. When figuring collections on Accounts Receivable, you will have to project the percentage of invoices that will be lost to bad debts and subtract it from your Accounts Receivable total.

3. **Miscellaneous income**

   Do you, or will you, have any monies out on loan or deposited in accounts that will yield interest income during the period in question?

4. **Sale of long-term assets**

   If you are expecting to sell any of your fixed assets such as land, buildings, vehicles, machinery, equipment, etc., be sure to include only the cash you will receive during the current period.

Important. At this point in your worksheet, add up all sources of cash. If you do not have an amount equal to your projected needs, you will have to plan sources of cash covered under numbers five and six below.

5. **Liabilities**

   This figure represents the amount you will be able to borrow from lending institutions such as banks, finance companies, the SBA, etc. Be reasonable about what you think you can borrow. If you have no collateral, have no business plan, or have a poor financial history, you will find it difficult, if not impossible, to find a lender. This source of cash requires preplanning.

6. **Equity**

   Sources of equity come from owner investments, contributed capital, sale of stock, or venture capital. Do you anticipate availability of personal funds? Does your business have potential for growth that might interest a venture capitalist? Be sure to be realistic. You cannot sell stock (or equity) to a nonexistent investor.

Sources of Cash Worksheet

Business Name: ABC Company

Time Period Covered: From January 1, 2002 to December 31, 2005

---

1. CASH ON HAND | $20,000

2. SALES (REVENUES)

Product sales income* | 90,000
Most of this sales revenue will not be received until Nov. or Dec.

Services income | 22,000

Deposits on sales or services | 0

Collections on accounts receivable | 3,000

3. MISCELLANEOUS INCOME

Interest income | 1,000

Payments to be received on loans | 0

4. SALE OF LONG-TERM ASSETS | 0

5. LIABILITIES | 40,000

Loan funds (to be received during current period; from banks,
through the SBA, or from other lending institutions)

6. EQUITY

Owner investments (sole proprietors/partners) | 10,000

Contributed capital (corporation) |

Sale of stock (corporation) |

Venture capital | 35,000

TOTAL CASH AVAILABLE

A. Without product sales = | **$131,000**

B. With product sales = | **$221,000**

Using the Worksheets

When you have completed the worksheets, you will have estimated how much cash will be needed for the year. You also know what sources are available. Now you will break each one-year projection into monthly segments, predicting when the cash will be needed to make the financial year flow smoothly.

Project sales on a monthly basis based on payment of invoices, demand for your particular product or service, and ability to fill that demand. Figure the cost-of-goods, fixed, and variable expenses in monthly increments. Most will vary. When do you plan to purchase the most inventory? What months will require the most advertising? Are you expecting a rent or insurance increase? When will commissions be due on expected sales? Determine your depreciable assets needs. How much will the payments be and when will they begin? Fill in as much of the cash flow statement as you can using any projections that you can comfortably determine.

Example. Follow ABC Company through January and February.

January Projections

1. ABC projects a beginning cash balance of $20,000.
2. Cash receipts. Product manufacturing will not be completed until February, so there will be no sales. However, service income of $4,000 is projected.
3. Interest on the $20,000 will amount to about $100 at current rate.
4. There are no long-term assets to sell. Enter a zero.
5. Adding 1, 2, 3, and 4 the Total Cash Available will be $24,100.
6. Cash payments. Product will be available from manufacturer in February and payment will not be due until pickup. However, there will be prototype costs of $5,000.
7. Variable (selling) expenses. Estimated at $1,140.
8. Fixed (administrative) expenses. Estimated at $1,215.
9. Interest expense. No outstanding debts or loans. Enter zero.
10. Taxes. No profit previous quarter. No estimated taxes would be due.
11. Payments on long-term assets. ABC plans to purchase office equipment to be paid in full at the time of purchase $1,139.
12. Loan repayments. No loans have been received. Enter zero.
13. Owner draws. Owner will need $2,000 for living expenses.
14. Total cash paid out. Add 6 through 13. Total $10,494.
15. Cash balance. Subtract Cash Paid Out from Total Cash Available ($13,606).
16. Loans to be received. Being aware of the $30,000 to be paid to the manufacturer in February, a loan of $40,000 is anticipated to increase Cash Available. (This requires advance planning.)
17. Equity deposit. Owner plans to add $5,000 from personal CD.
18. Ending cash balance. Adding 15, 16, and 17, the result is $58,606.

February Projections

1. February Beginning Cash Balance. January Ending Cash Balance ($58,606).
2. Cash receipts. Still no sales, but service income is $2,000.
3. Interest income. Projected at about $120.
4. Sale of long-term assets. None. Enter zero.
5. Total cash available. Add 1, 2, 3, and 4. The result is $60,726.
6. Cash payments. $30,000 due to manufacturer, $400 due on packaging design.
7. Continue as in January. Don't forget to include payments on your loan.

Partial Cash Flow Statement
for ABC Company

	Jan	Feb
BEGINNING CASH BALANCE	20,000	58,606
CASH RECEIPTS		
A. Sales/revenues	4,000	2,000
B. Receivables	0	0
C. Interest income	100	120
D. Sale of long-term assets	0	0
TOTAL CASH AVAILABLE	24,100	60,726
CASH PAYMENTS		
A. Cost of goods to be sold		
1. Purchases	0	30,000
2. Material	0	0
3. Labor	5,000	400
Total Cost of Goods	5,000	30,400
B. Variable Expenses (Selling)		
1. Advertising	300	
2. Freight	120	
3. Fulfillment of orders	0	
4. Packaging costs	270	
5. Sales/salaries	0	
6. Travel	285	
7. Miscellaneous selling expense	165	
Total Variable Expenses	1,140	
C. Fixed Expenses (Administrative)		
1. Financial administration	80	
2. Insurance	125	
3. License/permits	200	
4. Office salaries	500	
5. Rent expenses	110	
6. Utilities	200	
7. Miscellaneous administrative expense	0	
Total Fixed Expenses	1,215	
D. Interest expense	0	
E. Federal income tax	0	
F. Other uses	0	
G. Long-term asset payments	1,139	
H. Loan payments	0	
I. Owner draws	2,000	
TOTAL CASH PAID OUT	10,494	
CASH BALANCE/DEFICIENCY	13,606	
Loans to be received	40,000	
Equity deposits	5,000	
ENDING CASH BALANCE	58,606	

CONTINUE as in JANUARY

COMPLETING YOUR PRO FORMA CASH FLOW STATEMENT

This page contains instructions for completing the cash flow statement on the next page. A blank form for your own projections can be found in Appendix II.

- **Vertical columns** are divided by month and followed by a 6-month and 12-month "Total" column.

- **Horizontal positions** contain all sources of cash and cash to be paid out. Figures are retrieved from the two previous worksheets and from individual budgets.

To Project Figures for Each Month

Figures are projected for each month, reflecting the flow of cash in and out of your business for a one-year period. Begin with the first month of your business cycle and proceed as follows:

1. Project the Beginning Cash Balance. Enter under "January."

2. Project the Cash Receipts for January. Apportion your total year's revenues throughout the 12 months. Try to weight revenues as closely as you can to a realistic selling cycle for your industry.

3. Add Beginning Cash Balance and Cash Receipts to determine Total Cash Available.

4. Project cash payments to be made for cost of goods to be sold (inventory that you will purchase or manufacture). Apportion your total inventory budget throughout the year, being sure you are providing for levels of inventory that will fulfill your needs for sales projected.

5. Customize your Variable and Fixed Expense categories to match your business.

6. Project Variable, Fixed, and Interest Expenses for January. Fill out any that you can for 12 months.

7. Project cash to be paid out on Taxes, Long-Term Assets, Loan Repayments, and Owner Draws.

8. Calculate Total Cash Paid Out (Total of Cost of Goods to Be Sold, Variable, Fixed, Interest, Taxes, Long-Term Asset Payments, Loan Repayments, and Owner Draws).

9. Subtract Total Cash Paid Out from Total Cash Available. The result is entered under "Cash Balance/Deficiency." Be sure to bracket this figure if the result is a negative to avoid errors.

10. Look at Ending Cash Balance for each month and project Loans to be Received and Equity Deposits to be made. Add to Cash Balance/Deficiency to arrive at Ending Cash Balance each month.

11. Ending Cash Balance for January is carried forward to February's Beginning Cash Balance (as throughout the spreadsheet, each month's ending balance is the next month's beginning balance).

12. Go to February and input any numbers that are still needed to complete that month. The process is repeated until December is completed.

To Complete the Total Column

1. The Beginning Cash Balance for January is entered in the first space of the 6-month and 12-month "Total" column.

2. The monthly figures for each category (except Beginning Cash Balance, Total Cash Available, Cash Balance/Deficiency, and Ending Cash Balance) are added horizontally and the result entered in the corresponding Total category.

3. The 6- and 12-month Total column are then computed in the same manner as each of the individual months. If you have been accurate in your computations, the December Ending Cash Balance will be exactly the same as the Total Ending Cash Balance.

Note: If your business is new, you will have to base your projections solely on market research and industry trends. If you have an established business, you will also use your financial statements from previous years.

Pro Forma Cash Flow Statement for ABC Company

Year: 2005	Jan	Feb	Mar	Apr	May	Jun	6-MONTH PERIOD	Jul	Aug	Sep	Oct	Nov	Dec	12-MONTH PERIOD
BEGINNING CASH BALANCE	10,360	72,840	54,488	60,346	65,125	79,253	10,360	81,341	71,401	68,974	55,974	54,718	59,032	10,360
CASH RECEIPTS														
A. Sales/revenues	14,000	9,500	9,500	15,000	18,000	12,000	78,000	9,000	8,000	9,500	16,000	28,000	43,000	191,500
B. Receivables	400	400	300	500	450	300	2,475	500	750	650	600	1,250	8,000	14,225
C. Interest income	234	240	260	158	172	195	1,259	213	303	300	417	406	413	3,311
D. Sale of long-term assets	2,000	0	4,000	0	0	0	6,000	0	0	0	0	0	0	6,000
TOTAL CASH AVAILABLE	26,994	82,980	68,548	76,004	83,747	91,873	98,094	91,054	80,454	79,424	72,991	84,374	110,445	225,396
CASH PAYMENTS														
A. Cost of goods to be sold														
1. Purchases	800	16,500	3,700	200	200	300	21,700	9,000	430	540	6,700	14,000	12,000	64,370
2. Material	2,000	1,430	200	300	250	200	4,380	359	750	5,000	400	300	350	11,539
3. Labor	4,000	2,800	400	600	500	450	8,750	600	1,500	8,000	750	500	540	20,640
Total cost of goods	6,800	20,730	4,300	1,100	950	950	34,830	9,959	2,680	13,540	7,850	14,800	12,890	96,549
B. Variable expenses														
1. Advertising	900	300	900	250	300	700	3,350	350	300	640	1,300	1,200	1,400	8,540
2. Freight	75	75	75	75	180	70	550	75	75	90	180	300	560	1,830
3. Fulfillment of orders	300	300	300	400	350	300	1,950	300	280	325	450	600	975	4,880
4. Packaging costs	2,100	0	0	0	600	0	2,700	0	200	230	0	0	0	3,130
5. Sales/salaries	1,400	900	1,300	1,400	1,100	900	7,000	1,400	1,400	1,400	1,400	1,400	1,400	15,400
6. Travel	0	500	700	0	0	400	1,600	0	540	25	80	0	0	2,245
7. Misc. variable expense	100	100	100	100	100	100	600	100	100	100	100	100	100	1,200
Total variable expenses	4,875	2,175	3,375	2,225	2,630	2,470	17,750	2,225	2,895	2,810	3,510	3,600	4,435	37,225
C. Fixed expenses														
1. Financial administration	75	75	75	475	75	75	850	75	75	75	75	75	75	1,300
2. Insurance	1,564	0	0	0	0	0	1,564	1,563	0	0	0	0	0	3,127
3. License/permits	240	0	0	0	0	0	240	0	0	0	0	0	125	365
4. Office salaries	1,400	1,400	1,400	1,400	1,400	1,400	8,400	1,400	1,400	1,400	1,400	1,400	1,400	16,800
5. Rent expenses	700	700	700	700	700	700	4,200	700	700	700	700	700	700	8,400
6. Utilities	200	200	140	120	80	80	820	75	75	75	90	120	155	1,410
7. Misc. fixed expense	100	100	100	100	100	100	600	100	100	100	100	100	100	1,200
Total fixed expenses	4,279	2,475	2,415	2,795	2,355	2,355	16,674	3,913	2,350	2,350	2,365	2,395	2,555	32,602
D. Interest expense	0	0	0	234	233	232	699	231	230	225	223	222	220	2,050
E. Federal income tax	1,200	1	1	1,200	1	1,200	3,603	0	0	1,200	0	0	0	4,803
F. Other uses	0	0	0	0	0	0	0	0	0	0	0	0	0	0
G. Long-term asset payments	0	0	0	214	214	214	642	214	214	214	214	214	214	1,926
H. Loan payments	0	1,111	1,111	1,111	1,111	1,111	5,555	1,111	1,111	1,111	1,111	1,111	1,111	12,221
I. Owner draws	2,000	2,000	2,000	2,000	2,000	2,000	12,000	2,000	2,000	2,000	3,000	3,000	3,000	27,000
TOTAL CASH PAID OUT	19,154	28,492	13,202	10,879	9,494	10,532	91,753	19,653	11,480	23,450	18,273	25,342	24,425	214,376
CASH BALANCE/DEFICIENCY	7,840	54,488	55,346	65,125	74,253	81,341	6,341	71,401	68,974	55,974	54,718	59,032	86,020	11,020
LOANS TO BE RECEIVED	65,000	0	0	0	0	0	65,000	0	0	0	0	0	0	65,000
EQUITY DEPOSITS	0	0	5,000	0	5,000	0	10,000	0	0	0	0	0	0	10,000
ENDING CASH BALANCE	72,840	54,488	60,346	65,125	79,253	81,341	81,341	71,401	68,974	55,974	54,718	59,032	86,020	86,020

QUARTERLY BUDGET ANALYSIS

What Is a Quarterly Budget Analysis?

Your cash flow statement is of no value to you as a business owner unless there is some means to evaluate the actual performance of your company and measure it against your projections. A Quarterly Budget Analysis is used to compare projected cash flow (or budget) with your business's actual performance. Its purpose is to show you whether you are operating within your projections and to help you maintain control of all phases of your business operations. When your analysis shows that you are over or under budget in any area, it will be necessary to determine the reason for the deviation and implement changes that will enable you to get back on track.

Example. If you budgeted $1,000 in advertising funds for the first quarter and you spent $1,600, the first thing you should do is look to see if the increased advertising resulted in increased sales. If sales were over projections by an amount equal to or more than the $600, your budget will still be in good shape. If not, you will have to find expenses in your budget that can be revised to make up the deficit. You might be able to take a smaller draw for yourself or spend less on travel. You might even be able to increase your profits by adding a new product or service.

Format and Sources of Information

The Quarterly Budget Analysis needs the following seven columns. Information sources are listed for each column of entries. A blank form is located in Appendix II for your use.

1. **Budget Item.** The list of budget items is taken from headings on the Pro Forma Cash Flow Statement. All items in your budget should be listed.

2. **Budget this Quarter.** Fill in the amount budgeted for current quarter from your Pro Forma Cash Flow Statement.

3. **Actual this Quarter.** Fill in your actual income and expenditures for the quarter. These amounts are found in your Profit & Loss Statements, Fixed Assets Log, Owner Draw and Deposit Record, and Loan Repayment Records.

4. **Variation this Quarter.** Amount spent or received over or under budget. Subtract actual income and expenditures from amounts budgeted to arrive at variation.

5. **Year-to-Date Budget.** Amount budgeted from beginning of year through and including current quarter (from Cash Flow Statement).

6. **Actual Year-to-Date.** Actual amount spent or received from beginning of year through current quarter. Again, go to your General Records.

7. **Variation Year-to-Date.** Subtract amount spent or received year-to-date from the amount budgeted year-to-date and enter the difference.

Note: You will not have any information to input into columns 3, 4, 5, 6, and 7 until you have been in business for at least one quarter. To keep from running out of operating capital early in the year, make your projections, analyze quarterly, and revise your budget accordingly.

All items contained in the Budget are listed on this form. The second column is the amount budgeted for the current quarter. By subtracting the amount actually spent, you will arrive at the variation for the quarter. The last three columns are for year-to-date figures. If you analyze at the end of the 3rd quarter, figures will represent the first nine months of your tax year.

Making Calculations: When you calculate variations, the amounts are preceded by either a plus (+) or a minus (–), depending on whether the category is a revenue or an expense. If the actual amount is greater than the amount budgeted, (1) Revenue categories will represent the variation as a positive (+). (2) Expense categories will represent the variation as a negative (–).

Quarterly Budget Analysis

Business Name: ABC Company **For the Quarter Ending: September 30, 2004**

BUDGET ITEM	THIS QUARTER			YEAR-TO-DATE		
	Budget	Actual	Variation	Budget	Actual	Variation
SALES REVENUES	145,000	150,000	5,000	400,000	410,000	10,000
Less cost of goods	80,000	82,500	(2,500)	240,000	243,000	(3,000)
GROSS PROFITS	65,000	67,500	2,500	160,000	167,000	7,000
VARIABLE EXPENSES						
1. Advertising/marketing	3,000	3,400	(400)	6,000	6,200	(200)
2. Freight	6,500	5,750	750	16,500	16,350	150
3. Fulfillment of orders	1,400	950	450	3,800	4,100	(300)
4. Packaging	750	990	(240)	2,200	2,300	(100)
5. Salaries/commissions	6,250	6,250	0	18,750	18,750	0
6. Travel	500	160	340	1,500	1,230	270
7. Miscellaneous	0	475	(475)	0	675	(675)
FIXED EXPENSES						
1. Financial/administrative	1,500	1,500	0	4,500	4,700	(200)
2. Insurance	2,250	2,250	0	6,750	6,750	0
3. Licenses/permits	1,000	600	400	3,500	3,400	100
4. Office salaries	1,500	1,500	0	4,500	4,500	0
5. Rent	3,500	3,500	0	10,500	10,500	0
6. Utilities	750	990	(240)	2,250	2,570	(320)
7. Miscellaneous	0	60	(60)	0	80	(80)
NET INCOME FROM OPERATIONS	36,100	39,125	3,025	79,250	84,895	5,645
INTEREST INCOME	1,250	1,125	(125)	3,750	3,700	(50)
INTEREST EXPENSE	1,500	1,425	75	4,500	4,500	0
NET PROFIT (Pretax)	35,850	38,825	2,975	78,500	84,095	5,595
TAXES	8,500	9,500	(1,000)	25,500	28,500	(3,000)
NET PROFIT (After Tax)	27,350	29,325	1,975	53,000	55,595	2,595

NON-INCOME STATEMENT ITEMS

	Budget	Actual	Variation	Budget	Actual	Variation
1. Long-term asset repayments	2,400	3,400	(1,000)	7,200	8,200	(1,000)
2. Loan repayments	3,400	3,400	0	8,800	8,800	0
3. Owner draws	6,000	6,900	(900)	18,000	18,900	(900)

BUDGET DEVIATIONS

	This Quarter	Year-to-Date
1. Income statement items:	$1,975	$2,595
2. Nonincome statement items:	($1,900)	($1,900)
3. Total deviation	$75	$695

THREE-YEAR INCOME PROJECTION

What Is a Three-Year Income Projection?

The Pro Forma Income Statement (P&L Statement) differs from a cash flow statement in that the three-year projection includes only projected income and deductible expenses. It does not include nonincome statement projections. The following examples will illustrate the difference:

- **Example 1.** Your company plans to make loan repayments of $9,000 during the year, $3,000 of which will be interest. The full amount ($9,000) would be recorded on a cash flow statement. Only the interest ($3,000) is recorded on a projected income statement. The principal is not a deductible expense.

- **Example 2.** Your company plans to buy a vehicle for $15,000 cash. The full amount is recorded on your cash flow statement. The vehicle is a depreciable asset and only the projected depreciation for the year will be recorded on the projected income statement.

- **Example 3.** You plan to take owner draws of $2,000 per month. The draws will be recorded on your cash flow statement. They are not a deductible expense and will not be recorded on the projected income statement.

Account for Increases and Decreases

Increases in income and expenses are only realistic and should be reflected in your projections. Industry trends can also cause decreases in both income and expenses. An example of this might be in the computer industry, where constant innovation, heavy competition, and standardization of components have caused decreases in both cost and sale price of related products and services. The state of the economy will also be a contributing factor in the outlook for your business.

Sources of Information

Information for a three-year projection can be developed from your pro forma cash flow statement and your business and marketing analysis. The first year's figures can be transferred from the totals of income and expense items. The second and third years' figures are derived by combining these totals with projected trends in your particular industry. Again, if you are an established business, you will also be able to use past financial statements to help you determine what you project for the future of your business. Be sure to take into account fluctuations anticipated in costs, efficiency of operation, changes in your market, etc.

Sample Three-Year Income Projection form. On the next page is a sample form for your use. You may wish to compile all three years on a month-by-month basis. If you are diligent enough to do so, it will provide you with a more detailed annual projection that can be compared with actual monthly performance.

Three-Year Income Projection

Business Name: **Updated: September 26, 2004**

ABC Company

	YEAR 1 2001	YEAR 2 2002	YEAR 3 2003	TOTAL 3 YEARS
INCOME				
1. Sales revenues	500,000	540,000	595,000	1,635,000
2. Cost of goods sold (c – d)	312,000	330,000	365,000	1,007,000
a. Beginning inventory	147,000	155,000	175,000	147,000
b. Purchases	320,000	350,000	375,000	1,045,000
c. C.O.G. available Sale (a + b)	467,000	505,000	550,000	1,192,000
d. Less ending inventory (12/31)	155,000	175,000	185,000	185,000
3. GROSS PROFIT ON SALES (1 – 2)	188,000	210,000	230,000	628,000
EXPENSES				
1. Variable (selling) (a thru h)	67,390	84,300	89,400	241,090
a. Advertising/marketing	22,000	24,500	26,400	72,900
b. Freight	9,000	12,000	13,000	34,000
c. Fulfillment of orders	2,000	3,500	4,000	9,500
d. Packaging costs	3,000	4,000	3,500	10,500
e. Salaries/wages/commissions	25,000	34,000	36,000	95,000
f. Travel	1,000	1,300	1,500	3,800
g. Miscellaneous selling expense	390	0	0	390
h. Depreciation (prod/serv assets)	5,000	5,000	5,000	15,000
2. Fixed (administrative) (a thru h)	51,610	53,500	55,800	160,910
a. Financial administration	1,000	1,200	1,200	3,400
b. Insurance	3,800	4,000	4,200	12,000
c. Licenses and permits	2,710	1,400	1,500	5,610
d. Office salaries	14,000	17,500	20,000	51,500
e. Rent expense	22,500	22,500	22,500	67,500
f. Utilities	3,000	3,500	3,600	10,100
g. Miscellaneous fixed expense	0	0	0	0
h. Depreciation (office equipment)	4,600	3,400	2,800	10,800
TOTAL OPERATING EXPENSES (1 + 2)	119,000	137,800	145,200	402,000
NET INCOME OPERATIONS (GP – Exp)	69,000	72,200	84,800	226,000
OTHER INCOME (Interest income)	5,000	5,000	5,000	15,000
OTHER EXPENSE (Interest expense)	7,000	5,000	4,000	16,000
NET PROFIT (LOSS) BEFORE TAXES	67,000	72,200	85,800	225,000
TAXES 1. Federal, self-employment	21,700	24,200	28,500	74,400
2. State	4,300	4,800	5,700	14,800
3. Local	0	0	0	0
NET PROFIT (LOSS) AFTER TAXES	41,000	43,200	51,600	135,800

BREAKEVEN ANALYSIS

What Is a Breakeven Point?

This is the point at which a company's costs exactly match the sales volume and at which the business has neither made a profit nor incurred a loss. The breakeven point can be determined by mathematical calculation or by development of a graph. It can be expressed in:

Total dollars of revenue (exactly offset by total costs)

-or-

Total units of production (cost of which exactly equals the income derived by their sale).

To apply a Breakeven Analysis to an operation, you will need three projections:

1. **Fixed costs.** (Administrative overhead + Interest.) Many of these costs remain constant even during slow periods. Interest expense must be added to fixed costs for a breakeven analysis.

2. **Variable costs.** (Cost of goods + Selling expenses.) Usually varies with volume of business. The greater the sales volume, the higher the costs.

3. **Total sales volume.** (Projected sales for same period.)

Source of Information

All of your figures can be derived from your Three-Year Projection. Since breakeven is not reached until your total revenues match your total expenses, the calculation of your breakeven point will require that you add enough years' revenues and expenses together until you see that the total revenues are greater than the total expenses. Retrieve the figures and plug them into the following mathematical formula. (By now you should be able to see that each financial document in your business plan builds on the ones done previously.)

Mathematically

A firm's sales at breakeven point can be computed by using this formula:

BE Point (Sales) = Fixed Costs + [(Variable Costs/Est. Revenues) x Sales]

Terms used: a. **Sales** = volume of sales at Breakeven Point
b. **Fixed Costs** = administrative expense, depreciation, interest
c. **Variable Costs** = cost of goods and selling expenses
d. **Estimated Revenues** = income (from sales of goods/services)

Example: a. S (Sales at BE Point) = the unknown
b. FC (Fixed Costs) = $25,000
c. VC (Variable Costs) = $45,000
d. R (Estimated Revenues) = $90,000

Using the formula, the computation would appear as follows:
S (at BE Point) = $25,000 + [($45,000/$90,000) x S]
S = $25,000 + (1/2 x S)
S – 1/2 S = $25,000
S = $50,000 (BE Point in terms of dollars of revenue exactly offset by total costs)

Graphically

Breakeven point in graph form for the same business would be plotted as illustrated below. There is a blank form for your use in Appendix II.

Breakeven Analysis Graph

Business Name: ABC Company   **Date of Analysis: Sept 31, 2004**

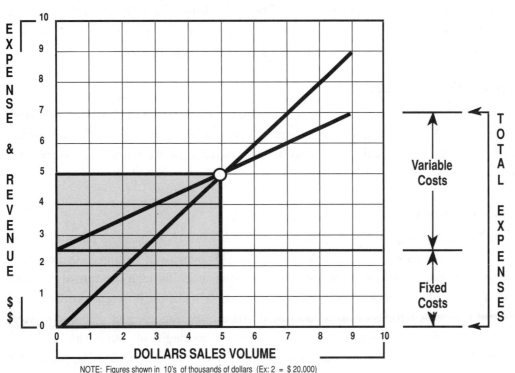

NOTE: Figures shown in 10's of thousands of dollars (Ex: 2 = $ 20,000)

To Complete the Graph. Determine the following projections'.

1. **Fixed costs for period.** Those costs that usually remain constant and must be met regardless of your sales volume (administrative, rent, insurance, depreciation, salaries, etc.). Also add interest expenses (i.e., $25,000).

2. **Variable costs.** Cost associated with the production and selling of your products or services. If you have a product, you will include cost of goods (inventory purchases, labor, materials) with your variable costs (freight, packaging, sales commissions, advertising, etc.). If you wish, these costs may be expressed by multiplying the unit cost by the units to be sold for a product (i.e., $1.50 per unit x 30,000 units = $45,000). For a service having no cost of goods, use total of projected selling expenses (variable).

3. **Total sales volume.** This is the figure representing your total projected revenues. You may also calculate revenues by multiplying projected units of product to be sold by sale price per unit. Example: 30,000 units @ $3.00 = $90,000; for a service, you can multiply your projected billable hours by your hourly rate (i.e., 900 hours x $100 = $90,000).

To Draw Graph Lines.

1. **Draw Horizontal Line** at point representing Fixed Costs (25).

2. **Draw Variable Cost Line** from left end of Fixed Cost Line sloping upward to point where Total Costs (Fixed + Variable) on vertical scale (7) meet Total Revenues on the horizontal scale (9).

3. **Draw Total Revenues Line** from zero through point describing total Revenues on both scales (where 9 meets 9).

Breakeven point. That point on the graph where the Variable Cost Line intersects the Total Revenue Line. This business estimates that it will break even at the time sales volume reaches $50,000. The triangular area below and to the left of that point represents company losses. The triangular area above and to the right of the point represents expected company profits.

· · · · ·

Congratulations!

You have now finished your study of financial statements and hopefully will at least feel a little more comfortable about developing a Pro Forma Cash Flow Statement, Profit & Loss Statement, and a Balance Sheet of your own from your General Records. These three records will be the backbone of your business. The rest of the financial statements you studied will also prove valuable, especially if you are in the process of writing a business plan.

It Takes Time to Learn

Don't expect to remember and absorb all of this information right now. I'm sure that you are overwhelmed. As you set up and work with your records, everything will fall into place. Recordkeeping is not difficult. It is simply a matter of repetitive work that will soon become habit.

Business Planning

Before I close this chapter, I would like to say another word about business planning. Every now and then, throughout the text, I have mentioned the benefits of writing a business plan. Most entrepreneurs shudder at the thought of having to go through the formal planning process. It is a difficult task, but one that may ultimately make the difference between success and failure. A business plan is required if you are seeking a lender or investor. More importantly, however, it is the guide you will follow during the life of your business. Having learned about recordkeeping and financial statements, you will have made a significant step in the planning process.

What's Next?

In the next chapter you will learn how to use the financial statements you have developed to analyze your business. Financial statement analysis is a very important tool that will enable you to make decisions, implement changes, and increase profitability.

CHAPTER 6

FINANCIAL STATEMENT ANALYSIS

written by
MARILYN J. BARTLETT, C.P.A.

Marilyn J. Bartlett is a CPA. Her success at helping businesses that are in trouble has been greatly enhanced by her ability to analyze financial statements and implement the appropriate changes. I would like to thank her for sharing her expertise with me through the contribution of this chapter. Because of her generosity, the user of this book has the opportunity not only to set up and maintain the proper records, but to gain the maximum benefits from those records through financial statement analysis.

• • • • •

FINANCIAL STATEMENTS

Your financial statements contain the information you need to help make decisions regarding your business. Many small business owners think of their financial statements as requirements for creditors, bankers, or tax preparers only, but they are much more than that. When analyzed, your financial statements can give you key information needed on the financial condition and the operations of your business.

Financial statement analysis requires measures to be expressed as ratios or percentages. For example, consider the situation where total assets on your balance sheet are $10,000. Cash is $2,000; Accounts Receivable are $3,000; and Fixed Assets are $5,000. The relationships would be expressed as follows:

	Ratio	**Ratio relationship**	**Percentages**
Cash:	.2	.2:1	20%
Accounts receivable:	.3	.3:1	30%
Fixed assets:	.5	.5:1	50%

Financial statement analysis involves the studying of relationships and comparisons of (1) items in a single year's financial statement, (2) comparative financial statements for a period of time, and (3) your statements with those of other businesses.

Many analytic tools are available, but this focus will be on the following measures that are of most importance to a small business owner in the business planning process:

Liquidity Analysis	**Measures of Investment**
Profitability Analysis	**Vertical Financial Statement Analysis**
Measures of Debit	**Horizontal Financial Statement Analysis**

Take a look, on the next few pages, at some ratios that may help you to evaluate your business. To illustrate, I will use the following statements from a small business. It is called Mary's Flower Shop, and I will use small figures that will be easy to examine.

Mary's Flower Shop
Comparative Balance
12/31/04 and 12/31/03

	2004	2003
Assets		
Current assets		
Cash	$2,000	$5,000
Accounts receivable	3,000	1,000
Inventory	5,000	3,000
Total current assets	$10,000	$9,000
Fixed assets	8,000	5,000
Total assets	**$18,000**	**$14,000**
Liabilities and Owner's equity		
Current liabilities		
Accounts payable	$4,000	$2,000
Taxes payable	220	300
Total current liabilities	$4,220	$2,300
Long-term liabilities	10,000	8,000
Total liabilities	**$14,220**	**$10,300**
Owner's equity	**$3,780**	**$3,700**
Total Liabilities + Equity	**$18,000**	**$14,000**

Mary's Flower Shop
Comparative Income Statement
For years ended 12/31/04 and 12/31/03

	2004	2003
Sales	$8,000	$6,000
Cost of goods sold	- 6,000	- 3,900
Gross profit	**$2,000**	**$2,100**
Expenses		
Selling (variable) expenses		
Advertising	$ 100	$ 50
Freight	50	40
Salaries	150	150
Total selling expenses	$ 300	$ 240
Administrative (fixed) expenses		
Rent	$ 450	$ 250
Insurance	150	125
Utilities	150	100
Total administrative expenses	$ 750	$ 475
Income from operations	**$ 950**	**$1,385**
Interest income	+ 0	+ 0
Interest expense	– 720	– 450
Net income before taxes	**$ 230**	**$ 935**
Taxes	– 150	– 180
NET PROFIT (LOSS) AFTER TAXES	**$ 80**	**$ 755**

* NOW YOU ARE READY TO *
ANALYZE MARY'S FINANCIAL STATEMENTS

—Turn the Page to Begin—

LIQUIDITY ANALYSIS

The liquidity of a business is the ability it has to meet financial obligations. The analysis focuses on the balance sheet relationships for the current assets and current liabilities.

Net Working Capital

The excess of current assets over current liabilities is net working capital. The more net working capital a business has, the less risky it is, as it has the ability to cover current liabilities as they come due. Take a look at the net working capital for Mary's Flower Shop.

	2004	2003
Current assets:	$10,000	$ 9,000
Current liabilities:	– 4,220	– 2,300
Net working capital:	$ 5,780	$ 6,700

In both years, net working capital was present, which would indicate a good position. But let's analyze this a bit more to get a clear picture of the liquidity of Mary's Flower Shop.

Current Ratio

The current ratio is a more dependable indication of liquidity than the net working capital. The current ratio is computed with the following formula:

$$\text{Current ratio} = \frac{\text{Current assets}}{\text{Current liabilities}}$$

For Mary's Flower Shop, the current ratios are:

$$2004: \quad \frac{\$10,000}{\$ 4,220} = 2.37$$

$$2003: \quad \frac{\$ 9,000}{\$ 2,300} = 3.91$$

As you can see, the business was in a more liquid position in 2003. In 2004, the business did experience an increase in current assets, but it also had an increase in current liabilities.

There is no set criteria for the **normal** current ratio, as that is dependent on the business you are in. If you have predictable cash flow, you can operate with a lower current ratio.

The ratio of 2.0 is considered acceptable for most businesses. A ratio of 2.0 would allow a company to lose 50% of its current assets and still be able to cover current liabilities. For most businesses, this is an adequate margin of safety.

For Mary's Flower Shop, the **decrease** in the current ratio would cause the owner to investigate further even though 2.37 is acceptable for the current year.

Quick Ratio

Since inventory is the most difficult current asset to dispose of quickly, it is subtracted from the current assets in the quick ratio to give a tougher test of liquidity. The quick ratio is computed as follows:

$$\text{Quick ratio} \ = \ \frac{\textbf{Current assets} - \textbf{Inventory}}{\textbf{Current liabilities}}$$

The quick ratios for our case are:

$$2004: \quad \frac{\$10,000 - 5,000}{\$4,220} \ = \ 1.18$$

$$2003: \quad \frac{\$ 9,000 - 3,000}{\$2,300} \ = \ 2.61$$

A quick ratio of 1.00 or greater is usually recommended, but that is dependent on the business you are in.

From the analysis of the liquidity measures (net working capital, current ratio, and quick ratio), the 2004 results are within acceptable limits. The business did experience a decrease in liquidity and is viewed as more risky than in 2003.

You can use these ratios to see if your business is in any risk of insolvency. You will also be able to assess your ability to increase or decrease current assets for your business strategy. How would these moves affect your liquidity?

Your creditors will use these ratios to determine whether to extend credit to you. They will compare the ratios for previous periods and with those of similar businesses.

PROFITABILITY ANALYSIS

A Profitability Analysis will measure the ability of a business to make a profit.

Gross Profit Margin

The gross profit margin indicates the percentage of each sales dollar remaining after a business has paid for its goods.

$$\text{Gross profit margin} \ = \ \frac{\text{Gross profit}}{\text{Sales}}$$

The higher the gross profit margin, the better. For Mary's Flower Shop, the gross profit margins were:

$$2004: \quad \frac{\$2,000}{\$8,000} \ = \ 25\%$$

$$2003: \quad \frac{\$2,100}{\$6,000} \ = \ 35\%$$

The normal rate is dependent on the business you are in. The Gross Profit Margin is the actual mark-up you have on the goods sold.

In 2004, this case has a 25% contribution margin, which means that 25 cents of every dollar in sales is left to cover the variable, fixed, and other expenses. Mary's Flower Shop can be viewed as "less profitable" in 2004 as compared to 2003.

Operating Profit Margin

This ratio represents the pure operations profits, ignoring interest and taxes. A high operating profit margin is preferred.

$$\text{Operating profit margin} \ = \ \frac{\text{Income from operations}}{\text{Sales}}$$

Mary's Flower Shop has the following ratios:

$$2004: \quad \frac{\$\,950}{\$\,8{,}000} \quad = \quad 11.88\%$$

$$2003: \quad \frac{\$\,1{,}385}{\$\,6{,}000} \quad = \quad 23.08\%$$

Again, this case is showing a less profitable position in 2004 than it did in 2003.

Net Profit Margin

The net profit margin is clearly the measure of a business's success with respect to earnings on sales.

$$\textbf{Net profit margin} \quad = \quad \frac{\textbf{Net profit}}{\textbf{Sales}}$$

A higher margin means the firm is more profitable. The net profit margin will differ according to your specific type of business. A 1% margin for a grocery store is not unusual due to the large quantity of items handled; while a 10% margin for a jewelry store would be considered low.

Mary's Flower Shop has the following net profit margins:

$$2004: \quad \frac{\$\,80}{\$\,8{,}000} \quad = \quad 1\%$$

$$2003: \quad \frac{\$\,755}{\$\,6{,}000} \quad = \quad 12.6\%$$

Clearly, Mary's Flower Shop is in trouble. All the ratios indicate a significant decrease in profitability from 2003. The next step is to determine reasons for that decrease.

As a business owner, you can see just how profitable your business is. If the ratios are too low, you will want to analyze why.

- **Did you have enough mark-up on your goods? Check your gross profit margin.**

- **Are your operating expenses too high? Check your operating profit margin.**

- **Are your interest expenses too high? Check your net profit margin.**

For Mary's Flower Shop, all of the above questions can be answered using the ratios computed. Your creditors will look at these ratios to see just how profitable your business is. Without profits, a business can't attract outside financing.

DEBT MEASURES

The debt position of a business indicates the amount of other people's money that is being used to generate profits. Many new businesses assume too much debt too soon in an attempt to grow too quickly. The measures of debt will tell a business how indebted it is and how able it is to service the debts. The more indebtedness, the greater the risk of failure.

Debt Ratio

This is a key financial ratio used by creditors.

$$\textbf{Debt ratio} \ = \ \frac{\textbf{Total liabilities}}{\textbf{Total assets}}$$

The higher this ratio, the more risk of failure. For Mary's Flower Shop, the debt ratios are:

$$\textbf{2004:} \quad \frac{\$\,14,200}{\$\,18,000} \ = \ 79\%$$

$$\textbf{2003:} \quad \frac{\$\,10,300}{\$\,14,000} \ = \ 74\%$$

The acceptable ratio is dependent upon the policies of your creditors and bankers. The rates of 79% and 74% above are excessively high and show a very high risk of failure. Clearly three-quarters of the company is being financed by others' money, and it does not put the business in a good position for acquiring new debt.

If your business plan includes the addition of long-term debt at a future point, you will want to monitor your debt ratio. Is it within the limits acceptable to your banker?

INVESTMENT MEASURES

As a small business owner, you have invested money to acquire assets, and you should be getting a return on these assets. Even if the owner is taking a salary from the business, he or she also should be earning an additional amount for the investment in the company.

Return On Investment (ROI)

The ROI measures your effectiveness as a business owner to generate profits from the available assets.

$$\text{ROI} = \frac{\text{Net profits}}{\text{Total assets}}$$

The higher the ROI, the better. The business owner should set a target for the ROI. What do you want your investment to earn?

For Mary's Flower Shop, the ROI is as follows:

$$2004: \quad \frac{\$\,80}{\$\,18,000} = .4\%$$

$$2003: \quad \frac{\$\,755}{\$\,14,000} = 5.4\%$$

We do not know Mary's target for ROI, but .4% would seem unacceptable. She could put her money in a savings account and earn 5%, so it doesn't appear that a .4% return on her investment is good.

Many small business owners have successfully created jobs for themselves, but still don't earn a fair return on their investment. Set your target for ROI, and work towards it.

VERTICAL FINANCIAL STATEMENT ANALYSIS

Percentage analysis is used to show the relationship of the components in a single financial statement.

- **For a balance sheet.** Each asset is stated as a percent of total assets, and each liability and equity item is stated as a percent of total liabilities and equity.

- **For an income statement.** In vertical analysis of the income statement, each item is stated as a percent of net sales.

A vertical analysis of the income statements for Mary's Flower Shop is shown below.

Mary's Flower Shop
Comparative Income Statement
For Years Ended 12/31/04 and 12/31/03

	2004		2003	
	Amount	**Percent**	**Amount**	**Percent**
Sales	$8,000	100.0%	$6,000	100.0%
Cost of goods sold	− 6,000	75.0%	− 3,900	65.0%
Gross profit	**$2,000**	**25.0%**	**$2,100**	**35.0%**
Selling (variable) expenses				
Advertising	$ 100	1.3%	$ 50	.8%
Freight	50	.6%	40	.7%
Salaries	150	1.9%	150	2.5%
Total selling expenses	**$ 300**	**3.8%**	**$ 240**	**4.0%**
Administrative (fixed) expenses				
Rent	$ 450	5.6%	$ 250	4.2%
Insurance	150	1.9%	125	2.1%
Utilities	150	1.9%	100	1.7%
Total administrative expenses	**$ 750**	**9.4%**	**$ 475**	**8.0%**
Income from operations	**$ 950**	**11.9%**	**$1,385**	**23.0%**
Interest income	+ 0	0.0%	+ 0	0.0%
Interest expense	− 720	9.0%	− 450	7.5%
Net income before taxes	**$ 230**	**2.9%**	**$ 935**	**15.5%**
Taxes	− 150	1.9%	− 180	3.0%
Net profit (loss) after taxes	**$ 80**	**1.0%**	**$ 755**	**12.5%**

Evaluation of Vertical Financial Statement

From the vertical analysis of Mary's income statements, you can see the following.

1. **The components of cost of goods sold and gross profit showed significant differences.**

    - Cost of goods sold increased from 65% of sales to 75% of sales. This should alert the owner to investigate.

        – Did the cost of the items really increase and the selling price stay the same?

        – Is there a possibility of theft that may have caused the variance?

    - The decrease in gross profit margin from 35% of sales to 25% of sales should also trigger the owner to look at the mark-up.

        – Is the mark-up too low? Will your customers still buy if you raise the selling price on your products?

2. **The composition of variable changed.**

    - The owner would want to evaluate the appropriateness of the increase in advertising and decrease in salaries.

3. **The composition of fixed expenses would alert the owner to evaluate the increase in rent.**

    - Why did this occur?

    - Is it necessary or are there other alternatives?

4. **The increase in interest should be analyzed.**

    - The most likely reason for the increase would probably be an increase in debt.

HORIZONTAL FINANCIAL STATEMENT ANALYSIS

Horizontal analysis is a percentage analysis of the increases and decreases in the items on comparative financial statements.

The increase or decrease of the item is listed, and the earlier statement is used as the base. The percentage of increase or decrease is listed in the last column.

A horizontal analysis of the income statements for Mary's Flower Shop can be seen below.

Mary's Flower Shop
Comparative Income Statement
For Years Ended 12/31/04 and 12/31/03

	2004 Amount	2003 Amount	Increase/Decrease Amount	Percent
Sales	$8,000	$6,000	$2,000	33.3%
Cost of goods sold	6,000	3,900	– 2,100	53.8%
Gross profit	**$2,000**	**$2,100**	**($ 100)**	**(4.8%)**
Selling (variable) expenses				
Advertising	$ 100	$ 50	$ 50	100.0%
Freight	50	40	10	25.0%
Salaries	150	150	same	same
Total selling expenses	**$ 300**	**$ 240**	**$ 60**	**25.0%**
Administrative (fixed) expenses				
Rent	$ 450	$ 250	$ 200	80.0%
Insurance	150	125	25	20.0%
Utilities	150	100	50	50.0%
Total administrative expenses	**$ 750**	**$ 475**	**$ 275**	**57.9%**
Income from operations	**$ 950**	**$1,385**	**(435)**	**(31.4%)**
Interest income	0	0	0	0.0%
Interest expense	720	450	270	60.0%
Net income before taxes	**$ 230**	**$ 935**	**($ 705)**	**(75.4%)**
Taxes	150	180	30	16.7%
Net profit (loss) after taxes	**$ 80**	**$ 755**	**($ 675)**	**(89.4%)**

Evaluation of Horizontal Financial Statement Analysis

From the horizontal analysis of Mary's income statements, you should evaluate the following:

1. **The 33.3% increase in sales resulted in only a 4.8% increase in gross profit.**
   - This would alert the owner that something was wrong.
   - Is the mark-up sufficient?
   - Was there an according adjustment?

2. **The 100% increase in advertising expense was steep.**
   - Did this expense increase sales?
   - Was it justified?

3. **The 80% rent increase and 50% utilities increase should be looked at.**
   - Are these increases justified?

4. **The 60% interest increase is most likely a result of increased debt.**
   - The owner would want to analyze the components.
   - Decide if the interest level is correct.
   - Decide if some debt should be retired.

5. **The 89.4% decrease in net profit is not acceptable.**
   - A serious decrease will require that the owner re-evaluate the business.

SUMMARY

Now, you can see how financial statement analysis can be a tool to help you manage your business.

- If the analysis produces results that don't meet your expectations or if the business is in danger of failure, you must analyze your expenses and your use of assets. Your first step should be to cut expenses and increase the productivity of your assets.

- If your return on investment is too low, examine how you could make your assets (equipment, machinery, fixtures, inventory, etc.) work better for your benefit.

- If your profit is low, be sure that your mark-up is adequate, analyze your operating expenses to see that they are not too high, and review your interest expenses.

- If your liquidity is low, you could have a risk of becoming insolvent. Examine the level and composition of current assets and current liabilities.

The vertical and horizontal financial statement analysis will reveal trends and compositions that signify trouble. Using your management skills, you can take corrective action.

TAXES AND BOOKKEEPING

Warning!
DISCLAIMER

The information in this chapter is presented with the understanding that I am in no way rendering legal, accounting, or other professional services. My purpose is to introduce you to some of the common tax forms and publications and to provide you with a general guide for use in recordkeeping. Detailed information, along with legal advice, will have to be obtained from your accountant, attorney, or the IRS.

. . . . .

BASIC UNDERSTANDING OF THE U.S. TAX SYSTEM

If you are going to be in command of your business bookkeeping, it will be necessary for you to have a good basic understanding of the relationship between your finances and income tax accounting. When the federal income tax came into being, it was structured according to accounting principles. This has served a double purpose. Your financial records enable you to retrieve the necessary information for filing taxes at the close of your tax year. By the same token, the tax forms that you will be required to submit will provide you with important clues as to how your accounting can be set up, not only in a usable format, but in a manner that will make it practical for you to analyze your financial statements and determine what changes will have to be implemented for future growth and profit.

The Relationship between Tax Forms and Business Analysis

In order for you to better comprehend the relationship between the tax system and analyzing your business, I will give you two examples of tax forms and how you can benefit from understanding those forms.

1. **Schedule C (Form 1040).** Entitled *Profit or Loss from Business (Sole Prorietorship)* (required tax reporting form for Sole Proprietors).

   - **IRS information required.** Gross receipts or sales, beginning and ending inventories, labor, materials, goods purchased, returns and allowances, deductible expenses, interest expense, interest income, and net profit or loss.

   - **Benefits of understanding.** In case you did not catch on, the required information listed above is exactly the same as the list of income and expenses on a Profit & Loss Statement. When the IRS has you fill out a business return, you are merely transferring information from the profit and loss. By understanding this, you can look through a Schedule C and see what categories of information are needed under expenses. This can help you to decide what categories you will use in your Revenue & Expense Journal. It will also help you after your accountant has sent your return back to you for submission to the IRS. Now you can put your knowledge of a P&L Statement to work and read and check it over for accuracy—a chore too frequently ignored by taxpayers. Since you have the final responsibility for the correctness of your return, knowing how to examine it can prevent mistakes that might prove costly.

   Note: Form 1065, *U.S. Return of Partnership Income*, and Form 1120 or Form 1120-A, *U.S. Corporation Income Tax Return*, are used for those legal structures.

2. **Schedule SE (Form 1040).** Entitled *Computation of Social Security Self-Employment Tax.*

   - **IRS information required.** Computation of contribution to Social Security.

   - **Benefits of understanding.** Failure to familiarize yourself with the requirements on how to compute this tax and know what percentage of your net income will be owed will result in a false picture as to the net profit of your business. Don't forget—the IRS is interested in your net profit before taxes. You are concerned with net profit after taxes.

As you can see from the two examples, examination of required tax forms can lead to the discovery of many types of records that you will need and profit from in your business.

FEDERAL TAXES FOR WHICH YOU MAY BE LIABLE

The next section of this chapter will be devoted to providing you with tax calendars and introducing you to the most common federal taxes for which a sole proprietor, partnership, or corporation may be liable.

I am not giving you complete information for filling out tax returns. What I am trying to do is make you aware of required reporting, familiarize you with some of the forms, and give you a frame of reference for any questions you have. To do this, I will give you a brief overview of each requirement and include the following:

- Tax to be reported.

- Forms used for reporting.

- IRS publications to be used for information.

- A sample of each reporting form.

Calendars of Federal Taxes

For your convenience, I have provided tax calendars on the next four pages. They will serve as a guide to tell you when tax and information returns must be filed. There is a calendar for each of the four legal structures (sole proprietor, partnership, S corporation, and corporation). Copy the calendar that is appropriate to your business and post it near your bookkeeping area to remind you to file on the appropriate dates.

It should be noted that these calendars are compiled according to specific dates. If your tax year is not January 1st through December 31st, there are footnoted dates listed below the calendar that you can transpose to figure out filing dates. These calendars will be especially useful combined with your Recordkeeping Schedule that will be presented in the next chapter.

Using the index. If you are looking for information on a specific tax or form, you will find that text and forms are indexed three ways in the back of the book: by form number, by subject matter, and by legal structure.

Sole Proprietor

Calendar of Federal Taxes for Which You May Be Liable

January	15	Estimated tax	Form 1040ES
	31	Social Security (FICA) tax and the withholding of income tax. Note: See IRS rulings for deposit—Pub. 334	Forms 941, 941E, 942, and 943
	31	Providing information on Social Security (FICA) tax and the withholding of income tax	Form W-2 (to employee)
	31	Federal unemployment (FUTA) tax	Form 940-EZ or 940
	31	Federal unemployment (FUTA) tax (only if liability for unpaid taxes exceeds $100)	Form 8109 (to make deposits)
	31	Information returns to nonemployees and transactions with other persons	Form 1099 (to recipients)
February	28	Information returns to nonemployees and transactions with other persons	Form 1099 (to IRS)
	28	Providing information on Social Security (FICA) tax and the withholding income tax	Forms W-2 and W-3 (to Social Security Admin.)
April	15	Income tax	Schedule C (Form 1040)
	15	Self-employment tax	Schedule SE (Form 1040)
	15	Estimated tax	Form 1040ES
	30	Social Security (FICA) tax and the withholding of income tax. Note: See IRS rulings for deposit—Pub. 334	Forms 941, 941E, 942, and 943
	30	Federal unemployment (FUTA) tax (only if liability for unpaid taxes exceeds $100)	Form 8109 (to make deposits)
June	15	Estimated tax	Form 1040ES
July	31	Social Security (FICA) tax and the withholding of income tax Note: See IRS rulings for deposit—Pub. 334	Forms 941, 941E, 942, and 943
	31	Federal unemployment (FUTA) tax (only if liability for unpaid taxes exceeds $100)	Form 8109 (to make deposits)
September	15	Estimated tax	Form 1040ES
October	31	Social Security (FICA) tax and the withholding of income tax. Note: See IRS rulings for deposit—Pub. 334	Forms 941, 941E, 942, and 943
	31	Federal unemployment (FUTA) tax (only if liability for unpaid taxes exceeds $100)	Form 8109 (to make deposits)

If your tax year is not January 1st through December 31st:

⊕ Schedule C (Form 1040) is due the 15th day of the 4th month after end of the tax year. Schedule SE is due same day as Form 1040.

⊕ Estimated tax (1040ES) is due the 15th day of 4th, 6th, and 9th months of tax year, and the 15th day of 1st month after the end of tax year.

Partnership

Calendar of Federal Taxes for Which You May Be Liable

January	15	Estimated tax (individual who is a partner)	Form 1040ES
	31	Social Security (FICA) tax and the withholding of income tax. Note: See IRS rulings for deposit—Pub. 334	Forms 941, 941E, 942, and 943
	31	Providing information on Social Security (FICA) tax and the withholding of income tax	Form W-2 (to employee)
	31	Federal unemployment (FUTA) tax	Form 940-EZ or 940
	31	Federal unemployment (FUTA) tax (only if liability for unpaid taxes exceeds $100).	Form 8109 (to make deposits)
	31	Information returns to nonemployees and transactions with other persons	Form 1099 (to recipients)
February	28	Information returns to nonemployees and transactions with other persons	Form 1099 (to IRS)
	28	Providing information on Social Security (FICA) tax and on withholding income tax	Forms W-2 and W-3 (to Social Security Admin.)
April	15	Income tax (individual who is a partner)	Schedule C (Form 1040)
	15	Annual return of income	Form 1065
	15	Self-employment tax (individual who is partner)	Schedule SE (Form 1040)
	15	Estimated tax (individual who is partner)	Form 1040ES
	30	Social Security (FICA) tax and the withholding of income tax. Note: See IRS rulings for deposit—Pub. 334	Forms 941, 941E, 942, and 943
	30	Federal unemployment (FUTA) tax (only if liability for unpaid taxes exceeds $100).	Form 8109 (to make deposits)
June	15	Estimated tax (individual who is a partner)	Form 1040ES
July	31	Social Security (FICA) tax and the withholding of income tax. Note: See IRS rulings for deposit—Pub. 334	Forms 941, 941E, 942, and 943
	31	Federal unemployment (FUTA) tax (only if liability for unpaid taxes exceeds $100).	Form 8109 (to make deposits)
September	15	Estimated tax (individual who is a partner)	Form 1040ES
October	31	Social Security (FICA) tax and the withholding of income tax. Note: See IRS rulings for deposit—Pub. 334	Forms 941, 941E, 942, and 943
	31	Federal unemployment (FUTA) tax (only if liability for unpaid taxes exceeds $100).	Form 8109 (to make deposits)

If your tax year is not January 1st through December 31st:

- Income tax is due the 15th day of the 4th month after end of tax year.
- Self-employment tax is due the same day as income tax (Form 1040).
- Estimated tax (1040ES) is due the 15th day of the 4th, 6th, and 9th month of the tax year and the 15th day of 1st month after end of the tax year.

S Corporation

Calendar of Federal Taxes for Which You May Be Liable

Month	Day	Description	Form
January	15	Estimated tax (individual S corp. shareholder)	Form 1040ES
	31	Social Security (FICA) tax and the withholding of income tax. Note: See IRS rulings for deposit—Pub. 334	Forms 941, 941E, 942, and 943
	31	Providing information on Social Security (FICA) tax and the withholding of income tax	Form W-2 (to employee)
	31	Federal unemployment (FUTA) tax	Form 940-EZ or 940
	31	Federal unemployment (FUTA) tax (only if liability for unpaid taxes exceeds $100)	Form 8109 (to make deposits)
	31	Information returns to nonemployees and transactions with other persons	Form 1099 (to recipients)
February	28	Information returns to nonemployees and transactions with other persons	Form 1099 (to IRS)
	28	Providing information on Social Security (FICA) tax and the withholding of income tax	Forms W-2 and W-3 (to Social Security Admin.)
March	15	Income tax	Form 1120S
April	15	Income tax (individual S corp. shareholder)	Form 1040
	15	Estimated tax (individual S corp. shareholder)	Form 1040ES
	30	Social Security (FICA) tax and the withholding of income tax. Note: See IRS rulings for deposit—Pub. 334	Forms 941, 941E, 942, and 943
	30	Federal unemployment (FUTA) tax (only if liability for unpaid taxes exceeds $100)	Form 8109 (to make deposits)
June	15	Estimated tax (individual S corp. shareholder)	Form 1040ES
July	31	Social Security (FICA) tax and the withholding of income tax. Note: See IRS rulings for deposit—Pub. 334	Forms 941, 941E, 942, and 943
	31	Federal unemployment (FUTA) tax (only if liability for unpaid taxes exceeds $100)	Form 8109 (to make deposits)
September	15	Estimated tax (individual S corp. shareholder)	Form 1040ES
October	31	Social Security (FICA) tax and the withholding of income tax. Note: See IRS rulings for deposit—Pub. 334	Forms 941, 941E, 942, and 943
	31	Federal unemployment (FUTA) tax (only if liability for unpaid taxes exceeds $100)	Form 8109 (to make deposits)

If your tax year is not January 1st through December 31st:

- ✦ S corporation income tax (1120S) and individual S corporation shareholder income tax (Form 1040) are due the 15th day of the 4th month after end of tax year.

- ✦ Estimated tax of individual shareholder (1040ES) is due the 15th day of 4th, 6th, and 9th months of tax year, and 15th day of 1st month after end of tax year.

Corporation

		Calendar of Federal Taxes for Which You May Be Liable		
January	31	Social Security (FICA) tax and the withholding of income tax. Note: See IRS rulings for deposit—Pub. 334	Forms 941, 941E, 942, and 943
	31	Providing information on Social Security (FICA) tax and the withholding of income tax	Form W-2 (to employee)
	31	Federal unemployment (FUTA) tax	Form 940-EZ or 940
	31	Federal unemployment (FUTA) tax (only if liability for unpaid taxes exceeds $100)	Form 8109 (to make deposits)
	31	Information returns to nonemployees and transactions with other persons	Form 1099 (to recipients)
February	28	Information returns to nonemployees and transactions with other persons	Form 1099 (to IRS)
	28	Providing information on Social Security (FICA) tax and the withholding of income tax	Forms W-2 and W-3 (to Social Security Admin.)
March	15	Income tax	Form 1120 or 1120-A
April	15	Estimated tax	Form 1120-W
	30	Social Security (FICA) tax and the withholding of income tax. Note: See IRS rulings for deposit—Pub. 334	Forms 941, 941E, 942, and 943
	30	Federal unemployment (FUTA) tax (only if liability for unpaid taxes exceeds $100)	Form 8109 (to make deposits)
June	15	Estimated tax	Form 1120-W
July	31	Social Security (FICA) tax and the withholding of income tax. Note: See IRS rulings for deposit—Pub. 334	Forms 941, 941E, 942, and 943
	31	Federal unemployment (FUTA) tax (only if liability for unpaid taxes exceeds $100)	Form 8109 (to make deposits)
September	15	Estimated tax	Form 1120-W
October	31	Social Security (FICA) tax and the withholding of income tax. Note: See IRS rulings for deposit—Pub. 334	Forms 941, 941E, 942, and 943
	31	Federal unemployment (FUTA) tax (only if liability for unpaid taxes exceeds $100)	Form 8109 (to make deposits)
December	15	Estimated tax	Form 1120-W

If your tax year is not January 1st through December 31st:

- Income tax (Form 1120 or 1120-A) is due on the 15th day of the 3rd month after the end of the tax year.
- Estimated tax (1120-W) is due the 5th day of the 4th, 6th, 9th, and 12th months of the tax year.

INCOME TAX (FOR SOLE PROPRIETORS)

File Schedule C (Form 1040), *Profit or Loss from Business (Sole Proprietorship).*

You are a sole proprietor if you are self-employed and are the sole owner of an unincorporated business.

If you are a sole proprietor, you report your income and expenses from your business or profession on Schedule C. File Schedule C with your Form 1040 and report the amount of net profit or (loss) from Schedule C on your 1040. If you operate more than one business as a sole proprietor, you prepare a separate Schedule C for each business.

Withdrawals. If you are a sole proprietor, there is no tax effect if you take money to or from your business, or transfer money to or from your business. You should set up a drawing account to keep track of amounts that are for personal use and not for business expenses.

Home office deductions. If you use part of your home exclusively and regularly as the principal place of business or as the place where you meet or deal with patients, clients, or customers you can deduct the expenses for that part of your home. If you claim a home office deduction, you must attach Form 8829. (Sample form is included after Schedule C.) For more information, see Publication 587, *Business Use of Your Home.*

Estimated tax. If you are a sole proprietor, you will have to make estimated tax payments if the total of your estimated income tax and self-employment tax for 2003 will exceed your total withholding and credits by $1,000 or more. Form 1040-ES is used to estimate your tax. See "Estimated Tax for Sole Proprietors."

Self-employment tax. Generally required if you are a sole proprietor. See "Self-Employment Tax," Schedule SE.

Schedule C and Form 1040

Forms are due by April 15th. If you use a fiscal year, your return is due by the 15th day of the 4th month after the close of your tax year.

IRS publication. See Publication 334, *Tax Guide for Small Business* for discussion on tax rules and for examples illustrating how to fill in these forms.

Sample. Schedule C (Form 1040) can be seen on the next two pages.

Form 1040 Schedule C
Profit or Loss from Business (Sole Proprietorship)

SCHEDULE C (Form 1040) Department of the Treasury Internal Revenue Service (99)	**Profit or Loss From Business** (Sole Proprietorship) ▶ Partnerships, joint ventures, etc., must file Form 1065 or 1065-B. ▶ Attach to Form 1040 or 1041. ▶ See Instructions for Schedule C (Form 1040).	OMB No. 1545-0074 20**03** Attachment Sequence No. 09

Name of proprietor		Social security number (SSN)

A	Principal business or profession, including product or service (see page C-2 of the instructions)	B Enter code from pages C-7, 8, & 9 ▶

C	Business name. If no separate business name, leave blank.	D Employer ID number (EIN), if any

E Business address (including suite or room no.) ▶ ....
   City, town or post office, state, and ZIP code

F Accounting method: (1) ☐ Cash   (2) ☐ Accrual   (3) ☐ Other (specify) ▶ ....
G Did you "materially participate" in the operation of this business during 2003? If "No," see page C-3 for limit on losses   ☐ Yes ☐ No
H If you started or acquired this business during 2003, check here . . . . ▶ ☐

Part I Income

1	Gross receipts or sales. Caution. If this income was reported to you on Form W-2 and the "Statutory employee" box on that form was checked, see page C-3 and check here ▶ ☐	1	
2	Returns and allowances	2	
3	Subtract line 2 from line 1	3	
4	Cost of goods sold (from line 42 on page 2)	4	
5	Gross profit. Subtract line 4 from line 3	5	
6	Other income, including Federal and state gasoline or fuel tax credit or refund (see page C-3) . . .	6	
7	Gross income. Add lines 5 and 6 . . . . ▶	7	

Part II Expenses. Enter expenses for business use of your home only on line 30.

8	Advertising	8		19 Pension and profit-sharing plans	19	
9	Car and truck expenses (see page C-3)	9		20 Rent or lease (see page C-5):		
10	Commissions and fees . .	10		a Vehicles, machinery, and equipment .	20a	
11	Contract labor (see page C-4)	11		b Other business property . .	20b	
12	Depletion	12		21 Repairs and maintenance . .	21	
13	Depreciation and section 179 expense deduction (not included in Part III) (see page C-4) . .	13		22 Supplies (not included in Part III) .	22	
				23 Taxes and licenses	23	
				24 Travel, meals, and entertainment:		
14	Employee benefit programs (other than on line 19) . . .	14		a Travel	24a	
15	Insurance (other than health) .	15		b Meals and entertainment		
16	Interest:			c Enter nondeductible amount included on line 24b (see page C-5) .		
a	Mortgage (paid to banks, etc.) .	16a				
b	Other	16b		d Subtract line 24c from line 24b	24d	
17	Legal and professional services	17		25 Utilities	25	
				26 Wages (less employment credits) .	26	
18	Office expense	18		27 Other expenses (from line 48 on page 2)	27	

28	Total expenses before expenses for business use of home. Add lines 8 through 27 in columns . ▶	28	

29	Tentative profit (loss). Subtract line 28 from line 7	29	
30	Expenses for business use of your home. Attach Form 8829	30	
31	Net profit or (loss). Subtract line 30 from line 29. • If a profit, enter on Form 1040, line 12, and also on Schedule SE, line 2 (statutory employees, see page C-6). Estates and trusts, enter on Form 1041, line 3. • If a loss, you must go to line 32.	31	
32	If you have a loss, check the box that describes your investment in this activity (see page C-6). • If you checked 32a, enter the loss on Form 1040, line 12, and also on Schedule SE, line 2 (statutory employees, see page C-6). Estates and trusts, enter on Form 1041, line 3. • If you checked 32b, you must attach Form 6198.	32a ☐ All investment is at risk. 32b ☐ Some investment is not at risk.	

For Paperwork Reduction Act Notice, see Form 1040 instructions.   Cat. No. 11334P   Schedule C (Form 1040) 2003

Form 1040 Schedule C
Profit or Loss from Business (Sole Proprietorship)

page 2

Schedule C (Form 1040) 2003

Page 2

Part III Cost of Goods Sold (see page C-6)

33 Method(s) used to value closing inventory: a ☐ Cost   b ☐ Lower of cost or market   c ☐ Other (attach explanation)

34 Was there any change in determining quantities, costs, or valuations between opening and closing inventory? If "Yes," attach explanation . . . . ☐ Yes   ☐ No

35 Inventory at beginning of year. If different from last year's closing inventory, attach explanation . .	35	
36 Purchases less cost of items withdrawn for personal use	36	
37 Cost of labor. Do not include any amounts paid to yourself	37	
38 Materials and supplies	38	
39 Other costs	39	
40 Add lines 35 through 39	40	
41 Inventory at end of year	41	
42 Cost of goods sold. Subtract line 41 from line 40. Enter the result here and on page 1, line 4 . .	42	

Part IV Information on Your Vehicle. Complete this part only if you are claiming car or truck expenses on line 9 and are not required to file Form 4562 for this business. See the instructions for line 13 on page C-4 to find out if you must file Form 4562.

43 When did you place your vehicle in service for business purposes? (month, day, year) ▶ .... / .... / ....

44 Of the total number of miles you drove your vehicle during 2003, enter the number of miles you used your vehicle for:

a Business .... b Commuting .... c Other ....

45 Do you (or your spouse) have another vehicle available for personal use? . . . . ☐ Yes   ☐ No

46 Was your vehicle available for personal use during off-duty hours? . . . . ☐ Yes   ☐ No

47a Do you have evidence to support your deduction? . . . . ☐ Yes   ☐ No

b If "Yes," is the evidence written? . . . . ☐ Yes   ☐ No

Part V Other Expenses. List below business expenses not included on lines 8 –26 or line 30.

--------------------------------------		
48 Total other expenses. Enter here and on page 1, line 27	48	

Schedule C (Form 1040) 2003

HOME OFFICE DEDUCTION

File Form 8829, *Expenses for Business Use of Your Home* (with Schedule C).

If you use your home for business, you may be able to deduct some of your expenses for its business use. But you cannot deduct more than you receive in gross income from its business use. The allowable deduction is computed on Form 8829.

Use Tests

To take a deduction for the use of part of your home in business, you must meet certain tests. That part of your home that you deduct must be used *exclusively* and *regularly* as (1) the principal place of business for the trade in which you engage, (2) as a place to meet and deal with customers in the normal course of your trade, or in connection with your trade if you are using a separate structure that is appurtenant to, but not attached to, your house or residence.

Note: The Taxpayer Relief Act of 1997 liberalized the Home Office Deduction for tax years beginning after December 31, 1998. The new law expanded the definition of "principal place of business." Home offices will qualify if: (1) the office is used to conduct administrative or management activities of the taxpayer's trade or business; and (2) there is no other fixed location of the trade or business where administrative or management activities are conducted.

Figure Business Percentage

To figure deductions for the business use of your home, you will have to divide the expenses of operating your home between personal and business use. Some expenses are divided on an area basis. Some are further divided on a time usage basis. To find the business percentage, divide the area used for the business by the total area of your home.

Deductible Expenses

Certain expenses are totally deductible, such as painting or repairs made to the specific area used for business. You can deduct indirect expenses based on percentage of usage, including real estate taxes, mortgage interest, casualty losses, utilities, telephone, insurance and security systems, and depreciation. Unrelated expenses cannot be deducted.

Form 8829

This form, entitled *Expenses for Business Use of Your Home*, is filed with Schedule C (Form 1040) on April 15th.

Sample. A copy of Form 8829 is provided on the next page.

Form 8829
Expenses for Business Use of Your Home

Form **8829**	Expenses for Business Use of Your Home	OMB No. 1545-1266
Department of the Treasury Internal Revenue Service (99)	▶ File only with Schedule C (Form 1040). Use a separate Form 8829 for each home you used for business during the year. ▶ See separate instructions.	**20**03 Attachment Sequence No. 66

Name(s) of proprietor(s)   Your social security number

Part I   Part of Your Home Used for Business

1	Area used regularly and exclusively for business, regularly for day care, or for storage of inventory or product samples (see instructions)	1
2	Total area of home	2
3	Divide line 1 by line 2. Enter the result as a percentage	3 %
	• For day-care facilities not used exclusively for business, also complete lines 4–6.	
	• All others, skip lines 4–6 and enter the amount from line 3 on line 7.	
4	Multiply days used for day care during year by hours used per day	4 hr.
5	Total hours available for use during the year (365 days × 24 hours) (see instructions)	5 8,760 hr.
6	Divide line 4 by line 5. Enter the result as a decimal amount	6 .
7	Business percentage. For day-care facilities not used exclusively for business, multiply line 6 by line 3 (enter the result as a percentage). All others, enter the amount from line 3 ▶	7 %

Part II   Figure Your Allowable Deduction

		(a) Direct expenses	(b) Indirect expenses	
8	Enter the amount from Schedule C, line 29, **plus** any net gain or (loss) derived from the business use of your home and shown on Schedule D or Form 4797. If more than one place of business, see instructions			8
	See instructions for columns (a) and (b) before completing lines 9–20.			
9	Casualty losses (see instructions)	9		
10	Deductible mortgage interest (see instructions)	10		
11	Real estate taxes (see instructions)	11		
12	Add lines 9, 10, and 11	12		
13	Multiply line 12, column (b) by line 7		13	
14	Add line 12, column (a) and line 13			14
15	Subtract line 14 from line 8. If zero or less, enter -0-			15
16	Excess mortgage interest (see instructions)	16		
17	Insurance	17		
18	Repairs and maintenance	18		
19	Utilities	19		
20	Other expenses (see instructions)	20		
21	Add lines 16 through 20	21		
22	Multiply line 21, column (b) by line 7	22		
23	Carryover of operating expenses from 2002 Form 8829, line 41	23		
24	Add line 21 in column (a), line 22, and line 23			24
25	Allowable operating expenses. Enter the smaller of line 15 or line 24			25
26	Limit on excess casualty losses and depreciation. Subtract line 25 from line 15			26
27	Excess casualty losses (see instructions)	27		
28	Depreciation of your home from Part III below	28		
29	Carryover of excess casualty losses and depreciation from 2002 Form 8829, line 42	29		
30	Add lines 27 through 29			30
31	Allowable excess casualty losses and depreciation. Enter the smaller of line 26 or line 30			31
32	Add lines 14, 25, and 31			32
33	Casualty loss portion, if any, from lines 14 and 31. Carry amount to Form 4684, Section B			33
34	Allowable expenses for business use of your home. Subtract line 33 from line 32. Enter here and on Schedule C, line 30. If your home was used for more than one business, see instructions ▶			34

Part III   Depreciation of Your Home

35	Enter the smaller of your home's adjusted basis or its fair market value (see instructions)	35
36	Value of land included on line 35	36
37	Basis of building. Subtract line 36 from line 35	37
38	Business basis of building. Multiply line 37 by line 7	38
39	Depreciation percentage (see instructions)	39 %
40	Depreciation allowable (see instructions). Multiply line 38 by line 39. Enter here and on line 28 above	40

Part IV   Carryover of Unallowed Expenses to 2004

41	Operating expenses. Subtract line 25 from line 24. If less than zero, enter -0-	41
42	Excess casualty losses and depreciation. Subtract line 31 from line 30. If less than zero, enter -0-	42

For Paperwork Reduction Act Notice, see page 4 of separate instructions.   Cat. No. 13232M   Form **8829** (2003)

INCOME TAX (PARTNERSHIPS)

File Form 1065, *U.S. Return of Partnership Income*.

A partnership is the relationship between two or more persons who join together to carry on a trade or business with each person contributing money, property, labor, or skill, and each expecting to share in the profits and losses of the business.

Every partnership doing business in or having income from sources within the United States is required to file Form 1065 for its tax year. This is mainly an information return. Partnership profits are not taxed to the partnership. Each partner must take into account his or her distributive share of partnership items and report it on his or her own income tax return (whether distributed or not).

Estimated tax. Tax is not withheld on partnership distributions and partners may have to make estimated tax payments. See Schedule SE (Form 1040) *Self-Employment Tax*.

Self-employment tax. A partner's distributive share of income is usually included in figuring net earnings from self-employment. See Schedule SE (Form 1040) *Self-Employment Tax*.

Schedules K and K-1 (Form 1065)

These forms are used to show partners distributive shares of reportable partnership items. Form 1065 and its Schedules K or K-1 are filed separately and not attached to your income tax return.

Schedule E (Form 1040)

Supplemental Income Schedule, Part II is used to report partnership items on your individual tax return. Failure to treat your individual and partnership returns consistently will allow the IRS to assess and take action to collect deficiencies and penalties.

IRS publication. See Publication 541, *Partnerships*, for information and for examples of filled-in forms.

Sample. Form 1065 and Schedule K-1 follow on the next two pages.

Form 1065
U.S. Return of Partnership Income

Form **1065**	U.S. Return of Partnership Income		OMB No. 1545-0099
Department of the Treasury Internal Revenue Service	For calendar year 2003, or tax year beginning ...., 2003, and ending ...., 20.... ▶ See separate instructions.		20**03**

A Principal business activity	Use the IRS label. Otherwise, print or type.	Name of partnership	D **Employer identification number**
B Principal product or service		Number, street, and room or suite no. If a P.O. box, see page 14 of the instructions.	E Date business started
C Business code number		City or town, state, and ZIP code	F Total assets (see page 14 of the instructions) $

G Check applicable boxes: (1) ☐ Initial return (2) ☐ Final return (3) ☐ Name change (4) ☐ Address change (5) ☐ Amended return

H Check accounting method: (1) ☐ Cash (2) ☐ Accrual (3) ☐ Other (specify) ▶ ....

I Number of Schedules K-1. Attach one for each person who was a partner at any time during the tax year ▶ ....

Caution: Include only trade or business income and expenses on lines 1a through 22 below. See the instructions for more information.

Income

1a Gross receipts or sales	1a	
b Less returns and allowances	1b	1c
2 Cost of goods sold (Schedule A, line 8)		2
3 Gross profit. Subtract line 2 from line 1c		3
4 Ordinary income (loss) from other partnerships, estates, and trusts (attach schedule)		4
5 Net farm profit (loss) (attach Schedule F (Form 1040))		5
6 Net gain (loss) from Form 4797, Part II, line 18		6
7 Other income (loss) (attach schedule)		7
8 Total income (loss). Combine lines 3 through 7		8

Deductions (see page 15 of the instructions for limitations)

9 Salaries and wages (other than to partners) (less employment credits)		9
10 Guaranteed payments to partners		10
11 Repairs and maintenance		11
12 Bad debts		12
13 Rent		13
14 Taxes and licenses		14
15 Interest		15
16a Depreciation (if required, attach Form 4562)	16a	
b Less depreciation reported on Schedule A and elsewhere on return	16b	16c
17 Depletion (Do not deduct oil and gas depletion.)		17
18 Retirement plans, etc.		18
19 Employee benefit programs		19
20 Other deductions (attach schedule)		20
21 Total deductions. Add the amounts shown in the far right column for lines 9 through 20		21
22 Ordinary income (loss) from trade or business activities. Subtract line 21 from line 8		22

Sign Here

Under penalties of perjury, I declare that I have examined this return, including accompanying schedules and statements, and to the best of my knowledge and belief, it is true, correct, and complete. Declaration of preparer (other than general partner or limited liability company member) is based on all information of which preparer has any knowledge.

May the IRS discuss this return with the preparer shown below (see instructions)? ☐ Yes ☐ No

▶ Signature of general partner or limited liability company member   ▶ Date

Paid Preparer's Use Only	Preparer's signature		Date		Check if self-employed ▶ ☐	Preparer's SSN or PTIN
	Firm's name (or yours if self-employed), address, and ZIP code	▶			EIN ▶	
					Phone no. ( )	

For Paperwork Reduction Act Notice, see separate instructions.   Cat. No. 11390Z   Form **1065** (2003)

Schedule K-1 (Form 1065)
Partner's Share of Income, Credits, Deductions, etc.

6511

SCHEDULE K-1 (Form 1065)	Partner's Share of Income, Credits, Deductions, etc.	OMB No. 1545-0099
Department of the Treasury Internal Revenue Service	▶ See separate instructions. For calendar year 2003 or tax year beginning , 2003, and ending , 20	2003

Partner's identifying number ▶

Partnership's identifying number ▶

Partner's name, address, and ZIP code

Partnership's name, address, and ZIP code

A This partner is a ☐ general partner ☐ limited partner
☐ limited liability company member

B What type of entity is this partner? ▶

C Is this partner a ☐ domestic or a ☐ foreign partner?

	(i) Before change or termination	(ii) End of year
D Enter partner's percentage of:		
Profit sharing	%	%
Loss sharing	%	%
Ownership of capital	%	%

E IRS Center where partnership filed return:

F Partner's share of liabilities (see instructions):
Nonrecourse . . . . $ ....
Qualified nonrecourse financing . $ ....
Other . . . . $ ....

G Tax shelter registration number . ▶ ....

H Check here if this partnership is a publicly traded partnership as defined in section 469(k)(2) . . . . . ☐

I Check applicable boxes: (1) ☐ Final K-1 (2) ☐ Amended K-1

J Analysis of partner's capital account:

(a) Capital account at beginning of year	(b) Capital contributed during year	(c) Partner's share of lines 3, 4, and 7, Form 1065, Schedule M-2	(d) Withdrawals and distributions	(e) Capital account at end of year (combine columns (a) through (d))
			( )	

	(a) Distributive share item		(b) Amount	(c) 1040 filers enter the amount in column (b) on:
Income (Loss)	1	Ordinary income (loss) from trade or business activities . . .	1	See page 6 of Partner's Instructions for Schedule K-1 (Form 1065).
	2	Net income (loss) from rental real estate activities	2	
	3	Net income (loss) from other rental activities	3	
	4	Portfolio income (loss):		
	a	Interest income	4a	Form 1040, line 8a
	b	(1) Qualified dividends	4b(1)	Form 1040, line 9b
		(2) Total ordinary dividends	4b(2)	Form 1040, line 9a
	c	Royalty income	4c	Sch. E, Part I, line 4
	d	(1) Net short-term capital gain (loss) (post-May 5, 2003) . . .	4d(1)	Sch. D, line 5, col. (g)
		(2) Net short-term capital gain (loss) (entire year)	4d(2)	Sch. D, line 5, col. (f)
	e	(1) Net long-term capital gain (loss) (post-May 5, 2003) . . .	4e(1)	Sch. D, line 12, col. (g)
		(2) Net long-term capital gain (loss) (entire year)	4e(2)	Sch. D, line 12, col. (f)
	f	Other portfolio income (loss) (attach schedule)	4f	
	5	Guaranteed payments to partner	5	See pages 6 and 7 of Partner's Instructions for Schedule K-1 (Form 1065).
	6a	Net section 1231 gain (loss) (post-May 5, 2003).	6a	
	b	Net section 1231 gain (loss) (entire year)	6b	
	7	Other income (loss) (attach schedule)	7	
Deductions	8	Charitable contributions (see instructions) (attach schedule) . .	8	Sch. A, line 15 or 16
	9	Section 179 expense deduction	9	See page 8 of Partner's Instructions for Schedule K-1 (Form 1065).
	10	Deductions related to portfolio income (attach schedule) . . .	10	
	11	Other deductions (attach schedule).	11	
Credits	12a	Low-income housing credit: (1) From section 42(j)(5) partnerships	12a(1)	Form 8586, line 5
		(2) Other than on line 12a(1)	12a(2)	
	b	Qualified rehabilitation expenditures related to rental real estate activities	12b	See page 9 of Partner's Instructions for Schedule K-1 (Form 1065).
	c	Credits (other than credits shown on lines 12a and 12b) related to rental real estate activities	12c	
	d	Credits related to other rental activities	12d	
	13	Other credits	13	

For Paperwork Reduction Act Notice, see Instructions for Form 1065.   Cat. No. 11394R   Schedule K-1 (Form 1065) 2003

INCOME TAX (S CORPORATIONS)

File Form 1120S, *U.S. Income Tax Return for an S Corporation.*

Some corporations may elect not to be subject to income tax. If a corporation qualifies and chooses to become an S corporation, its income usually will be taxed to the shareholders.

The formation of an S corporation is only allowable under certain circumstances.

- It must be a domestic corporation either organized in the United States or organized under federal or state law.

- It must have only one class of stock.

- It must have no more than 75 shareholders.

- It must have as shareholders only individuals, estates, and certain trusts. Partnerships and corporations cannot be shareholders in an S corporation.

- It must have shareholders who are citizens or residents of the United States. Nonresident aliens cannot be shareholders.

The formation of an S corporation can be an advantageous form of legal structure, but if entered into without careful planning, it can result in more taxes instead of less, as anticipated.

Form 1120S

This form is used to file an income tax return for an S corporation. Schedule K and K-1 are extremely important parts of Form 1120S. Schedule K summarizes the corporation's income, deductions, credits, etc., reportable by the shareholders. Schedule K-1 shows each shareholder's separate share. The individual shareholders report their income taxes on Form 1040. Form 1120S is due on the 15th day of the third month after the end of the tax year.

IRS publication. If you need information about S corporations, see Instructions for Form 1120S.

Sample. A copy of Form 1120S follows.

Form 1120S
U.S. Income Tax Return for an S Corporation

Form **1120S** Department of the Treasury Internal Revenue Service	U.S. Income Tax Return for an S Corporation ▶ Do not file this form unless the corporation has timely filed Form 2553 to elect to be an S corporation. ▶ See separate instructions.	OMB No. 1545-0130 20**03**

For calendar year 2003, or tax year beginning , 2003, and ending , 20

A Effective date of election as an S corporation	Use the IRS label. Other-wise, print or type.	Name	C Employer identification number
		Number, street, and room or suite no. (If a P.O. box, see page 12 of the instructions.)	D Date incorporated
B Business code number (see pages 31–33 of the Insts.)		City or town, state, and ZIP code	E Total assets (see page 12 of instructions) $

F Check applicable boxes: (1) ☐ Initial return (2) ☐ Final return (3) ☐ Name change (4) ☐ Address change (5) ☐ Amended return
G Enter number of shareholders in the corporation at end of the tax year . . . . ▶

Caution: Include only trade or business income and expenses on lines 1a through 21. See page 12 of the instructions for more information.

Income

1a	Gross receipts or sales	b Less returns and allowances c Bal ▶	1c
2	Cost of goods sold (Schedule A, line 8)		2
3	Gross profit. Subtract line 2 from line 1c		3
4	Net gain (loss) from Form 4797, Part II, line 18 (attach Form 4797)		4
5	Other income (loss) (attach schedule) . . . . ▶		5
6	Total income (loss). Add lines 3 through 5. . . . . ▶		6

Deductions (see page 13 of the instructions for limitations)

7	Compensation of officers		7
8	Salaries and wages (less employment credits)		8
9	Repairs and maintenance		9
10	Bad debts		10
11	Rents.		11
12	Taxes and licenses		12
13	Interest		13
14a	Depreciation (Attach Form 4562)	14a	
b	Depreciation claimed on Schedule A and elsewhere on return . .	14b	
c	Subtract line 14b from line 14a		14c
15	Depletion (Do not deduct oil and gas depletion.)		15
16	Advertising		16
17	Pension, profit-sharing, etc., plans		17
18	Employee benefit programs		18
19	Other deductions (attach schedule) . . . . ▶		19
20	Total deductions. Add the amounts shown in the far right column for lines 7 through 19 . ▶		20
21	Ordinary income (loss) from trade or business activities. Subtract line 20 from line 6 . . .		21

Tax and Payments

22	Tax: a Excess net passive income tax (attach schedule) . . .	22a	
b	Tax from Schedule D (Form 1120S)	22b	
c	Add lines 22a and 22b (see page 17 of the instructions for additional taxes)		22c
23	Payments: a 2003 estimated tax payments and amount applied from 2002 return	23a	
b	Tax deposited with Form 7004	23b	
c	Credit for Federal tax paid on fuels (attach Form 4136)	23c	
d	Add lines 23a through 23c		23d
24	Estimated tax penalty (See page 17 of instructions). Check if Form 2220 is attached ▶ ☐		24
25	Tax due. If line 23d is smaller than the total of lines 22c and 24, enter amount owed. . . .		25
26	Overpayment. If line 23d is larger than the total of lines 22c and 24, enter amount overpaid ▶		26
27	Enter amount of line 26 you want: Credited to 2004 estimated tax ▶ Refunded ▶		27

Sign Here

Under penalties of perjury, I declare that I have examined this return, including accompanying schedules and statements, and to the best of my knowledge and belief, it is true, correct, and complete. Declaration of preparer (other than taxpayer) is based on all information of which preparer has any knowledge.

▶		▶	May the IRS discuss this return with the preparer shown below (see instructions)? ☐ Yes ☐ No
Signature of officer	Date	Title	

Paid Preparer's Use Only

Preparer's signature ▶		Date	Check if self-employed ☐	Preparer's SSN or PTIN
Firm's name (or yours if self-employed), address, and ZIP code ▶			EIN	
			Phone no. ( )	

For Paperwork Reduction Act Notice, see the separate instructions. Cat. No. 11510H Form **1120S** (2003)

INCOME TAX (CORPORATIONS)

File Form 1120 or 1120-A, *U.S. Corporation Income Tax Return*, or *U.S. Corporation Short-Form Income Tax Return*.

Forming a corporation involves a transfer of either money, property, or both by the prospective shareholders in exchange for capital stock in the corporation.

Every corporation, unless it is specifically exempt or has dissolved, must file a tax return even if it has no taxable income for the year and regardless of the amount of its gross income. Corporate profits normally are taxed to the corporation. When the profits are distributed as dividends, the dividends are then taxed to the shareholders.

Estimated tax. Every corporation whose tax is expected to be $500 or more must make estimated tax payments. If a corporation's estimated tax is $500 or more, its estimated tax payments are deposited with an authorized financial institution or Federal Reserve. Each deposit must be accompanied by Form 8109.

Contributions to the capital of a corporation. Contributions are "paid in capital" and are not taxable income to the corporation.

Form 1120 or 1120-A

The income tax return for ordinary corporations is Form 1120. Form 1120-A is for companies having gross receipts, total income, and total assets that are all under $500,000. In addition, there are other requirements that must be met.

Corporation returns are due on March 15th. A corporation using a fiscal year not beginning January 1st and ending December 31st will have to file the return on or before the 15th day of the third month following the close of its fiscal year.

IRS publication. See Publication 542, *Corporations*, for explanation of the application of various tax provisions to corporations (filing requirements, tax computations, estimated tax payments, corporate distribution and retained earnings, discussion of corporation taxation, as well as liquidations and stock redemptions). Publication 542 also has filled-in examples.

Sample. See Forms 1120 and 1120-A on the following pages.

Form 1120
U.S. Corporation Income Tax Return

Form **1120** Department of the Treasury Internal Revenue Service	U.S. Corporation Income Tax Return	OMB No. 1545-0123
	For calendar year 2003 or tax year beginning ...., 2003, ending ...., 20.... ▶ Instructions are separate. See page 20 for Paperwork Reduction Act Notice.	**2003**

A Check if a:	Use IRS label. Other- wise, print or type.	Name	B Employer identification number
1 Consolidated return (attach Form 851) ☐			
2 Personal holding co. (attach Sch. PH) ☐		Number, street, and room or suite no. (If a P.O. box, see page 7 of instructions.)	C Date incorporated
3 Personal service corp. (as defined in Regulations sec. 1.441-3(c)— see instructions) ☐		City or town, state, and ZIP code	D Total assets (see page 8 of instructions)

E Check applicable boxes: (1) ☐ Initial return   (2) ☐ Final return   (3) ☐ Name change   (4) ☐ Address change $

Income	1a	Gross receipts or sales [____] b Less returns and allowances [____] c Bal ▶	1c
	2	Cost of goods sold (Schedule A, line 8)	2
	3	Gross profit. Subtract line 2 from line 1c	3
	4	Dividends (Schedule C, line 19)	4
	5	Interest	5
	6	Gross rents	6
	7	Gross royalties	7
	8	Capital gain net income (attach Schedule D (Form 1120))	8
	9	Net gain or (loss) from Form 4797, Part II, line 18 (attach Form 4797)	9
	10	Other income (see page 9 of instructions—attach schedule)	10
	11	Total income. Add lines 3 through 10 . . . . ▶	11

Deductions (See instructions for limitations on deductions.)	12	Compensation of officers (Schedule E, line 4)	12
	13	Salaries and wages (less employment credits)	13
	14	Repairs and maintenance	14
	15	Bad debts	15
	16	Rents	16
	17	Taxes and licenses	17
	18	Interest	18
	19	Charitable contributions (see page 11 of instructions for 10% limitation) . .	19
	20	Depreciation (attach Form 4562)	20	
	21	Less depreciation claimed on Schedule A and elsewhere on return . .	21a	21b
	22	Depletion	22
	23	Advertising	23
	24	Pension, profit-sharing, etc., plans	24
	25	Employee benefit programs	25
	26	Other deductions (attach schedule)	26
	27	Total deductions. Add lines 12 through 26 . . . . ▶	27
	28	Taxable income before net operating loss deduction and special deductions. Subtract line 27 from line 11	28
	29	Less: a Net operating loss (NOL) deduction (see page 13 of instructions)	29a	
		b Special deductions (Schedule C, line 20)	29b	29c

Tax and Payments	30	Taxable income. Subtract line 29c from line 28	30
	31	Total tax (Schedule J, line 11)	31
	32	Payments: a 2002 overpayment credited to 2003	32a	
	b	2003 estimated tax payments . .	32b	
	c	Less 2003 refund applied for on Form 4466	32c ( )	d Bal ▶	32d
	e	Tax deposited with Form 7004	32e
	f	Credit for tax paid on undistributed capital gains (attach Form 2439) . . .	32f
	g	Credit for Federal tax on fuels (attach Form 4136). See instructions . .	32g	32h
	33	Estimated tax penalty (see page 14 of instructions). Check if Form 2220 is attached . . . ▶ ☐	33
	34	Tax due. If line 32h is smaller than the total of lines 31 and 33, enter amount owed	34
	35	Overpayment. If line 32h is larger than the total of lines 31 and 33, enter amount overpaid	35
	36	Enter amount of line 35 you want: Credited to 2004 estimated tax ▶ Refunded ▶	36

Sign Here	Under penalties of perjury, I declare that I have examined this return, including accompanying schedules and statements, and to the best of my knowledge and belief, it is true, correct, and complete. Declaration of preparer (other than taxpayer) is based on all information of which preparer has any knowledge.	May the IRS discuss this return with the preparer shown below (see instructions)? ☐ Yes ☐ No
	▶ _____ _____ ▶ _____ Signature of officer Date Title	

Paid Preparer's Use Only	Preparer's signature ▶	Date	Check if self-employed ☐	Preparer's SSN or PTIN
	Firm's name (or yours if self-employed), address, and ZIP code ▶		EIN	
			Phone no. ( )	

Cat. No. 11450Q   Form **1120** (2003)

Form 1120-A
U.S. Corporation Short-Form Income Tax Return

Form **1120-A** Department of the Treasury Internal Revenue Service	U.S. Corporation Short-Form Income Tax Return	OMB No. 1545-0890
	For calendar year 2003 or tax year beginning ...., 2003, ending ...., 20...... See separate instructions to make sure the corporation qualifies to file Form 1120-A.	2003

A Check this box if the corp. is a personal service corp. (as defined in Regulations section 1.441-3(c)—see instructions) ☐

Use IRS label. Otherwise, print or type.

Name

Number, street, and room or suite no. (If a P.O. box, see page 7 of instructions.)

City or town, state, and ZIP code

B Employer identification number

C Date incorporated

D Total assets (see page 8 of instructions)
$

E Check applicable boxes: (1) ☐ Initial return (2) ☐ Name change (3) ☐ Address change

F Check method of accounting: (1) ☐ Cash (2) ☐ Accrual (3) ☐ Other (specify) ►

Income

1a Gross receipts or sales | b Less returns and allowances | c Balance ► **1c**
2 Cost of goods sold (see page 14 of instructions) **2**
3 Gross profit. Subtract line 2 from line 1c **3**
4 Domestic corporation dividends subject to the 70% deduction **4**
5 Interest **5**
6 Gross rents **6**
7 Gross royalties **7**
8 Capital gain net income (attach Schedule D (Form 1120)) **8**
9 Net gain or (loss) from Form 4797, Part II, line 18 (attach Form 4797) **9**
10 Other income (see page 9 of instructions) **10**
11 Total income. Add lines 3 through 10 ► **11**

Deductions (See instructions for limitations on deductions.)

12 Compensation of officers (see page 10 of instructions) **12**
13 Salaries and wages (less employment credits) **13**
14 Repairs and maintenance **14**
15 Bad debts **15**
16 Rents **16**
17 Taxes and licenses **17**
18 Interest **18**
19 Charitable contributions (see page 11 of instructions for 10% limitation) **19**
20 Depreciation (attach Form 4562) **20**
21 Less depreciation claimed elsewhere on return **21a** **21b**
22 Other deductions (attach schedule) **22**
23 Total deductions. Add lines 12 through 22 ► **23**
24 Taxable income before net operating loss deduction and special deductions. Subtract line 23 from line 11 **24**
25 Less: a Net operating loss deduction (see page 13 of instructions) **25a**
b Special deductions (see page 13 of instructions) **25b** **25c**

Tax and Payments

26 Taxable income. Subtract line 25c from line 24 **26**
27 Total tax (from page 2, Part I, line 6) **27**
28 Payments:
a 2002 overpayment credited to 2003 **28a**
b 2003 estimated tax payments **28b**
c Less 2003 refund applied for on Form 4466 **28c** ( ) Bal ► **28d**
e Tax deposited with Form 7004 **28e**
f Credit for tax paid on undistributed capital gains (attach Form 2439) **28f**
g Credit for Federal tax on fuels (attach Form 4136). See instructions **28g**
h Total payments. Add lines 28d through 28g ► **28h**
29 Estimated tax penalty (see page 14 of instructions). Check if Form 2220 is attached ► ☐ **29**
30 Tax due. If line 28h is smaller than the total of lines 27 and 29, enter amount owed **30**
31 Overpayment. If line 28h is larger than the total of lines 27 and 29, enter amount overpaid **31**
32 Enter amount of line 31 you want: **Credited to 2004 estimated tax** ► | Refunded ► **32**

Sign Here

Under penalties of perjury, I declare that I have examined this return, including accompanying schedules and statements, and to the best of my knowledge and belief, it is true, correct, and complete. Declaration of preparer (other than taxpayer) is based on all information of which preparer has any knowledge.

Signature of officer | Date | Title

May the IRS discuss this return with the preparer shown below (see instructions)? ☐ Yes ☐ No

Paid Preparer's Use Only

Preparer's signature | Date | Check if self-employed ☐ | Preparer's SSN or PTIN

Firm's name (or yours if self-employed), address, and ZIP code | EIN | Phone no. ( )

For Paperwork Reduction Act Notice, see page 20 of the instructions. Cat. No. 11456E Form **1120-A** (2003)

ESTIMATED TAX (FOR SOLE PROPRIETOR, INDIVIDUAL WHO IS A PARTNER, OR AN S CORPORATION SHAREHOLDER)

File Form 1040-ES, *Estimated Tax for Individuals.*

If you are a sole proprietor, an individual who is a partner, or a shareholder in an S corporation, you probably will have to make estimated tax payments if the total of your estimated income tax and self-employment tax is in excess of a certain amount (in 2003, if it exceeds your total withholding and credits by $1,000 or more).

Underpayment of tax. If you do not pay enough income tax and self-employment tax for the current year by withholding or by making estimated tax payments, you may have to pay a penalty on the amount not paid. IRS will figure the penalty and send you a bill.

Form 1040-ES

IRS Form 1040-ES is used to estimate your tax. There are four vouchers and they are filed on April 15th, June 15th, September 15th, and January 15th. (Notice that there are only two months between the first and second payments and four months between the third and fourth payments.)

Your estimated tax payments include both federal income tax and self-employment tax liabilities.

Estimated Tax Worksheet

You can use the Estimated Tax Worksheet to figure your estimated tax liability. Keep it for your own records and revise if your actual income is very far over or under your estimate. After the first filing, Form 1040-ES will be sent to you each year.

IRS publications. See Publication 505, *Tax Withholding and Estimated Tax*, for information. Also see instructions accompanying Form 1040-ES.

Sample. Samples of an Estimated Tax Worksheet and a 1040-ES can be seen on the following pages.

2003
Estimated Tax Worksheet

2003 Estimated Tax Worksheet   (keep for your records)

1	Adjusted gross income you expect in 2003 (see instructions above)	1	
2	• If you plan to itemize deductions, enter the estimated total of your itemized deductions. Caution: If line 1 above is over $139,500 ($69,750 if married filing separately), your deduction may be reduced. See Pub. 505 for details. • If you do not plan to itemize deductions, enter your standard deduction from page 2.	2	
3	Subtract line 2 from line 1	3	
4	Exemptions. Multiply $3,050 by the number of personal exemptions. If you can be claimed as a dependent on another person's 2003 return, your personal exemption is not allowed. Caution: See Pub. 505 to figure the amount to enter if line 1 above is over: $209,250 if married filing jointly or qualifying widow(er); $174,400 if head of household; $139,500 if single; or $104,625 if married filing separately	4	
5	Subtract line 4 from line 3	5	
6	Tax. Figure your tax on the amount on line 5 by using the 2003 Tax Rate Schedules on page 2. Caution: If you have a net capital gain, see Pub. 505 to figure the tax	6	
7	Alternative minimum tax from Form 6251	7	
8	Add lines 6 and 7. Also include any tax from Forms 4972 and 8814 and any recapture of the education credits (see instructions above)	8	
9	Credits (see instructions above). Do not include any income tax withholding on this line . . .	9	
10	Subtract line 9 from line 8. If zero or less, enter -0-	10	
11	Self-employment tax (see instructions above). Estimate of 2003 net earnings from self-employment $_____ ; if $87,000 or less, multiply the amount by 15.3%; if more than $87,000, multiply the amount by 2.9%, add $10,788.00 to the result, and enter the total. Caution: If you also have wages subject to social security tax, see Pub. 505 to figure the amount to enter	11	
12	Other taxes (see instructions on page 5)	12	
13a	Add lines 10 through 12	13a	
b	Earned income credit, additional child tax credit, and credits from Form 4136 and Form 8885	13b	
c	Total 2003 estimated tax. Subtract line 13b from line 13a. If zero or less, enter -0- . . . ▶	13c	
14a	Multiply line 13c by 90% (66⅔% for farmers and fishermen) . . .	14a	
b	Enter the tax shown on your 2002 tax return (110% of that amount if you are not a farmer or fisherman and the adjusted gross income shown on line 36 of that return is more than $150,000 or, if married filing separately for 2003, more than $75,000)	14b	
c	Required annual payment to avoid a penalty. Enter the smaller of line 14a or 14b . . ▶	14c	
	Caution: Generally, if you do not prepay (through income tax withholding and estimated tax payments) at least the amount on line 14c, you may owe a penalty for not paying enough estimated tax. To avoid a penalty, make sure your estimate on line 13c is as accurate as possible. Even if you pay the required annual payment, you may still owe tax when you file your return. If you prefer, you may pay the amount shown on line 13c. For details, see Pub. 505.		
15	Income tax withheld and estimated to be withheld during 2003 (including income tax withholding on pensions, annuities, certain deferred income, etc.)	15	
16	Subtract line 15 from line 14c. (Note: If zero or less or line 13c minus line 15 is less than $1,000, stop here. You are not required to make estimated tax payments.)	16	
17	If the first payment you are required to make is due April 15, 2003, enter ¼ of line 16 (minus any 2002 overpayment that you are applying to this installment) here, and on your payment voucher(s) if you are paying by check or money order. (Note: Household employers, see instructions on page 5.)	17	

2003 Tax Rate Schedules

Caution. Do not use these Tax Rate Schedules to figure your 2002 taxes. Use only to figure your 2003 estimated taxes.

Single —Schedule X

If line 5 is:		The tax is:	of the amount
Over—	But not over—		over—
$0	$ 6,000	.... 10%	$0
6,000	28,400	$600.00 + 15%	6,000
28,400	68,800	3,960.00 + 27%	28,400
68,800	143,500	14,868.00 + 30%	68,800
143,500	311,950	37,278.00 + 35%	143,500
311,950	....	96,235.50 + 38.6%	311,950

Head of household —Schedule Z

If line 5 is:		The tax is:	of the amount
Over—	But not over—		over—
$0	$10,000	.... 10%	$0
10,000	38,050	$1,000.00 + 15%	10,000
38,050	98,250	5,207.50 + 27%	38,050
98,250	159,100	21,461.50 + 30%	98,250
159,100	311,950	39,716.50 + 35%	159,100
311,950	....	93,214.00 + 38.6%	311,950

Married filing jointly or Qualifying widow(er) —Schedule Y-1

If line 5 is:		The tax is:	of the amount
Over—	But not over—		over—
$0	$12,000	.... 10%	$0
12,000	47,450	$1,200.00 + 15%	12,000
47,450	114,650	6,517.50 + 27%	47,450
114,650	174,700	24,661.50 + 30%	114,650
174,700	311,950	42,676.50 + 35%	174,700
311,950	....	90,714.00 + 38.6%	311,950

Married filing separately —Schedule Y-2

If line 5 is:		The tax is:	of the amount
Over—	But not over—		over—
$0	$ 6,000	.... 10%	$0
6,000	23,725	$600.00 + 15%	6,000
23,725	57,325	3,258.75 + 27%	23,725
57,325	87,350	12,330.75 + 30%	57,325
87,350	155,975	21,338.25 + 35%	87,350
155,975	....	45,357.00 + 38.6%	155,975

Form 1040–ES
Estimated Tax Payment Record and Sample Voucher

Payment Due Dates

You may pay all of your estimated tax by April 15, 2003, or in four equal amounts by the dates shown below.

1st payment	April 15, 2003
2nd payment	June 16, 2003
3rd payment	Sept. 15, 2003
4th payment	Jan. 15, 2004*

*You do not have to make the payment due January 15, 2004, if you file your 2003 tax return by February 2, 2004, and pay the entire balance due with your return.

Note. Payments are due by the dates indicated whether or not you are outside the United States and Puerto Rico.

Where To File Your Payment Voucher if Paying by Check or Money Order

Mail your payment voucher and check or money order to the Internal Revenue Service at the address shown below for the place where you live. Do not mail your tax return to this address or send an estimated tax payment without a payment voucher. Also, do not mail your estimated tax payments to the address shown in the Form 1040 or 1040A instructions. If you need more payment vouchers, use another Form 1040-ES package.

Note: For proper delivery of your estimated tax payment to a P.O. box, you must include the box number in the address. Also, note that only the U.S. Postal Service can deliver to P.O. boxes.

IF you live in . . .	THEN use . . .
New York (New York City and counties of Nassau, Rockland, Suffolk, and Westchester)	P.O. Box 162 Newark, NJ 07101-0162
New York (all other counties), Maine, New Hampshire, Vermont	P.O. Box 1219 Charlotte, NC 28201-1219
Massachusetts, Michigan, Rhode Island	P.O. Box 37001 Hartford, CT 06176-0001

Connecticut, Delaware, District of Columbia, Maryland, New Jersey, Pennsylvania	P.O. Box 80102 Cincinnati, OH 45280-0002
Florida, Georgia, Mississippi, North Carolina, South Carolina, West Virginia	P.O. Box 105900 Atlanta, GA 30348-5900
Alabama, Arkansas, Ohio, Tennessee, Virginia	P.O. Box 105225 Atlanta, GA 30348-5225
Illinois, Indiana, Iowa, Kansas, Minnesota, Missouri, Nebraska, North Dakota, South Dakota, Utah, Wisconsin	P.O. Box 970006 St. Louis, MO 63197-0006
Arizona, Idaho, Washington	P.O. Box 54919 Los Angeles, CA 90054-0919
Alaska, California, Hawaii, Nevada, Oregon	P.O. Box 510000 San Francisco, CA 94151-5100
Colorado, Kentucky, Louisiana, Montana, New Mexico, Oklahoma, Texas, Wyoming	P.O. Box 660406 Dallas, TX 75266-0406

All APO and FPO addresses, American Samoa, the Commonwealth of the Northern Mariana Islands, nonpermanent residents of Guam or the Virgin Islands, Puerto Rico (or if excluding income under section 933), dual-status aliens, a foreign country: U.S. citizens and those filing Form 2555, 2555-EZ, or 4563)	P.O. Box 80102 Cincinnati, OH 45280-0002
Permanent residents of Guam*	Department of Revenue and Taxation Government of Guam P.O. Box 23607 GMF, GU 96921
Permanent residents of the Virgin Islands*	V.I. Bureau of Internal Revenue 9601 Estate Thomas Charlotte Amalie St. Thomas, VI 00802

* Permanent residents must prepare separate vouchers for estimated income tax and self-employment tax payments. Send the income tax vouchers to the address for permanent residents and the self-employment tax vouchers to the address for nonpermanent residents.

----- Tear off here -----

Form **1040-ES** Department of the Treasury Internal Revenue Service	**2003** Payment Voucher **4**		OMB No. 1545-0087

File only if you are making a payment of estimated tax by check or money order. Mail this voucher with your check or money order payable to the "United States Treasury. " Write your social security number and "2003 Form 1040-ES" on your check or money order. Do not send cash. Enclose, but do not staple or attach, your payment with this voucher.

	Calendar year —Due Jan. 15, 2004		
	Amount of estimated tax you are paying by check or money order.	Dollars	Cents

Type or print	Your first name and initial	Your last name	Your social security number
	If joint payment, complete for spouse		
	Spouse's first name and initial	Spouse's last name	Spouse's social security number
	Address (number, street, and apt. no.)		
	City, state, and ZIP code (If a foreign address, enter city, province or state, postal code, and country.)		

For Privacy Act and Paperwork Reduction Act Notice, see instructions on page 5.

ESTIMATED TAX (CORPORATIONS)

File Form 1120-W, *Estimated Tax for Corporations* (Worksheet).

Every corporation whose tax is expected to be $500 or more must make estimated tax payments. A corporation's estimated tax is the amount of its expected tax liability (including alternative minimum tax and environmental tax) less its allowable tax credits.

Deposits

If a corporation's estimated tax is $500 or more, its estimated tax payments must be deposited with an authorized financial institution or a Federal Reserve Bank. Each deposit must be accompanied by a federal tax deposit coupon and deposited according to the instructions in the coupon book.

The due dates of deposits are the 15th day of the 4th, 6th, 9th, and 12th months of the tax year. Depending on when the $500 requirement is first met, a corporation will make either four, three, two, or one installment deposit. Amounts of estimated tax should be refigured each quarter and amended to reflect changes.

Penalty. A corporation that fails to pay in full a correct installment of estimated tax by the due date is generally subject to a penalty. The penalty is figured at a rate of interest published quarterly by the IRS in the *Internal Revenue Bulletin*.

Form 1120-W (Worksheet)

This form is filled out as an aid in determining the estimated tax and required deposits. The form should be retained and not filed with the IRS. As an aid in determining its estimated alternative minimum tax and environmental tax, a corporation should get a copy of Form 4626-W. Retain this form and do not file with the IRS.

IRS publication. See Publication 542, *Corporations*. This publication includes discussion of corporation taxation, as well as liquidations and stock redemptions.

Sample. See sample of Form 1120-W (Worksheet) on the next page.

Form 1120-W
Estimated Tax for Corporations Worksheet

Form **1120-W** (WORKSHEET) Department of the Treasury Internal Revenue Service	Estimated Tax for Corporations For calendar year 2003, or tax year beginning .... , 2003, and ending .... , 20 ..... (Keep for the corporation's records—Do not send to the Internal Revenue Service.)	OMB No. 1545-0975 2003

1	Taxable income expected for the tax year . . . . (Qualified personal service corporations (defined in the instructions), skip lines 2 through 13 and go to line 14.)	1
2	Enter the smaller of line 1 or $50,000. (Members of a controlled group, see instructions.) . .	2
3	Subtract line 2 from line 1	3
4	Enter the smaller of line 3 or $25,000. (Members of a controlled group, see instructions.) . .	4
5	Subtract line 4 from line 3	5
6	Enter the smaller of line 5 or $9,925,000. (Members of a controlled group, see instructions.) .	6
7	Subtract line 6 from line 5	7
8	Multiply line 2 by 15%	8
9	Multiply line 4 by 25%	9
10	Multiply line 6 by 34%	10
11	Multiply line 7 by 35%	11
12	If line 1 is greater than $100,000, enter the smaller of (a) 5% of the excess over $100,000 or (b) $11,750. Otherwise, enter -0-. (Members of a controlled group, see instructions.)	12
13	If line 1 is greater than $15 million, enter the smaller of (a) 3% of the excess over $15 million or (b) $100,000. Otherwise, enter -0-. (Members of a controlled group, see instructions.) . .	13
14	Subtotal. Add lines 8 through 13. (Qualified personal service corporations, multiply line 1 by 35%.).	14
15	Alternative minimum tax (see instructions)	15
16	Total. Add lines 14 and 15	16
17	Tax credits (see instructions)	17
18	Subtract line 17 from line 16	18
19	Other taxes (see instructions)	19
20	Total. Add lines 18 and 19	20
21	Credit for Federal tax paid on fuels (see instructions)	21
22	Subtract line 21 from line 20. Note. If the result is less than $500, the corporation is not required to make estimated tax payments	22
23a	Enter the tax shown on the corporation's 2002 tax return (see instructions). Caution: If zero or the tax year was for less than 12 months, skip this line and enter the amount from line 22 on line 23b	23a
b	Enter the smaller of line 22 or line 23a. If the corporation is required to skip line 23a, enter the amount from line 22 on line 23b	23b

		(a)	(b)	(c)	(d)
24	Installment due dates (see instructions) . . . . . ▶	24			
25	Required installments. Enter 25% of line 23b in columns (a) through (d) unless the corporation uses the annualized income installment method, the adjusted seasonal installment method, or is a "large corporation" (see instructions)	25			

For Paperwork Reduction Act Notice, see the instructions on page 6. Cat. No. 11525G Form **1120-W** (2003)

SELF-EMPLOYMENT TAX
(FOR SOLE PROPRIETOR, INDIVIDUAL
WHO IS A PARTNER, OR AN S CORPORATION SHAREHOLDER)

File Schedule SE (Form 1040), *Self-Employment Tax.*

The self-employment tax is a Social Security and Medicare tax for individuals who work for themselves. Social Security benefits are available to the self-employed individual just as they are to wage earners. Your payments of self-employment tax contribute to your coverage under the Social Security system. That coverage provides you with retirement benefits and with medical insurance (Medicare) benefits.

Note: You may be liable for paying self-employment tax even if you are now fully insured under Social Security and are now receiving benefits.

Who Must Pay the Tax?

If you carry on a trade or business, except as an employee, you will have to pay self-employment tax on your self-employment income. A trade or business is generally an activity that is carried on for a livelihood, or in good faith to make a profit. The business does not need to actually make a profit, but the profit motive must exist and you must be making ongoing efforts to further your business. Regularity of activities and transactions and the production of income are key elements.

You are self-employed if you are a (1) sole proprietor, (2) independent contractor, (3) member of a partnership, or (4) are otherwise in business for yourself. You do not have to carry on regular full-time business activities to be self-employed. Part-time work, including work you do on the side in addition to your regular job, may also be self-employment.

Income Limits

You must pay self-employment tax if you have net earnings from self-employment of $400 or more. The self-employment tax rate for 2003 is 15.3% (a total of 12.4% for Social Security on net earnings up to a maximum of $87,000 for 2003 and $87,900 for 2004, and 2.9% for Medicare on total net earnings). If you are also a wage earner and those earnings were subject to Social Security tax, you will not be taxed on that amount under self-employment income.

Figuring Self-Employment Tax

There are three steps to figure the amount of self-employment tax you owe: (1) determine your net earnings from self-employment, (2) determine the amount that is subject to the tax, and (3) multiply that amount by the tax rate.

Note: There are two tax deductions on your income tax return relating to self-employment tax. Both deductions result in a reduction of your total income tax burden.

1. **On Schedule SE.** A deduction of **7.65%** of your net earnings from self-employment is taken directly on Schedule SE, reducing the self-employment tax itself by that percentage.

2. **On Form 1040.** There is a deduction that reduces your adjusted gross income on Form 1040 by allowing one-half the amount of your self-employment tax liability to be deducted as a business expense. This is an income tax adjustment only. It does not affect your net earnings from self-employment or your Schedule SE tax.

Joint Returns

You may not file a joint Schedule SE (Form 1040) even if you file a joint income tax return. Your spouse is not considered self-employed just because you are. If you both have self-employment income, each of you must file a separate Schedule SE (Form 1040).

Social Security Number

You must have a Social Security number if you have to pay self-employment tax. You may apply for one at the nearest Social Security Office. Form SS-5, *Application for a Social Security Card*, may be obtained from any Social Security office.

Schedule SE (Form 1040)

Schedule SE, *Self-Employment Tax*, is used to compute self-employment tax. If you are required to pay estimated income tax (see Estimated Tax section) you must also figure any self-employment tax you owe and include that amount when you send in your 1040-ES vouchers. If you are not required to pay estimated taxes, the full payment is remitted with your annual tax return.

IRS publications. See Publication 334, *Tax Guide for Small Business*. For more detailed information, read Publication 533, *Self-Employment Tax*. Included in the publication is an illustrated Schedule SE.

Sample. A sample of Schedule SE (Form 1040) can be seen on the next page. For information on 1040-ES, refer back to page 127 to the information on Estimated Tax for your legal structure.

Schedule SE (Form 1040)
Computation of Self-Employment Tax

SCHEDULE SE		OMB No. 1545-0074
(Form 1040)	**Self-Employment Tax**	20**03**
Department of the Treasury Internal Revenue Service (99)	▶ Attach to Form 1040. ▶ See Instructions for Schedule SE (Form 1040).	Attachment Sequence No. **17**

Name of person with self-employment income (as shown on Form 1040)	Social security number of person with self-employment income ▶	

Who Must File Schedule SE

You must file Schedule SE if:

- You had net earnings from self-employment from other than church employee income (line 4 of Short Schedule SE or line 4c of Long Schedule SE) of $400 or more or

- You had church employee income of $108.28 or more. Income from services you performed as a minister or a member of a religious order is not church employee income (see page SE-1).

Note. Even if you had a loss or a small amount of income from self-employment, it may be to your benefit to file Schedule SE and use either "optional method" in Part II of Long Schedule SE (see page SE-3).

Exception. If your only self-employment income was from earnings as a minister, member of a religious order, or Christian Science practitioner and you filed Form 4361 and received IRS approval not to be taxed on those earnings, do not file Schedule SE. Instead, write "Exempt–Form 4361" on Form 1040, line 55.

May I Use Short Schedule SE or Must I Use Long Schedule SE?

Did You Receive Wages or Tips in 2003?

No → Are you a minister, member of a religious order, or Christian Science practitioner who received IRS approval not to be taxed on earnings from these sources, but you owe self-employment tax on other earnings? — Yes →

No ↓

Are you using one of the optional methods to figure your net earnings (see page SE-3)? — Yes →

No ↓

Did you receive church employee income reported on Form W-2 of $108.28 or more? — Yes →

No ↓

You May Use Short Schedule SE Below

Yes → Was the total of your wages and tips subject to social security or railroad retirement tax plus your net earnings from self-employment more than $87,000? — Yes →

No ↓

No ← Did you receive tips subject to social security or Medicare tax that you did not report to your employer? — Yes →

You Must Use Long Schedule SE on page 2

Section A—Short Schedule SE. Caution. Read above to see if you can use Short Schedule SE.

1	Net farm profit or (loss) from Schedule F, line 36, and farm partnerships, Schedule K-1 (Form 1065), line 15a	1	
2	Net profit or (loss) from Schedule C, line 31; Schedule C-EZ, line 3; Schedule K-1 (Form 1065), line 15a (other than farming); and Schedule K-1 (Form 1065-B), box 9. Ministers and members of religious orders, see page SE-1 for amounts to report on this line. See page SE-2 for other income to report	2	
3	Combine lines 1 and 2	3	
4	Net earnings from self-employment. Multiply line 3 by 92.35% (.9235). If less than $400, do not file this schedule; you do not owe self-employment tax . . . . ▶	4	
5	Self-employment tax. If the amount on line 4 is: • $87,000 or less, multiply line 4 by 15.3% (.153). Enter the result here and on Form 1040, line 55. • More than $87,000, multiply line 4 by 2.9% (.029). Then, add $10,788.00 to the result. Enter the total here and on Form 1040, line 55.	5	
6	Deduction for one-half of self-employment tax. Multiply line 5 by 50% (.5). Enter the result here and on Form 1040, line 28	6	

For Paperwork Reduction Act Notice, see Form 1040 instructions. Cat. No. 11358Z Schedule SE (Form 1040) 2003

SOCIAL SECURITY (FICA) TAX AND WITHHOLDING OF INCOME TAX

File Form 941 (941E, 942, or 943), *Employers Quarterly Federal Tax Return*. Also, Forms W-2, W-3, and W-4.

If you have one or more employees, you will be required to withhold federal income tax from their wages. You also must collect and pay the employee's part and your matching share of Social Security (FICA) and Medicare taxes.

You are liable for the payment of these taxes to the federal government whether or not you collect them from your employees. See "Liability for Tax Withheld" on page 137.

Who Are Employees?

Under common law rules, every individual who performs services that are subject to the will and control of an employer, as to both what must be done and how it must be done, is an employee. Two of the usual characteristics of an employer-employee relationship are that the employer has the right to discharge the employee and the employer supplies tools and a place to work. It does not matter if the employee is called an employee, a partner, co-adventurer, agent, or independent contractor. It does not matter how the payments are measured, how they are made, or what they are called. Nor does it matter whether the individual is employed full-time or part-time.

Note: For an in-depth discussion and examples of employer-employee relationships, see Publication 15-A, *Employer's Supplemental Tax Guide*. If you want the IRS to determine whether a worker is an employee, file Form SS-8 with the District Director for the area in which your business is located.

Social Security and Medicare Taxes

The Federal Insurance Contributions Act (FICA) provides for a federal system of old-age, survivors, disability, and hospital insurance. The old-age, survivors, and disability part is financed through Social Security taxes. The hospital part is financed by the Medicare tax. Each of these taxes is reported separately. Social Security taxes are levied on both you and your employees. You as an employer must collect and pay the employee's part of the tax. You must withhold it from wages. You are also liable for your own (employer's) matching share of Social Security taxes.

Tax Rate

The tax rate for Social Security is 6.2% each for employers and employees (12.4% total), and the wage base for 2003 is $87,000 ($87,900 for 2004). The tax rate for Medicare is 1.45% each for employers and employees (2.9% total). There is no wage base limit for

Medicare tax. All covered wages are subject to the tax. Social Security taxes and withheld income taxes are reported and paid together. For more detailed information, read Publication 334, *Tax Guide for Small Business*, and Publication 15, *Circular E, Employer's Tax Guide*.

Withholding of Income Tax

Generally, you must withhold income from wages you pay employees if their wages for any payroll period are more than the dollar amount of their withholding allowances claimed for that period. The amount to be withheld is figured separately for each payroll period. You should figure withholding on gross wages before any deductions for Social Security tax, pension, union dues, insurance, etc. are made. *Circular E, Employer's Tax Guide*, contains the applicable tables and detailed instructions for using withholding methods.

Tax Forms

The following are the forms used to report Social Security taxes and withheld income tax.

Form 941, *Employer's Quarterly Federal Tax Return*

Generally, Social Security (FICA) and Medicare taxes and withheld income tax are reported together on Form 941. Forms 942, 943, and 945 are used for other than the usual type of employee. (See Publication 334.) Form 943 (for Agricultural Employees) is an annual return due one month after the end of the calendar year. The other forms are quarterly returns and are due one month after the end of each calendar quarter. Due dates are April 30, July 31, October 31, and January 31. An extra 10 days are given if taxes are deposited on time and in full.

Form 8109, *Federal Tax Deposit Coupon*

You generally will have to make deposits of Social Security and Medicare taxes and withheld income taxes before the return is due. Deposits are not required for taxes reported on Form 942. You must deposit both your part and your employee's part of Social Security taxes in an authorized financial institution or a Federal Reserve Bank. See Publication 15, *Circular E, Employer's Tax Guide* for detailed information on deposits. Forms 8109, *Federal Tax Deposit Coupons*, are used to make deposits.

Form W-2

You must furnish copies of Form W-2 to each employee from whom income tax or Social Security tax has been withheld. Form W-2 shows the total wages and other compensations paid. Total wages subject to Social Security and Medicare taxes, amounts deducted for income, Social Security, and Medicare taxes, and any other information required on the statement. Detailed information for preparation of this form is contained in the instructions for Form W-2. Furnish copies of Form W-2 to employees as soon as possible after December 31, so they may file their income tax returns early. It must be sent to the employee no later than January 31st. W-2s must also be transmitted annually to the Social Security Administration.

Form W-3

Employers must file Form W-3 annually to transmit forms W-2 and W-2P to the Social Security Administration. These forms will be processed by the Social Security Administration, which will then furnish the Internal Revenue Service with the income tax data that it needs from the forms. Form W-3 and its attachments must be filed separately from Form 941 by the last day of February, following the calendar year for which the Form W-2 is prepared.

Form W-4

In general, an employee can claim withholding allowances equal to the number of exemptions he or she is entitled to claim on an income tax return. Each new employee should give you a form W-4, *Employee's Withholding Allowance Certificate*, on or before the first day of work. The certificates must include the employee's Social Security number. Copies of W-4 that are required to be submitted because of a large number of allowances or claims of exemption from income tax withholding are sent in with quarterly employment tax returns (Form 941 and 941E). Withholding is then figured on gross wages before deductions for Social Security, tax pension, insurance, etc.

Liability for Tax Withheld

You are required by law to deduct and withhold income tax from the salaries and wages of your employees. You are liable for payment of that tax to the federal government whether or not you collect it from your employees.

IRS publication. For detailed information, refer to Publication 15, *Circular E, Employer's Tax Guide*.

Sample. You will find samples of Form 941, W-2, W-3, and W-4 on the following pages.

Form 941
Employer's Quarterly Federal Tax Return

Form 941
(Rev. January 2003)
Department of the Treasury
Internal Revenue Service (99)

Employer's Quarterly Federal Tax Return

▶ See separate instructions revised January 2003 for information on completing this return.

Please type or print.

Enter state code for state in which deposits were made only if different from state in address to the right ▶ ☐ (see page 2 of separate instructions).

Name (as distinguished from trade name)	Date quarter ended
Trade name, if any	Employer identification number
Address (number and street)	City, state, and ZIP code

OMB No. 1545-0029

| T |
| FF |
| FD |
| FP |
| I |
| T |

If address is different from prior return, check here ▶ ☐

IRS Use

1 1 1 1 1 1 1 1 1 1   2   3 3 3 3 3 3 3   4 4 4   5 5 5
6   7   8 8 8 8 8 8 8   9 9 9 9 9   10 10 10 10 10 10 10 10 10

A If you do not have to file returns in the future, check here ▶ ☐ and enter date final wages paid ▶

B If you are a seasonal employer, see Seasonal employers on page 1 of the instructions and check here ▶ ☐

1	Number of employees in the pay period that includes March 12th . ▶	1		
2	Total wages and tips, plus other compensation		2	
3	Total income tax withheld from wages, tips, and sick pay		3	
4	Adjustment of withheld income tax for preceding quarters of this calendar year		4	
5	Adjusted total of income tax withheld (line 3 as adjusted by line 4)		5	
6	Taxable social security wages	6a	× 12.4% (.124) =	6b	
	Taxable social security tips	6c	× 12.4% (.124) =	6d	
7	Taxable Medicare wages and tips . . .	7a	× 2.9% (.029) =	7b	
8	Total social security and Medicare taxes (add lines 6b, 6d, and 7b). Check here if wages are not subject to social security and/or Medicare tax . . . . . ▶ ☐		8	
9	Adjustment of social security and Medicare taxes (see instructions for required explanation) Sick Pay $_____ ± Fractions of Cents $_____ ± Other $_____ =		9	
10	Adjusted total of social security and Medicare taxes (line 8 as adjusted by line 9)		10	
11	Total taxes (add lines 5 and 10)		11	
12	Advance earned income credit (EIC) payments made to employees (see instructions) . . .		12	
13	Net taxes (subtract line 12 from line 11). If $2,500 or more, this must equal line 17, column (d) below (or line D of Schedule B (Form 941))		13	
14	Total deposits for quarter, including overpayment applied from a prior quarter		14	
15	Balance due (subtract line 14 from line 13). See instructions		15	
16	Overpayment. If line 14 is more than line 13, enter excess here ▶ $_____			

and check if to be: ☐ Applied to next return or ☐ Refunded.

- All filers: If line 13 is less than $2,500, do not complete line 17 or Schedule B (Form 941).
- Semiweekly schedule depositors: Complete Schedule B (Form 941) and check here . . . . ▶ ☐
- Monthly schedule depositors: Complete line 17, columns (a) through (d), and check here. . . . . ▶ ☐

17	Monthly Summary of Federal Tax Liability. (Complete Schedule B (Form 941) instead, if you were a semiweekly schedule depositor.)			
	(a) First month liability	(b) Second month liability	(c) Third month liability	(d) Total liability for quarter

Third Party Designee

Do you want to allow another person to discuss this return with the IRS (see separate instructions)? ☐ Yes. Complete the following. ☐ No

Designee's name ▶

Phone no. ▶ ( )

Personal identification number (PIN) ▶ ☐☐☐☐☐

Sign Here

Under penalties of perjury, I declare that I have examined this return, including accompanying schedules and statements, and to the best of my knowledge and belief, it is true, correct, and complete.

Signature ▶

Print Your Name and Title ▶

Date ▶

For Privacy Act and Paperwork Reduction Act Notice, see back of Payment Voucher.   Cat. No. 17001Z   Form **941** (Rev. 1-2003)

Form W-2
Wage and Tax Statement 2003

a Control number	22222	Void ☐	For Official Use Only ▶ OMB No. 1545-0008		

b Employer identification number	1 Wages, tips, other compensation $	2 Federal income tax withheld $

c Employer's name, address, and ZIP code	3 Social security wages $	4 Social security tax withheld $
	5 Medicare wages and tips $	6 Medicare tax withheld $
	7 Social security tips $	8 Allocated tips $

d Employee's social security number	9 Advance EIC payment $	10 Dependent care benefits $

e Employee's first name and initial Last name	11 Nonqualified plans $	12a See instructions for box 12 $
	13 Statutory employee ☐ Retirement plan ☐ Third-party sick pay ☐	12b $
	14 Other	12c $
		12d $

f Employee's address and ZIP code					
15 State Employer's state ID number	16 State wages, tips, etc. $	17 State income tax $	18 Local wages, tips, etc. $	19 Local income tax $	20 Locality name
	$	$	$	$	

Form **W-2** Wage and Tax Statement (99)   **2003**

Department of the Treasury—Internal Revenue Service
For Privacy Act and Paperwork Reduction Act Notice, see separate instructions.

Copy A For Social Security Administration— Send this entire page with Form W-3 to the Social Security Administration; photocopies are not acceptable.   Cat. No. 10134D

Do Not Cut, Fold, or Staple Forms on This Page — Do Not Cut, Fold, or Staple Forms on This Page

---

a Control number	22222	Void ☐	For Official Use Only ▶ OMB No. 1545-0008		

b Employer identification number	1 Wages, tips, other compensation $	2 Federal income tax withheld $

c Employer's name, address, and ZIP code	3 Social security wages $	4 Social security tax withheld $
	5 Medicare wages and tips $	6 Medicare tax withheld $
	7 Social security tips $	8 Allocated tips $

d Employee's social security number	9 Advance EIC payment $	10 Dependent care benefits $

e Employee's first name and initial Last name	11 Nonqualified plans $	12a See instructions for box 12 $
	13 Statutory employee ☐ Retirement plan ☐ Third-party sick pay ☐	12b $
	14 Other	12c $
		12d $

f Employee's address and ZIP code					
15 State Employer's state ID number	16 State wages, tips, etc. $	17 State income tax $	18 Local wages, tips, etc. $	19 Local income tax $	20 Locality name
	$	$	$	$	

Form **W-2** Wage and Tax Statement (99)   **2003**

Department of the Treasury—Internal Revenue Service
For Privacy Act and Paperwork Reduction Act Notice, see separate instructions.

Copy A For Social Security Administration— Send this entire page with Form W-3 to the Social Security Administration; photocopies are not acceptable.   Cat. No. 10134D

Do Not Cut, Fold, or Staple Forms on This Page — Do Not Cut, Fold, or Staple Forms on This Page

Form W-3
Transmittal of Income and Tax Statements 2003

DO NOT STAPLE OR FOLD

a Control number 33333 For Official Use Only ▶ OMB No. 1545-0008		

b Kind of Payer	941 ☐ Military ☐ 943 ☐ CT-1 ☐ Hshld. emp. ☐ Medicare govt. emp. ☐ **Third-party sick pay** ☐	**1** Wages, tips, other compensation $	**2** Federal income tax withheld $

3 Social security wages $	**4** Social security tax withheld $
c Total number of Forms W-2 **d** Establishment number	**5** Medicare wages and tips $	**6** Medicare tax withheld $
e Employer identification number	**7** Social security tips $	**8** Allocated tips $
f Employer's name	**9** Advance EIC payments $	**10** Dependent care benefits $
	11 Nonqualified plans $	**12** Deferred compensation $
	13 For third-party sick pay use only	
	14 Income tax withheld by payer of third-party sick pay $	
g Employer's address and ZIP code		
h Other EIN used this year		
15 State Employer's state ID number	**16** State wages, tips, etc. $	**17** State income tax $
	18 Local wages, tips, etc. $	**19** Local income tax $
Contact person	Telephone number ( )	For Official Use Only
E-mail address	Fax number ( )	

Under penalties of perjury, I declare that I have examined this return and accompanying documents, and, to the best of my knowledge and belief, they are true, correct, and complete.

Signature ▶   Title ▶   Date ▶

Form **W-3** Transmittal of Wage and Tax Statements   **2003**   Department of the Treasury Internal Revenue Service

Send this entire page with the entire Copy A page of Form(s) W-2 to the Social Security Administration. Photocopies are not acceptable.

Do not send any payment (cash, checks, money orders, etc.) with Forms W-2 and W-3.

An Item To Note

Separate instructions. See the separate **2003 Instructions for Forms W-2 and W-3** for information on completing this form.

Purpose of Form

Use this form to transmit Copy A of **Form(s) W-2,** Wage and Tax Statement. Make a copy of Form W-3, and keep it with Copy D (For Employer) of Form(s) W-2 for your records. Use Form W-3 for the correct year. **File Form W-3 even if only one Form W-2 is being filed.** If you are filing Form(s) W-2 on magnetic media or electronically, **do not** file Form W-3.

When To File

File Form W-3 with Copy A of Form(s) W-2 by March 1, 2004.

Where To File

Send this entire page with the entire Copy A page of Form(s) W-2 to:

**Social Security Administration
Data Operations Center
Wilkes-Barre, PA 18769-0001**

Note: If you use "Certified Mail" to file, change the ZIP code to "18769-0002." If you use an IRS approved private delivery service, add "ATTN: W-2 Process, 1150 E. Mountain Dr." to the address and change the ZIP code to "18702-7997." See **Circular E,** Employer's Tax Guide (Pub. 15), for a list of IRS approved private delivery services.

Do **not** send magnetic media to the address shown above.

For Privacy Act and Paperwork Reduction Act Notice, see the 2003 Instructions for Forms W-2 and W-3.

Cat. No. 10159Y

Form W-4
Employee's Withholding Allowance Certificate

Form W-4 (2003)

Purpose. Complete Form W-4 so that your employer can withhold the correct Federal income tax from your pay. Because your tax situation may change, you may want to refigure your withholding each year.

Exemption from withholding. If you are exempt, complete only lines 1, 2, 3, 4, and 7 and sign the form to validate it. Your exemption for 2003 expires February 16, 2004. See Pub. 505, Tax Withholding and Estimated Tax.

Note: You cannot claim exemption from withholding if: (a) your income exceeds $750 and includes more than $250 of unearned income (e.g., interest and dividends) and (b) another person can claim you as a dependent on their tax return.

Basic instructions. If you are not exempt, complete the Personal Allowances Worksheet below. The worksheets on page 2 adjust your withholding allowances based on itemized deductions, certain credits, adjustments to income, or two-earner/two-job situations. Complete all worksheets that apply. However, you may claim fewer (or zero) allowances.

Head of household. Generally, you may claim head of household filing status on your tax return only if you are unmarried and pay more than 50% of the costs of keeping up a home for yourself and your dependent(s) or other qualifying individuals. See line E below.

Tax credits. You can take projected tax credits into account in figuring your allowable number of withholding allowances. Credits for child or dependent care expenses and the child tax credit may be claimed using the Personal Allowances Worksheet below. See Pub. 919, How Do I Adjust My Tax Withholding? for information on converting your other credits into withholding allowances.

Nonwage income. If you have a large amount of nonwage income, such as interest or dividends, consider making estimated tax payments using Form 1040-ES, Estimated Tax for Individuals. Otherwise, you may owe additional tax.

Two earners/two jobs. If you have a working spouse or more than one job, figure the total number of allowances you are entitled to claim on all jobs using worksheets from only one Form W-4. Your withholding usually will be most accurate when all allowances are claimed on the Form W-4 for the highest paying job and zero allowances are claimed on the others.

Nonresident alien. If you are a nonresident alien, see the Instructions for Form 8233 before completing this Form W-4.

Check your withholding. After your Form W-4 takes effect, use Pub. 919 to see how the dollar amount you are having withheld compares to your projected total tax for 2003. See Pub. 919, especially if your earnings exceed $125,000 (Single) or $175,000 (Married).

Recent name change? If your name on line 1 differs from that shown on your social security card, call 1-800-772-1213 for a new social security card.

Personal Allowances Worksheet (Keep for your records.)

A   Enter "1" for yourself if no one else can claim you as a dependent . . . .   A _____

B   Enter "1" if:
- You are single and have only one job; or
- You are married, have only one job, and your spouse does not work; or
- Your wages from a second job or your spouse's wages (or the total of both) are $1,000 or less.

  . .   B _____

C   Enter "1" for your spouse. But, you may choose to enter "-0-" if you are married and have either a working spouse or more than one job. (Entering "-0-" may help you avoid having too little tax withheld.) . . . .   C _____

D   Enter number of dependents (other than your spouse or yourself) you will claim on your tax return . . . .   D _____

E   Enter "1" if you will file as head of household on your tax return (see conditions under Head of household above) .   E _____

F   Enter "1" if you have at least $1,500 of child or dependent care expenses for which you plan to claim a credit . .   F _____

  (Note: Do not include child support payments. See Pub. 503, Child and Dependent Care Expenses, for details.)

G   Child Tax Credit (including additional child tax credit).
- If your total income will be between $15,000 and $42,000 ($20,000 and $65,000 if married), enter "1" for each eligible child plus 1 additional if you have three to five eligible children or 2 additional if you have six or more eligible children.
- If your total income will be between $42,000 and $80,000 ($65,000 and $115,000 if married), enter "1" if you have one or two eligible children, "2" if you have three eligible children, "3" if you have four eligible children, or "4" if you have five or more eligible children.   G _____

H   Add lines A through G and enter total here. Note: This may be different from the number of exemptions you claim on your tax return. ▶   H _____

For accuracy, complete all worksheets that apply.
- If you plan to itemize or claim adjustments to income and want to reduce your withholding, see the Deductions and Adjustments Worksheet on page 2.
- If you have more than one job or are married and you and your spouse both work and the combined earnings from all jobs exceed $35,000, see the Two-Earner/Two-Job Worksheet on page 2 to avoid having too little tax withheld.
- If neither of the above situations applies, stop here and enter the number from line H on line 5 of Form W-4 below.

-   Cut here and give Form W-4 to your employer. Keep the top part for your records.   - - - - - - - - - - - - -

Form W-4

Department of the Treasury
Internal Revenue Service

Employee's Withholding Allowance Certificate

▶ For Privacy Act and Paperwork Reduction Act Notice, see page 2.

OMB No. 1545-0010

20**03**

1 Type or print your first name and middle initial	Last name		2 Your social security number

Home address (number and street or rural route)	3 ☐ Single ☐ Married ☐ Married, but withhold at higher Single rate.
	Note: If married, but legally separated, or spouse is a nonresident alien, check the "Single" box.
City or town, state, and ZIP code	4 If your last name differs from that shown on your social security card, check here. You must call 1-800-772-1213 for a new card. ▶ ☐

5   Total number of allowances you are claiming (from line H above or from the applicable worksheet on page 2)   **5** _____

6   Additional amount, if any, you want withheld from each paycheck . . . .   **6** $ _____

7   I claim exemption from withholding for 2003, and I certify that I meet both of the following conditions for exemption:
- Last year I had a right to a refund of all Federal income tax withheld because I had no tax liability and
- This year I expect a refund of all Federal income tax withheld because I expect to have no tax liability.

If you meet both conditions, write "Exempt" here . . . . ▶   **7** _____

Under penalties of perjury, I certify that I am entitled to the number of withholding allowances claimed on this certificate, or I am entitled to claim exempt status.

Employee's signature
(Form is not valid unless you sign it.) ▶   Date ▶

8 Employer's name and address (Employer: Complete lines 8 and 10 only if sending to the IRS.)	9 Office code (optional)	10 Employer identification number

Cat. No. 10220Q

FEDERAL UNEMPLOYMENT (FUTA) TAX

File Form 940, *Employer's Annual Federal Unemployment (FUTA) Tax Return*. Also, use Form 8109 to make deposits.

The federal unemployment tax system, together with the state systems, provides for payments of unemployment compensation to workers who have lost their jobs. This tax applies to wages you pay your employees. Most employers pay both a state and the federal unemployment tax.

In general you are subject to FUTA tax on the wages you pay employees who are not farm workers or household workers if: (1) in any calendar quarter, the wages you paid to employees in this category totaled $1,500 or more; or (2) in each of 20 different calendar weeks, there was at least a part of a day in which you had an employee in this category. See *Circular E, Employer's Tax Guide*, for lists of payments excluded from FUTA and types of employment not subject to the tax.

Figuring the Tax

The federal unemployment tax is figured on the first $7,000 in wages paid to each employee annually. The tax is imposed on you as the employer. You must not collect it or deduct it from the wages of your employees.

Tax Rate

The gross federal unemployment tax rate is 6.2%. However, you are given a credit of up to 5.4% for the state unemployment tax you pay providing you have paid your state unemployment liability by the due date. The net tax rate, therefore, can be as low as 0.8% (6.2% minus 5.4%) if your state is subject to a credit reduction. Study rules applying to liability for this tax (i.e., credit reduction, success of employer, concurrent employment by related corporations). For information on figuring federal unemployment tax, including special rules for a "successor employer," see Publication 15, *Circular E, Employer's Tax Guide*.

Form 940

Employer's annual FUTA tax return, Form 940, is used for reporting. This form covers one calendar year and is generally due one month after the year ends. However, you may have to make deposits of this tax before filing the return. If you deposit the tax on time and in full, you have an extra ten days to file—until February 10th.

Deposits

If at the end of any calendar quarter, you owe but have not yet deposited, more than $100 in federal unemployment (FUTA) tax for the year, you must make a deposit by the end of the next month.

Due dates are:

If your undeposited FUTA tax is more than $100 on:	Deposit full amount by:
March 31	April 30
June 30	July 31
September 30	October 31
December 31	January 31

If the tax is $100 or less at the end of the quarter, you need not deposit it, but you must add it to the tax for the next quarter and deposit according to the $100 rule. (See Publication 15, *Circular E, Employer's Tax Guide*.) Use a federal Tax Deposit Coupon Book containing Form 8109 federal tax deposit coupons to deposit taxes to an authorized financial institution or Federal Reserve Bank.

Form 8109

Federal tax deposit coupons are used to make deposits to an authorized financial institution or Federal Reserve Bank. You can get the names of authorized institutions from a Federal Reserve Bank. Each deposit must be accompanied by a federal tax deposit (FTD) coupon. Clearly mark the correct type of tax and tax period on each deposit coupon. The FUTA tax must be deposited separately from the Social Security and withheld income tax deposits. A federal tax deposit coupon book containing Form 8109 coupons and instructions will automatically be sent to you after you apply for an employer identification member (EIN) (see page 148).

IRS publications. Form 940, *FUTA Tax Return* (Instructions); Publication 15, *Circular E, Employer's Tax Guide*; and Form 8109, *Federal Tax Deposit Coupon* (instructions).

Sample. The next page shows a sample Form 940, *Employer's Annual Federal Unemployment (FUTA) Tax Return*.

Form 940, Employer's Annual Federal Unemployment (FUTA) Tax Return

Form **940**	Employer's Annual Federal Unemployment (FUTA) Tax Return	OMB No. 1545-0028
Department of the Treasury Internal Revenue Service (99)	▶ See separate Instructions for Form 940 for information on completing this form.	20**03**

			T
	Name (as distinguished from trade name)	Calendar year	FF
You must complete this section. ▶			FD
	Trade name, if any	Employer identification number (EIN)	FP
			I
	Address (number and street)	City, state, and ZIP code	T

A Are you required to pay unemployment contributions to only one state? (If "No," skip questions B and C.) . ☐ Yes ☐ No

B Did you pay all state unemployment contributions by February 2, 2004? ((1) If you deposited your total FUTA tax when due, check "Yes" if you paid all state unemployment contributions by February 10, 2004. (2) If a 0% experience rate is granted, check "Yes." (3) If "No," skip question C.) . . . . ☐ Yes ☐ No

C Were all wages that were taxable for FUTA tax also taxable for your state's unemployment tax? . . . . . ☐ Yes ☐ No

If you answered "No" to any of these questions, you must file Form 940. If you answered "Yes" to all the questions, you may file Form 940-EZ, which is a simplified version of Form 940. (Successor employers, see Special credit for successor employers on page 3 of the separate instructions.) You can get Form 940-EZ by calling 1-800-TAX-FORM (1-800-829-3676) or from the IRS website at www.irs.gov.

If you will not have to file returns in the future, check here (see Who Must File in the separate instructions) and complete and sign the return . . . . ▶ ☐

If this is an Amended Return, check here (see Amended Returns in the separate instructions) . . . . . . ▶ ☐

Part I	Computation of Taxable Wages

1	Total payments (including payments shown on lines 2 and 3) during the calendar year for services of employees	1	
2	Exempt payments. (Explain all exempt payments, attaching additional sheets if necessary.) ▶ _____ _____	2	
3	Payments of more than $7,000 for services. Enter only amounts over the first $7,000 paid to each employee (see separate instructions). Do not include any exempt payments from line 2. The $7,000 amount is the Federal wage base. Your state wage base may be different. Do not use your state wage limitation	3	
4	Add lines 2 and 3 . . . . ▶	4	
5	Total taxable wages (subtract line 4 from line 1) . . . . ▶	5	

Be sure to complete both sides of this form, and sign in the space provided on the back.

For Privacy Act and Paperwork Reduction Act Notice, see separate instructions. ▼ DETACH HERE ▼ Cat. No. 112340 Form **940** (2003)

Form **940-V**	Payment Voucher	OMB No. 1545-0028
Department of the Treasury Internal Revenue Service	Use this voucher only when making a payment with your return.	20**03**

Complete boxes 1, 2, and 3. Do not send cash, and do not staple your payment to this voucher. Make your check or money order payable to the "United States Treasury." Be sure to enter your employer identification number (EIN), "Form 940," and "2003" on your payment.

1 Enter your employer identification number (EIN).	2 Enter the amount of your payment. ▶	Dollars	Cents
	3 Enter your business name (individual name for sole proprietors).		
	Enter your address.		
	Enter your city, state, and ZIP code.		

PAYMENT TO NONEMPLOYEES FOR SERVICES RENDERED

File Form 1099-MISC, *Statement to Recipients of Miscellaneous Income* together with Form 1096, *Annual Summary and Transmittal of U.S. Information Returns.*

Payments made by you in your trade or business activities that are not for wages must be reported to the IRS. Payments include fees, commissions, prizes, awards, or other forms of compensation for services rendered to your company by an individual who is not your employee. This also includes fair market value of exchanges (bartering) of property or services between individuals in the course of a trade or business. Exempt payments include payments for inventory, payments of rent to a real estate agent, payments for telephone services, utilities, telephone, employee travel expense reimbursements, and payments to corporations.

If the following four conditions are met, a payment is generally reported as nonemployee compensation: (1) You made the payment to a nonemployee; (2) you made the payment for services rendered in your business; (3) you made the payment to a payee who is not a corporation; and (4) you made payments to the payee totaling $600 or more during the year.

Form 1099-MISC

Statement to Recipient of Miscellaneous Income is an information form used to report payments in the course of your trade or business to nonemployees (or for which you were a nominee/middleman, or from which you withheld federal income tax or foreign tax).

When and How to File

File 1099-MISC on or before the last day of February. Transmit these forms to your IRS Service Center with Form 1096, *Annual Summary and Transmittal of U.S. Information Returns.* A 1099-MISC copy must be sent to the recipient by January 31st. For payments in the form of barter, file Form 1099-B, *Proceeds From Broker and Barter Exchange.*

IRS publications. Publication 15-A, *Employer's Supplemental Tax Guide.* For more information on 1099s, see the current year's instructions for Forms 1099 and 1096.

Samples. The following pages show samples of Form 1099-MISC and 1096.

Independent Contractors
Facts versus Myths

Appendix I of *Keeping the Books* will provide you with comprehensive information regarding independent contractors. That section, entitled "Independent Contractors: Facts versus Myths," includes:

- The "List of 20 Common Law Factors."
- Basic rules regarding independent contractor status.
- Benefits and risks of hiring independent contractors.
- Benefits and risks to the independent contractor.

Form 1099-MISC
Statement to Recipients of Miscellaneous Income

9595 ☐ VOID ☐ CORRECTED

PAYER'S name, street address, city, state, ZIP code, and telephone no.	1 Rents $	OMB No. 1545-0115	Miscellaneous Income
	2 Royalties $	20**03** Form 1099-MISC	
	3 Other income $	4 Federal income tax withheld $	Copy A For Internal Revenue Service Center
PAYER'S Federal identification number / RECIPIENT'S identification number	5 Fishing boat proceeds $	6 Medical and health care payments $	File with Form 1096.
RECIPIENT'S name	7 Nonemployee compensation $	8 Substitute payments in lieu of dividends or interest $	For Privacy Act and Paperwork Reduction Act Notice, see the 2003 General Instructions for Forms 1099, 1098, 5498, and W-2G.
Street address (including apt. no.)	9 Payer made direct sales of $5,000 or more of consumer products to a buyer (recipient) for resale ▶ ☐	10 Crop insurance proceeds $	
City, state, and ZIP code	11	12	
Account number (optional) 2nd TIN not. ☐	13 Excess golden parachute payments $	14 Gross proceeds paid to an attorney $	
15	16 State tax withheld $ $	17 State/Payer's state no.	18 State income $ $

Form 1099-MISC   Cat. No. 14425J   Department of the Treasury - Internal Revenue Service

Do Not Cut or Separate Forms on This Page — Do Not Cut or Separate Forms on This Page

---

9595 ☐ VOID ☐ CORRECTED

PAYER'S name, street address, city, state, ZIP code, and telephone no.	1 Rents $	OMB No. 1545-0115	Miscellaneous Income
	2 Royalties $	20**03** Form 1099-MISC	
	3 Other income $	4 Federal income tax withheld $	Copy A For Internal Revenue Service Center
PAYER'S Federal identification number / RECIPIENT'S identification number	5 Fishing boat proceeds $	6 Medical and health care payments $	File with Form 1096.
RECIPIENT'S name	7 Nonemployee compensation $	8 Substitute payments in lieu of dividends or interest $	For Privacy Act and Paperwork Reduction Act Notice, see the 2003 General Instructions for Forms 1099, 1098, 5498, and W-2G.
Street address (including apt. no.)	9 Payer made direct sales of $5,000 or more of consumer products to a buyer (recipient) for resale ▶ ☐	10 Crop insurance proceeds $	
City, state, and ZIP code	11	12	
Account number (optional) 2nd TIN not. ☐	13 Excess golden parachute payments $	14 Gross proceeds paid to an attorney $	
15	16 State tax withheld $ $	17 State/Payer's state no.	18 State income $ $

Form 1099-MISC   Cat. No. 14425J   Department of the Treasury - Internal Revenue Service

Do Not Cut or Separate Forms on This Page — Do Not Cut or Separate Forms on This Page

Form 1096, Annual Summary
and Transmittal of U.S. Information Returns

Do Not Staple 6969

Form **1096** Department of the Treasury Internal Revenue Service	Annual Summary and Transmittal of U.S. Information Returns	OMB No. 1545-0108 20**03**

FILER'S name

Street address (including room or suite number)

City, state, and ZIP code

Name of person to contact	Telephone number ( )	For Official Use Only
E-mail address	Fax number ( )	

1 Employer identification number	2 Social security number	3 Total number of forms	4 Federal income tax withheld $	5 Total amount reported with this Form 1096 $

Enter an "X" in only one box below to indicate the type of form being filed.   If this is your final return , enter an "X" here . . . ▶ ☐

W-2G 32	1098 81	1098-E 84	1098-T 83	1099-A 80	1099-B 79	1099-C 85	1099-CAP 73	1099-DIV 91	1099-G 86	1099-H 71	1099-INT 92	1099-LTC 93	1099-MISC 95
☐	☐	☐	☐	☐	☐	☐	☐	☐	☐	☐	☐	☐	☐

1099-MSA 94	1099-OID 96	1099-PATR 97	1099-Q 31	1099-R 98	1099-S 75	5498 28	5498-ESA 72	5498-MSA 27
☐	☐	☐	☐	☐	☐	☐	☐	☐

Return this entire page to the Internal Revenue Service. Photocopies are not acceptable.

Under penalties of perjury, I declare that I have examined this return and accompanying documents, and, to the best of my knowl edge and belief, they are true, correct, and complete.

Signature ▶   Title ▶   Date ▶

Instructions

Purpose of form. Use this form to transmit paper Forms 1099, 1098, 5498, and W-2G to the Internal Revenue Service. Do not use Form 1096 to transmit electronically or magnetically.   For magnetic media, see Form 4804, Transmission of Information Returns Reported Magnetically; for electronic submissions, see Pub. 1220, Specifications for Filing Forms 1098, 1099, 5498 and W-2G Electronically or Magnetically.

Who must file. The name, address, and TIN of the filer on this form must be the same as those you enter in the upper left area of Forms 1099, 1098, 5498, or W-2G.   A filer includes a payer; a recipient of mortgage interest payments (including points) or student loan interest; an educational institution; a broker; a barter exchange; a creditor; a person reporting real estate transactions; a trustee or issuer of any individual retirement arrangement, a Coverdell ESA, an Archer MSA (including a Medicare+Choice MSA); certain corporations; and a lender who acquires an interest in secured property or who has reason to know that the property has been abandoned.

Preaddressed Form 1096. If you received a preaddressed Form 1096 from the IRS with Package 1099, use it to transmit paper Forms 1099, 1098, 5498, and W-2G to the Internal Revenue Service. If any of the preprinted information is incorrect, make corrections on the form.

If you are not using a preaddressed form, enter the filer's name, address (including room, suite, or other unit number), and TIN in the spaces provided on the form.

When to file. File Form 1096 with Forms 1099, 1098, or W-2G by March 1, 2004. File Form 1096 with Forms 5498, 5498-ESA, and 5498-MSA by May 31, 2004.

Where To File

Send all information returns filed on paper with Form 1096 to the following:

If your principal business, office or agency, or legal residence in the case of an individual, is located in	Use the following Internal Revenue Service Center address
Alabama, Arizona, Florida, Georgia, Louisiana, Mississippi, New Mexico, North Carolina, Texas, Virginia	Austin, TX 73301
Arkansas, Connecticut, Delaware, Kentucky, Maine, Massachusetts, New Hampshire, New Jersey, New York, Ohio, Pennsylvania, Rhode Island, Vermont, West Virginia	Cincinnati, OH 45999
Illinois, Indiana, Iowa, Kansas, Michigan, Minnesota, Missouri, Nebraska, North Dakota, Oklahoma, South Carolina, South Dakota, Tennessee, Wisconsin	Kansas City, MO 64999

For more information and the Privacy Act and Paperwork Reduction Act Notice, see the 2003 General Instructions for Forms 1099, 1098, 5498, and W-2G.

Cat. No. 14400O   Form **1096** (2003)

TAXPAYER IDENTIFICATION NUMBER (EIN)

Form SS-4, *Application for Employer Identification Number.*

Social Security Number

If you are a sole proprietor, you will generally use your Social Security number as your taxpayer identification number. You must put this number on each of your individual income tax forms, such as Form 1040 and its schedules.

Employer Identification Number (EIN)

Every partnership, S corporation, corporation, and certain sole proprietors must have an employer identification number (EIN) to use as a taxpayer identification number.

Sole proprietors must have EINs if they pay wages to one or more employees or must file pension or excise tax returns. Otherwise they can use their Social Security numbers.

New EIN

You may need to get a new EIN if either the form or the ownership of your business changes.

- **Change in organization.** A new EIN is required if: a sole proprietor incorporates; a sole proprietorship takes in partners and operates as a partnership; a partnership incorporates; a partnership is taken over by one of the partners and is operated as a sole proprietorship; or a corporation changes to a partnership or to a sole proprietorship.

- **Change in ownership.** A new EIN is required if: you buy or inherit an existing business that you will operate as a sole proprietorship; you represent an estate that operates a business after the owner's death; or you terminate an old partnership and begin a new one.

Application for an EIN or Social Security Number

To apply for an EIN, use Form SS-4, *Application for Employer Identification Number.* This form is available from the IRS and Social Security Administration offices. You can also download the form online. To do so, go to http://www.irs.gov, type Form SS-4 in the search box, and this will take you to the page where the form can be downloaded as a pdf file. There is a copy of this form in Appendix II on page 195.

Form SS-5 is used to apply for a Social Security number card. These forms are available from Social Security Administration offices. If you are under 18 years of age, you must furnish evidence, along with this form, of age, identity, and U.S. citizenship. If you are 18 or older, you must appear in person with this evidence at a Social Security office. If you are an alien, you must appear in person and bring your birth certificate and either your alien registration card or your U.S. immigration form.

FREE TAX PUBLICATIONS AVAILABLE FROM THE IRS

The following is a list of IRS publications that may prove helpful to you in the course of your business. Make it a point to keep a file of tax information. Send for these publications and update your file with new publications at least once a year. The United States government has spent a great deal of time and money to make this information available to you for preparation of income tax returns.

By phone or mail. You may call IRS toll free at **1-800-TAX-FORM (1-800-829-3676)** between 8 AM and 5 PM weekdays and 9 AM to 3 PM on Saturdays. If you wish to order publications or forms by mail, you will find an order form for the publications on page 151.

By computer and modem. If you subscribe to an online service, ask if IRS information is available and, if so, how to access it. The IRS offers the ability to download electronic print files of current tax forms, instructions, and taxpayer information publications (TIPs) in three different file formats. Internal Revenue Information Services (IRIS) is housed within Fed-World, known also as the Electronic Marketplace of U.S. government information, a broadly accessible electronic bulletin board system. FedWorld offers direct dial-up access, as well as Internet connectivity, and provides "gateway" access to more than 140 different government bulletin boards.

IRIS at FedWorld can be reached by any of the following means:

1. Modem (dial-up) The Internal Revenue Information Services bulletin board at 703-321-8020 (not toll free)

2. Telnet—http://iris.irs.ustreas.gov

3. File Transfer Protocol (FTP)—connect to http://ftp.irs.ustreas.gov

4. World Wide Web—http://www.irs.gov

Tax Guide for Small Business
(For Individuals Who Use Schedule S or S-EZ)

Sole proprietors should begin by reading Publication 334, *Tax Guide for Small Business.* It is a general guide to all areas of small business and will give you comprehensive information.

Listing of Publications for Small Business

If you are a small business owner, the following IRS publications are good to have on hand as reference material and will give you fairly detailed information on specific tax-related topics.

   1 - *Your Rights as a Taxpayer*

  15 - *Circular E, Employer's Tax Guide*

15-A - *Employer's Supplemental Tax Guide*

17 - *Your Federal Income Tax*

463 - *Travel, Entertainment, Gift, and Car Expenses*

505 - *Tax Withholding and Estimated Tax*

509 - *Tax Calendars for 2003*

533 - *Self-Employment Tax*

535 - *Business Expenses*

536 - *Net Operating Losses*

538 - *Accounting Periods and Methods*

541 - *Partnerships*

542 - *Corporations*

S Corporations get instructions for 1120S

544 - *Sales and Other Dispositions of Assets*

551 - *Basis of Assets*

553 - *Highlights of Tax Changes*

556 - *Examination of Returns, Appeal Rights, and Claims for Refund*

560 - *Retirement Plans for the Small Business*

583 - *Starting a Business and Keeping Records*

587 - *Business Use of Your Home (including Use by Day-Care Providers)*

594 - *The IRS Collection Process*

908 - *Bankruptcy Tax Guide*

910 - *Guide to Free Tax Services*

911 - *Direct Sellers*

925 - *Passive Activity and At Risk Rules*

946 - *How to Depreciate Property*

947 - *Practice Before the IRS and Power of Attorney*

1066 - *Small Business Tax Workshop Workbook*

1544 - *Reporting Cash Payments of Over $10,000 (Received in a Trade or Business)*

1546 - *The Taxpayer Advocate Service of the IRS*

1853 - *Small Business Talk*

Order Information for IRS Forms and Publications

How to Get IRS Forms and Publications (Resource: Pub. 334, Tax Guide for Small Business)

You can download forms, visit your local IRS office, or order tax forms and publications from the IRS Forms Distribution Center listed for your state at the address on this page. Or, if you prefer, you can photocopy tax forms from reproducible copies kept at participating public libraries. In addition, many of these libraries have reference sets of IRS publications that you can read or copy.

Where to Mail Your Order Blank for Free Forms and Publications

If you live in:	Mail to:	Other locations:
Alaska, Arizona, California, Colorado, Hawaii, Idaho, Montana, Nevada, New Mexico, Oregon, Utah, Washington Wyoming, Guam, Northern Marianas American Samoa	Western Area Distribution Center Rancho Cordova, CA 95743-0001	**Foreign Addresses:** Taxpayers with mailing addresses in foreign countries should mail this order blank to either: Eastern Area Distribution Center, P.O. Box 25866, Richmond, VA 23286-8107; or Western Area Distribution Center, Rancho Cordova, CA 95743-0001, whichever is closer. Mail letter requests for other forms and publications to: Eastern Area Distribution Center, P.O. Box 25866, Richmond, VA 23286-8107
Alabama, Arkansas, Illinois, Indiana, Iowa, Kansas, Kentucky, Louisiana, Michigan, Minnesota, Mississippi, Missouri, Nebraska North Dakota, Ohio, Oklahoma, South Dakota, Tennessee, Texas, Wisconsin	Central Area Distribution Center P.O. Box 8903 Bloomington, IL 61702-8903	**Puerto Rico:** Eastern Area Distribution Center, P.O. Box 25866, Richmond, VA 23286-8107
Connecticut, Delaware, District of Columbia, Florida, Georgia, Maine, Maryland, Masssachusetts, New Hampshire New Jersey, New York, North Carolina Pennsylvania, Rhode Island, South Carolina, Vermont, Virginia, West Virginia	Eastern Area Distribution Center P.O. Box 85074 Richmond, VA 23261-5074	**Virgin Islands:** V.I. Bureau of Internal Revenue, Lockhart Gardens, No. 1-A, Charlotte Amalie, St. Thomas, VI 00802

-------------------------------- **Order Blank** --------------------------------

1040	Schedule F (1040)	Schedule 3 (1040A) & Instructions	2210 & Instructions	8606 & Instructions	Pub.502	Pub. 550	Pub. 929
Instructions for 1040 & Schedules	Schedule H (1040)	1040EZ	2441 & Instructions	8822 & Instructions	Pub. 509	Pub.544	Pub. 910
Schedules A&B (1040)	Schedule R (1040) & Instructions	Instructions for 1040EZ	3903 & Instructions	8829 & Instructions	Pub. 533	Pub. 551	Pub. 911
Schedule C (1040)	Schedule SE (1040)	1040-ES (1996) & Instructions	4562 & Instructions	Pub. 1	Pub. 535	Pub. 553	Pub. 946
Schedule C-EZ (1040)	1040A	1040X & Instructions	4868 & Instructions	Pub. 17	Pub. 536	Pub. 556	Pub. 1066
Schedule D (1040)	Instructions for 1040A & Schedules	2106 & Instructions	5329 & Instructions	Pub. 334	Pub. 538	Pub. 560	Pub. 1853
Schedule E (1040)	Schedule 1 (1040A)	2106-EZ & Instructions	8283 & Instructions	Pub. 463	Pub. 541	Pub. 583	
Schedule EIC (1040A or 1040)	Schedule 2 (1040A)	2119 & Instructions	8582 & Instructions	Pub. 505	Pub. 542	Pub. 587	

You will be sent 2 copies of each form and 1 copy of each publication or set of instructions you circle. Please cut the order blank on the dotted line above. Be sure to print or type your name and address accurately in the space below. Also complete the address information on your envelope, mailing to the IRS address shown above for your state. Be sure to affix proper postage. Order only the forms, instructions and publications you think you will need to prepare your return. Use the blank spaces to order items not listed. You should receive your order or notification of status of your order within 7-15 working days after receipt of your request.

Name _____

Number and street _____

City or town _____ State_____ ZIP code_____

SUMMARY

The purpose of this chapter has been to introduce you to the tax requirements pertaining to your business. It is important to keep abreast of revisions in the tax laws that will affect your business.

IRS Workshops

The IRS holds tax seminars on a regular basis for small business owners who would like to learn more about current regulations and requirements. You can call the local IRS office and ask it to mail you a schedule of coming workshops.

Know What Is Happening

Planning for your business is an ongoing process requiring the implementation of many changes. You may rest assured that many of those changes will be a direct result of new tax laws. Today, many small businesses are having to examine their hiring policies because of the regulatory legislation that is being passed or considered regarding employee benefits, workers' compensation, contract services, etc. Business owners need to understand what is happening and take active positions to impact legislation that is pertinent to their operations and can ultimately lead to their success or failure.

You have taken the first step. You would not be reading this book unless you had already committed yourself to organizing and understanding your recordkeeping. You are one of the lucky ones—the entrepreneurs who know that every decision makes an impact on the bottom line.

What's Next?

Now that you are familiar with basic records, financial statements, and tax returns, it is time to combine your information and utilize it to formulate recordkeeping and tax reporting schedules for your business. Setting up your records and keeping them current are two different pieces of the same pie.

To help you get started, the next chapter will be devoted to providing you with written guides to follow while you are getting into the habit of doing all the unfamiliar chores required to keep your records current.

CHAPTER 8

RECORDKEEPING AND TAX REPORTING SCHEDULES

You should now have a basic understanding of the interrelationship of each of the phases of record-keeping. Up to this point, you have been introduced to the following:

Basics of recordkeeping
- Functions and types of recordkeeping
- When recordkeeping begins and who should do it

Essential records for small business
- What records are required
- What their purposes are
- Format for recording information

Development of financial statements
- What they are
- How they are developed
- Information sources

Taxes and recordkeeping
- Federal taxes for which you may be liable
- Forms to be used for reporting
- Publications available as tax aids

ORGANIZING YOUR RECORDKEEPING

Just as timing is important to all other phases of your business, it also is important when you deal with recordkeeping. You cannot haphazardly throw all of your paperwork into a basket and deal with it in a sporadic nature. You will have to organize your recordkeeping into a system that will allow you to proceed through the tax year in an orderly fashion. That system will have to provide for retrieval and verification of tax information and, at the same time, form a picture of your business that will help you to analyze trends and implement changes to make your venture grow and become more profitable.

BUILDING YOUR SYSTEM

The information in this book has been presented in a particular order for a specific reason. Just as a home builder must first lay the foundation, do the framing, put up the walls, and then do the finish work, you, too, must build your foundation first and learn the basics of recordkeeping. The frame can be likened to your General Records. They are the underlying material without which there could be no walls. In the same way, General Records are the basis (source of information) for forming Financial Statements. At last, the builder finishes the home and makes some rooms into a limited space for each family member and other rooms into common areas where the whole family will meet. This is Tax Accounting, with different legal structures functioning within their limited areas, but meeting in areas common to all businesses. The house is complete—and so is your recordkeeping. Now a schedule needs to be made to maintain your home or it will soon be a shambles. To keep your business in a maintained state, it too must have scheduled upkeep. To keep maintenance at an optimum, you will need to set up a Recordkeeping and Tax Reporting Schedule.

Proceeding on the assumption that you have never done recordkeeping and that you have no idea in what order it must be done, I will give you a basic format to follow while you learn this task.

Doing Tasks in Sequence

There is a specific order to recordkeeping, and you must follow that order if your records are going to be effective. Because the two goals of recordkeeping are retrieval for tax purposes and the analyzing of information for internal planning, your schedule will have to provide for the reaching of those goals.

We have provided a General Recordkeeping and Tax Reporting Schedule on the following pages that will do just that if you will follow it. There are two things that you must keep in mind to ensure success:

1. **Do not fail to do any of the tasks.**
2. **Be sure to do them on time.**

POST your schedule on the wall in your office and refer to it every day for what needs to be done. Before long, those chores will become automatic. All of the information presented in this book will have assimilated in your mind and you will begin to see the overall picture. At the end of the year, if you have followed the schedule, you will have every piece of financial information at your fingertips. It can be done—and you can do it!

Schedule Format

The General Recordkeeping Schedule is divided into tasks according to frequency. There are two basic divisions:

1. **General recordkeeping**
   - **Daily**. Tasks you should be aware of and do every day.
   - **Weekly.** The tasks you do when you do your regular bookkeeping. Timing may vary according to the needs of your business.
   - **Monthly.** Closing out your books at the end of the month.
   - **Quarterly.** Analysis of past quarter and revision of budget.
   - **End of year.** Closing out your books for the year and setting up records for the new year.

2. **Tax reporting**
   - **Monthly.** Payroll reporting and deposits, Sales Tax Reporting (sales tax may be monthly, quarterly, or annually).
   - **Quarterly.** Sending in required tax reports.
   - **Annually**. Filing information and tax returns.

Every business has individual needs. You may have to shift the frequency of some tasks. To begin with, however, follow the progression in the schedule we have provided, and it should adequately cover most of your needs.

Note for different legal structures. Because some recordkeeping tasks are different for different legal structures (i.e., sole proprietorship, partnership, S corporation, and corporation), it will be noted as to which apply. If there is no notation accompanying the task, it applies to all legal structures.

If you need help, refer back. Keep in mind when you are using the General Recordkeeping Schedule that all the items on the schedule have been covered in one of the previous sections. You need only refer back to the appropriate record, statement, or tax return information to refresh your memory and complete your task. Be sure to keep reference materials mentioned in those sections close at hand in case you need more detailed information.

Sample schedule. The next five pages contain a General Recordkeeping and Tax Reporting Schedule. Copy it! Post it!

USE THESE SCHEDULES!

The following schedules are meant to serve as guides for you until you are familiar with the recordkeeping process. There may be other jobs for you to do, but this should get you off to a good start.

RECORDKEEPING SCHEDULE
Daily

1. Go through mail and file for appropriate action.

2. Unpack and put away incoming inventory.

3. Record inventory information in Inventory Record.

4. Pay any invoices necessary to meet discount deadlines.

5. Record daily invoices sent out in Accounts Receivable. **Note:** It would be a good idea to keep invoice copies in an envelope or folder behind the corresponding Accounts Receivable record.*

   ***Accounting software.** Invoices generated from within your software will be automatically posted to the proper accounts.

Weekly

1. Prepare bank deposit for income received and take it to the bank.

2. Enter deposit in checkbook and Revenue & Expense Journal.*

3. Enter sales information in Inventory Record.*

4. Enter week's checking transactions in Revenue & Expense Journal.*

5. Record petty cash purchases in Petty Cash Record and file receipts.*

6. Pay invoices due. Be aware of discount dates.

7. Record any depreciable purchases in your Fixed Asset Log.*

   ***Accounting software.** Enter deposits, checks written, and petty cash expenditures for the week.

Monthly

1. Balance checkbook (reconcile with bank statement).*

2. Enter any interest earned and any bank charges in checkbook and in your Revenue & Expense Journal.

3. Total and balance all Revenue & Expense Journal columns.*

4. Enter monthly income and expense totals on 12-month P&L Statement. Prepare a separate one-month Profit & Loss if you wish.*

5. If you wish to look at assets and liabilities, prepare a Balance Sheet. It is only required at year end for those who are not sole proprietors or filers of Schedule C (see End of the Year).

6. Check Accounts Payable and send statements to open accounts.

    ***Accounting software.** Perform bank reconciliation. Generate a monthly and year-to-date P&L Statement and a current Balance Sheet.

Quarterly

1. Do a Quarterly Budget Analysis. Compare actual income and expenses with projections.

2. Revise your cash flow statement (budget) accordingly.

End of Tax Year

1. Pay all invoices, sales taxes, and other expenses that you wish to use as deductions for the current tax year.

2. Prepare annual Profit & Loss Statement. (Add income and expense totals from the 12 monthly reports.)*

3. Prepare a Balance Sheet for your business. A Balance Sheet is required for all but sole proprietors or filers of Schedule C.*

4. Prepare a Pro Forma Cash Flow Statement (budget) for next year. Use your Profit & Loss information from the current year to help you make decisions.

5. Set up your new records for the coming year. It is a good idea to buy new journals and files early before the supply runs out. Begin recordkeeping in the first week. Do not get behind.*

    ***Accounting software.** Generate an annual Profit & Loss Statement and an end-of-year Balance Sheet. Accounting for new year does not need to be set up again. It will continue from previous year.

TAX REPORTING SCHEDULE

Warning!

The following Tax Reporting Schedule is not meant for use as a final authority. Requirements may change. Also you may be responsible for reports and returns that are not listed below. This is meant only to be used as a general guide to help keep you on track until you become familiar with the specific requirements for your business.

Note: This schedule refers to tax reports and reporting dates. In the tax chapter, there are tax reporting calendars for all legal structures. Post your calendar with this schedule and refer to it for required forms and dates. Also refer to information on individual forms that are listed in the index by subject and by form number.

Monthly

1. **Check your payroll tax liability.** If it will exceed $2,500 for any quarter, a deposit is due on the 15th of each month for the taxes of the previous month. (If you work with an accountant or payroll service, information on payments and withholding amounts needs to be provided to them as early in the month as possible so you can receive information back as to what your deposits should be.) See information on "Payroll Records" in Chapter 4.

2. **Sales tax reports.** You may be required to file monthly, quarterly, or annually, according to your sales volume. In some cases, you may be required to be bonded or prepay sales tax. Fill out and send in your sales tax report to the State Board of Equalization (or in some states sales tax may be administered through the Department of Revenue) with a check for monies collected (or due) for the sale of taxable goods or services for the previous period. This is for those businesses holding a Seller's Permit. The subject of sales tax is not covered in this book. (See our business start-up book, *Steps to Small Business Start-Up*, Dearborn Trade.) Report forms are furnished by the collecting agency and will generally be due somewhere about 30 days after the end of the reporting period.

Quarterly

1. **Estimated taxes (Form 1040ES).** File estimated taxes with the Internal Revenue Service. You must also file with your state, if applicable.

   • Sole proprietor, individual who is a partner, or S corporation shareholder file on 15th day of the 4th, 6th, and 9th months of tax year, and 15th day of the 1st month after the end of tax year. For most businesses the due dates would be April 15, June 15, September 15, and January 15. If the due date falls on a weekend day, the due date will be the following Monday.

   • Corporations file the 15th day of the 4th, 6th, 9th, and 12th months of the tax year. For most businesses this will be April 15, June 15, September 15, and December 15; the same weekend rules apply.

   Note: Take special note that only two months lapse between 1st and 2nd quarter filing. There will be four months between the third and fourth quarter finals.

2. **FICA and withholding returns (Form 941).** File *Employer's Quarterly Federal Tax Returns* reporting Social Security (FICA) tax and the withholding of income tax. Check early to see if you are required to make deposits.

3. **FUTA deposits (Form 8109).** Make Federal Unemployment (FUTA) tax deposits. Make deposits on April 30th, July 31st, October 31st, and January 31st, but only if the liability for unpaid tax is more than $100.

4. **Sales tax reports.** If you are on a quarterly reporting basis, reports will be due by April 30th, July 31st, October 31st, and January 31st for the previous quarter. If you are only required to file annually, it will generally be due on January 31st for the previous calendar year.

Annually

1. **FICA and withholding information returns.** Provide information on Social Security (FICA) tax and the withholding of income tax. (Also, make it your business to be aware of any additional state requirements.)

   • W-2 to employees on January 31st.

   • W-2 and W-3 to Social Security Administration on the last day of February.

2. **1099 information returns.** Send information for payments to nonemployees and transactions with other persons.

   • Forms 1099 due to recipient by January 31st.

   • Forms 1099 and transmittals 1096 due to IRS on the last day of February.

3. **FUTA tax returns.** File federal unemployment (FUTA) tax returns with the IRS. Due date is January 31st.

4. **Income tax returns (Form 1040).** File income tax returns with the IRS (and your state, if applicable).

   • Sole proprietor, individual who is a partner, or S Corporation shareholder file on the 15th day of the 4th month after end of tax year (generally April 15th, Schedule C, Form 1040).

   • Partnership returns due on the 15th day of the 4th month after the end of tax year (generally April 15th, Form 1065).

   • S corporations (Form 1120S) and corporations (Form 1120) file on the 15th day of the 3rd month after end of the tax year (generally March 15th).

5. **Self-employment tax forms (Form SE).** Self-employment tax forms are filed with Form 1040 (see above).

   • For sole proprietors or individuals who are partners.

   • Self-employment forms are only applicable if your business shows a taxable profit in excess of $400.

CHAPTER 9

PREPARING FOR UNCLE SAM

This book would not be complete without giving you information on getting ready to prepare your income tax returns. As was stated earlier, one of the two main purposes of recordkeeping is for income tax retrieval and verification.

· · · · ·

When all your end-of-the-year work has been done, it is time to begin work on income taxes. By no means am I suggesting that you do it all yourself. As a matter of fact, I strongly suggest that you hire a CPA, Enrolled Agent, or other tax professional to do the final preparation and aid you in maximizing your tax benefits. Not very many of us are well enough informed to have a good command of all the tax regulations and changes. However, you can do a great deal of the preliminary work. This will be of benefit to you in two different ways: (1) You will save on accounting fees, and (2) you will learn a lot about your business by working on your taxes.

There will be a great deal of variation in what you can do yourself, due not only to the complexity of your particular business, but also to the abilities of the individual doing your recordkeeping. For this reason, we will not attempt to give directions for preliminary tax preparations. However, there is some sound advice that we can give you at this point.

You have spent the year keeping general records and developing financial statements. These are the records that provide all the information you need for income tax accounting. In fact, if the IRS regulations weren't so fast changing and complicated, you could probably fill out your own tax return.

However, because you will need a professional preparer to make sure that your return is correct and to maximize your benefits, your task is to gather and pass on the information that is needed to get the job done.

Many tax preparers complain that the assignment is made difficult because customers do not prepare their material. They bring in bags full of receipts and disorganized information. What do you need in order to be prepared for the accountant?

WHAT TO GIVE YOUR ACCOUNTANT

The information needed by your accountant will come from sources that you should already have if you have kept your general records and generated financial statements as presented in Chapters 3 and 4.

All Businesses

There are two things that your accountant will need from you regardless of your type of business:

1. **Annual Profit & Loss Statement.** This gives your accountant a list of all of the income and expenses your business has had for the tax year. If you are in a product industry, your accountant will need to compute your cost of goods sold for your return. You are required to do a beginning and ending inventory every year. Before you complete your P&L Statement, you will need the following items:

   * **Beginning inventory.** Inventory as of January 1st of the current year. It must match the figure you listed as "Ending Inventory" last year.
   * **Ending inventory.** Inventory as of December 31st of this year. This is done by physical inventory. It will become your beginning inventory for next year.
   * **Amount of inventory purchased.** List the cost of all inventory purchased by your company during the tax year.

Note: If you develop your own P&L Statement, you can compute "Cost of Goods Sold." However, giving your accountant a list of the above three items will help in checking your understanding and accuracy. If you use software, your P&L Statement will probably not include beginning and ending inventory. You will still need to give these numbers to your accountant for computation of "Cost of Goods Sold."

2. **Copy of your Fixed Asset Log.** This document lists all of the depreciable assets your company has purchased during the current year, with date purchased, purchase price, etc. Your accountant needs to know whether you have listed any of these costs as expenses (instead of cost of goods) in your P&L Statement. Both of you can then decide whether to depreciate these items or expense them under Section 179.

Home-Based Businesses

List of Home-Office Expenses. Because these items are generally paid with personal checks, you will have to gather information on taxes, insurance, and interest paid (rent, if you are not a homeowner). You will also need amounts on maintenance and utilities. Before you decide to depreciate your home as a home-office deduction, ask your accountant to explain the recapture if you subsequently sell. You must also measure your office space and calculate the percentage of your home that is used exclusively for your business. Your accountant will need this information to fill out the required form that must accompany your income tax return if you are claiming a home-office deduction.

Partnerships, S Corporations, and Full Corporations

Record of Owner Equity Deposits and Owner Draws. The three legal structures listed are required to have a balance sheet as part of the return, listing the equity of each owner. In order to compute equity, your accountant will have to have the total contributed and withdrawn by each owner. Using last year's equity account balances as a base, deposits will be added and withdrawals subtracted to arrive at the owners' new balances. These totals will be automatically generated by software users.

It is best to provide the accountant with the above information as soon as possible after the new year. This allows extra time for any questions that might arise while your returns are being prepared. It also allows you to forget about income taxes and get on with the new business year.

THE LAST CHORE

The IRS, in general, requires us to keep all income tax information for a period of three years from the date the return is filed. During that time (and longer, in come cases, such as fraud) past returns are subject to audit. In addition, several records are retained for longer periods, mostly determined by administrative decision. It is a good idea to keep many of them for the life of your business. Remember that the other purpose of records is that of analyzing trends and implementing changes. They are only useful if they are still in your possession.

I have found it to be very effective to file all of the information together for one year. Put the following things in your file, mark it with the year date, and put it away.

- Income tax returns
- All receipts
- Bank statements
- Revenue & Expense Journal
- Petty Cash Record
- Fixed Assets Record, Inventory Record, etc.
- All information pertinent to verification of your return

Records retention schedule. The schedule on the next page will help you to decide what records you should retain and how long you should keep them.

Records Retention Schedule

RETENTION PERIOD	AUTHORITY TO DISPOSE
1-10 - No. Years to be Retained **PR** - Retain Permanently **EOY**- Retain Until End of Year **CJ** - Retain Until Completion of Job **EXP**- Retain Until Expiration **ED** - Retain Until Equipment Disposal	**AD** - Administrative Decision **FLSA** - Fair Labor Standards Act **CFR** - Code of Federal Regulators **IR** - Insurance Regulation

TYPE OF RECORD	RETAIN FOR	BY WHOSE AUTHORITY
BANK DEPOSIT RECORDS	7	AD
BANK STATEMENTS	7	AD
BUSINESS LICENSES	EXP	AD
CATALOGS	EXP	AD
CHECK REGISTER	PR	AD
CHECKS (CANCELLED)	3	FLSA, STATE
CONTRACTS	EXP	AD
CORRESPONDENCE	5	AD
DEPRECIATION RECORDS	PR	CFR
ESTIMATED TAX RECORDS	PR	AD
EXPENSE RECORDS	7	AD
INSURANCE (CLAIMS RECORDS)	11	IR
INSURANCE POLICIES	EXP	AD
INVENTORY RECORDS	10	AD
INVENTORY REPORTS	PR	CFR
INVOICES (ACCT. PAYABLE)	3	FLSA, STATE
INVOICES (ACCT. RECEIVABLE)	7	AD
LEDGER (GENERAL)	PR	CFR
MAINTENANCE RECORDS	ED	AD
OFFICE EQUIPMENT RECORDS	5	AD
PATENTS	PR	AD
PETTY CASH RECORD	PR	AD
POSTAL RECORDS	1	AD, CFR
PURCHASE ORDERS	3	CFR
SALES TAX REPORTS TO STATE	PR	STATE
SHIPPING DOCUMENTS	2-10	AD, CFR
TAX BILLS & STATEMENTS	PR	AD
TAX RETURNS (FED. & STATE)	PR	AD
TRADEMARKS & COPYRIGHTS	PR	AD
TRAVEL RECORDS	7	AD
WORK PAPERS (PROJECTS)	CJ	AD
YEAR-END REPORTS	PR	AD

INDEPENDENT CONTRACTORS:
FACTS VERSUS MYTHS © 2004

JUDEE SLACK, ENROLLED AGENT

Judee Slack *is a designated Enrolled Agent (licensed by the IRS). She is the owner of SlackTax, Inc., a tax accounting firm in Fountain Valley, California. Ms. Slack has been active on both the federal and state (CA) level promoting changes in legislation that will clarify and simplify the classification process regarding independent contractors.*

• • • • •

Independent contractors are independent business people who are hired to perform specific tasks. They are just like any other vendor, except they perform services rather than provide tangible goods. Independent contractors are in business for themselves. Thus, they are not the hiring firm's employees. They are not eligible for unemployment, disability, or workers' compensation benefits. The hiring firm does not have to pay employee-employer taxes or provide workers' compensation insurance, and usually is not liable for the contractor's actions.

BENEFITS AND RISKS OF HIRING INDEPENDENT CONTRACTORS
Benefits

1. **Save money—hiring firms don't have to pay:**
   - Social Security taxes (2003 rate: 6.2% of an employee's wages, up to $87,000 and 1.45% of an employee's total wages. In 2004 the rate will be 6.2% of $87,900).
   - Workers' compensation premiums.

- Unemployment insurance (rate for new businesses, state and federal taxes total 6.2% of an employee's wages, up to $434 per employee).
- California Employment Training taxes (currently $7 per employee).
- Health insurance and retirement benefits.

2. **Avoid a long-term employee commitment.**

3. **Avoid liability for the workers' actions.**

4. **Avoid dealing with labor unions and their accompanying demands for union scale wages, benefits, and hiring/firing practices.**

Risks

1. **Government fines.**

- The government looks negatively at the misclassification of bona fide employees as independent contractors for two reasons. Independent contractors can contribute to the underground economy by not paying taxes. They are responsible for withholding their own taxes and Social Security. Many do not report their earnings and thus rob the system and the other taxpayers of tax dollars.

- The government also wants to protect workers. The Social Security, disability, and unemployment insurance programs were all designed to protect average workers. The government does not want businesses to circumvent these programs (and their costs) simply by calling their workers independent contractors.

2. **Lawsuits from independent contractors.**

- When workers are injured, employees can usually only receive workers' compensation benefits. However, independent contractors may sue their hiring firm.

3. **No control over the work.**

- A hiring firm cannot control an independent contractor's work. If it does, the worker's legal status will automatically convert to an employer-employee relationship and the hiring firm will be liable for employment taxes and benefits. Because hiring firms can't control their contracts, deadlines may be missed, customers may become angry, or other situations may arise that are detrimental to the hiring firm.

4. **Limited right to fire independent contractors.**

- Hiring firms can fire independent contractors only if they breach their contract or if the completed work is unacceptable. If a hiring firm keeps the right to fire the worker at will, the worker's legal status usually converts to an employer-employee relationship.

BENEFITS AND RISKS TO INDEPENDENT CONTRACTORS

Benefits

1. **Personal flexibility; they are their own boss.**

2. **Business expenses are tax deductible.**

Risks

1. **No disability or workers' compensation insurance.**

   - If independent contractors are injured, they can't collect disability or workers' compensation insurance.

2. **No unemployment insurance.**

   - Independent contractors may develop tax troubles.

   - Independent contractors must pay quarterly income tax and Social Security self-employment taxes. Social Security self-employment tax is currently 15.3% of net taxable income; a big shock to people who don't plan ahead. When you add federal income tax (10 to 35%), state income tax, and self-employment tax, the total bill can be huge. If independent contractors spend that money before tax time, they get into BIG trouble with the government.

3. **Independent contractors can be held liable.**

   - Independent contractors can be held liable for their actions, instead of being protected by the hiring firm (or its insurance).

THE BASIC RULES

Government Rules Determine If a Worker Is an Independent Contractor, Not Written Agreements

- The IRS' rules and laws of individual states determine whether a worker is an independent contractor or an employee, not the written or oral agreement between the hiring firm and the person hired. A contract in a file is not proof of an independent contractor relationship.

Workers Are Employees, Unless a Hiring Firm Can Prove Otherwise

Statutory Employees

- According to IRS Code Section 3121(d), the following workers are automatically employees:

  – Officers of corporations who provide services to that corporation.

  – Food and laundry drivers.

  – Full-time traveling or city salespeople who sell goods to people (or firms) for resale.

  – Full-time life insurance agents, working mainly for one company (IRS only).

  – At-home workers who are supplied with materials or goods and are given specifications for the work to be done.

Statutory Nonemployees

- The 1982 TEFRA (Tax Equity and Fiscal Responsibility Act) created new Code Section 3508 that defines two categories of workers who are statutorily not to be treated as employees:

  – Direct sellers who sell a product to the final user. Basically, this applies to door-to-door and home demonstration salespeople.

  – Licensed real estate agents.

20 Common Law Factors (Rev Rul 87–41)

- If workers don't fall into the special categories above, the 20 Common Law Factors should be used. Independent contractors do not have to satisfy all 20 common law factors. The courts have given different weights for each factor according to the industry and job and the courts have not always been consistent in weighing these factors.

What Are the
"20 Common Law Factors?"

At the end of this appendix, you will find a list of the "20 Common Law Factors" that are used to determine whether a worker is an employee or an independent contractor. It would be wise to familiarize yourself with the 20 factors and refer to them when you are considering the hiring of independent contractors. The list may help you to avoid misclassification and costly penalties.

Federal Safe Harbor Rules (IRS Code Section 530)

- The IRS has special independent contractors' rules that "exempt" certain workers from the 20 common law factors if all of the following three statements are true:

  - Since December 31, 1977, the hiring firm and its predecessors have consistently treated individuals doing similar work as independent contractors.

  - The hiring firm and its predecessors have never treated the current independent contractors as employees and have filed all the required federal tax returns (Form 1099-MISC) for independent contractors.

  - There was a reasonable basis for treating the worker as an independent contractor. Reasonable basis means:

    > A reliance on judicial rulings, IRS rulings, or IRS technical advice;

    > - or -

    > In a prior audit, no penalties were assessed for treating workers doing a similar type of work as independent contractors;

    > - or -

    > It is a recognized practice for a large segment of the industry to treat certain types of workers as independent contractors.

Note: *If a firm cannot meet the three safe harbor rules, it may still be entitled to exemption if it can demonstrate, in some other manner, a reasonable basis for not treating the individual as an employee. IRS Rev Proc 85-18 indicates that agents should liberally construe what constitutes a "reasonable basis" in favor of the taxpayer.*

Penalties for Misclassification

1. **TEFRA** added a new Section 3509 that sets rules for any assessments after 1982 resulting from a reclassification of an independent contractor to employee status. The employer will be assessed a liability for:

   - 1.5% of the gross wages (federal withholding)

     - and -

   - 20% of the amount that would have been the employee's share of FICA taxes

     - and -

   - The appropriate employer's share of FICA.

     PROVIDING:

   - Information returns (Form 1099-MISC) were filed.

     - and -

   - Such failure to deduct was not intentional disregard of the requirement.

2. **Employer disregard**.

- In the case of an employer who fails to file information returns, fails to file information returns on services rendered and direct sellers, or fails to provide W-2s to employees, the penalty is doubled to:

    – 3% of the gross wages (federal withholding); and

    – 40% of the amount that would have been the employee's share of FICA taxes; and

    – The appropriate employer's share of FICA.

Relief from retroactive assessment. *IRS Code Section 3402(d)(1) offers an employer relief from a retroactive assessment of income tax withholding liability if the employer can adequately demonstrate that the worker reported the income covered by the assessment on his Form 1040 return and paid the tax. Form 4669 is designed for this purpose. This relief is not available if the special tax rates (employer disregard) apply.*

• • • • •

SUMMARIZED VERSION
20 COMMON LAW FACTORS (REV RUL 87–41)

1. **No instructions.** Contractors are not required to follow, nor are they furnished with instructions to accomplish a job. They can be provided job specifications by the hiring firm.

2. **No training.** Contractors typically do not receive training by the hiring firm. They use their own methods to accomplish the work.

3. **Services don't have to be rendered personally.** Contractors are hired to provide a result and usually have the right to hire others to do the actual work.

4. **Work not essential to the hiring firm.** A company's success or continuation should not depend on the service of outside contractors. An example violating this would be a law firm which called their lawyers independent contractors.

5. **Own work hours.** Contractors set their own work hours.

6. **Not a continuing relationship.** Usually contractors don't have a continuing relationship with a hiring company. The relationship can be frequent, but it must be at irregular intervals, on call, or whenever work is available. Warning: Part-time, seasonal, or short duration relationships have nothing to do with independent contractor status.

7. **Control their own assistants.** Contractors shouldn't hire, supervise, or pay assistants at the direction of the hiring company. If assistants are hired, it should be at the contractor's sole discretion.

8. **Time to pursue other work.** Contractors should have enough time available to pursue other gainful work.

9. **Job location.** Contractors control where they work. If they work on the premises of the hiring company, it is not under that company's direction or supervision.

10. **Order of work set.** Contractors determine the order and sequence that they will perform their work.

11. **No interim reports.** Contractors are hired for the final result and therefore should not be asked for progress or interim reports.

12. **Payment timing.** Contractors are paid by the job, not by time. Payment by the job can include periodic payments based on a percentage of job completed. Payment can be based on the number of hours needed to do the job times a fixed hourly rate. However, this should be determined before the job commences.

13. **Working for multiple firms.** Contractors often work for more than one firm at a time.

14. **Business expenses.** Contractors are generally responsible for their incidental expenses.

15. **Own tools.** Usually contractors furnish their own tools. Some hiring firms have leased equipment to their independent contractors, so that they could show the contractor had their own tools and an investment in their business (see #16). This strategy won't work if the lease is for a nominal amount or can be voided by the hiring firm at will. In short, the lease must be equivalent to what an independent business person could have obtained in the open market.

16. **Significant investment.** Contractors should be able to perform their services without the hiring company's facilities (equipment, office furniture, machinery, etc.). The contractor's investment in the trade must be real, essential, and adequate. (Please see #15 above.)

17. **Services available to general public.** Contractors make their services available to the general public by one or more of the following:
    - Having an office and assistants
    - Having business signs
    - Having a business license
    - Listing their services in a business directory
    - Advertising their services

18. **Limited right to discharge.** Contractors can't be fired so long as they produce a result that meets the contract specifications.

19. **No compensation for noncompletion.** Contractors are responsible for the satisfactory completion of a job or they may be legally obligated to compensate the hiring firm for failure to complete.

20. **Possible profit or loss.** Contractors should be able to make a profit or a loss. Employees can't suffer a loss. Five circumstances show that a profit or loss is possible:
    - If the contractor hires, directs, and pays assistants
    - If the contractor has his own office, equipment, materials, or facilities
    - If the contractor has continuing and reoccurring liabilities
    - If the contractor has agreed to perform specific jobs for prices agreed upon in advance
    - If the contractor's services affect his or her own business reputation

WORKSHEETS

These blank forms and worksheets are for you to fill out and use.

Beginning Journal

Date	1. Check # 2. Cash 3. C/Card	Paid To or Received From	Explanation of Income or Expense	Income		Expense	
Total Income and Expenses							

Revenue & Expense Journal

Month: _____ 20___, page ___

—— Customize headings to match the business ——

CHECK NO.	DATE	TRANSACTION	REVENUE	EXPENSE												MISC
		Balance forward----														
TOTALS																

Petty Cash Record

PETTY CASH - 20___					Page ___
DATE	PAID TO WHOM	EXPENSE ACCOUNT DEBITED	DEPOSIT	AMOUNT OF EXPENSE	BALANCE
	BALANCE FORWARD				

Inventory Record
Identifiable Stock

WHOLESALER:_____					Page___

PURCH DATE	INVENTORY PURCHASED		PURCH. PRICE	DATE SOLD	SALE PRICE	NAME OF BUYER (Optional)
	Stock #	Description				

Inventory Record
Non-Identifiable Stock

DEPARTMENT/CATEGORY: _____

PRODUCTION OR PURCHASE DATE	INVENTORY PURCHASED OR MANUFACTURED		NUMBER OF UNITS	UNIT COST	VALUE ON DATE OF INVENTORY (Unit Cost X Units on Hand)	
	Stock #	Description			Value	Date

Fixed Assets Log

COMPANY NAME: _____

ASSET PURCHASED	DATE PLACED IN SERVICE	COST OF ASSET	% USED FOR BUSINESS	RECOVERY PERIOD	METHOD OF DEPRECIATION	DEPRECIATION PREVIOUSLY ALLOWED	DATE SOLD	SALE PRICE

Accounts Receivable
Account Record

CUSTOMER: _____

ADDRESS: _____

_____

TEL. NO: _____   ACCOUNT NO._____

INVOICE DATE	INVOICE NO.	INVOICE AMOUNT		TERMS	DATE PAID	AMOUNT PAID	INVOICE BALANCE

Accounts Payable
Account Record

CREDITOR: _____

ADDRESS: _____

_____

TEL. NO: _____   ACCOUNT NO._____

INVOICE DATE	INVOICE NO.	INVOICE AMOUNT	TERMS	DATE PAID	AMOUNT PAID	INVOICE BALANCE

Mileage Log

NAME: _____

DATED: From_____To_____

DATE	CITY OF DESTINATION	NAME OR OTHER DESIGNATION	BUSINESS PURPOSE	NO. OF MILES
		TOTAL MILES THIS SHEET		

Entertainment Expense Record

NAME: _____

DATED: From_____To_____

DATE	PLACE OF ENTERTAINMENT	BUSINESS PURPOSE	NAME OF PERSON ENTERTAINED	AMOUNT SPENT	

Travel Record

TRIP TO: _____

Dated From: _____ **To:** _____

Business Purpose: _____

No. Days Spent on Business _____

DATE	LOCATION	EXPENSE PAID TO	MEALS			HOTEL	TAXIS, ETC.	AUTOMOBILE			MISC EXP
			Breakfast	Lunch	Dinner	Misc.			Gas	Parking	Tolls	
TOTALS →												

Balance Sheet

Business Name: _____ **Date:** _____ ___, _____

ASSETS

Current assets
Cash	$ _____
Petty cash	$ _____
Accounts receivable	$ _____
Inventory	$ _____
Short-term investments	$ _____
Prepaid expenses	$ _____

Long-term investments
$ _____

Fixed assets
Land (valued at cost) $ _____

Buildings $ _____
1. Cost _____
2. Less acc. depr. _____

Improvements $ _____
1. Cost _____
2. Less acc. depr. _____

Equipment $ _____
1. Cost _____
2. Less acc. depr. _____

Furniture $ _____
1. Cost _____
2. Less acc. depr. _____

Autos/vehicles $ _____
1. Cost _____
2. Less acc. depr. _____

Other assets
1. $ _____
2. $ _____

TOTAL ASSETS $ _____

LIABILITIES

Current liabilities
Accounts payable	$ _____
Notes payable	$ _____
Interest payable	$ _____

Taxes payable
Federal income tax	$ _____
Self-employment tax	$ _____
State income tax	$ _____
Sales tax accrual	$ _____
Property tax	$ _____

Payroll accrual $ _____

Long-term liabilities
Notes payable $ _____

TOTAL LIABILITIES $ _____

NET WORTH (EQUITY)

Proprietorship $ _____
or
Partnership
(name)_____, ___% equity $ _____
(name)_____, ___% equity $ _____
or
Corporation
Capital stock $ _____
Surplus paid in $ _____
Retained earnings $ _____

TOTAL NET WORTH $ _____

Assets – Liabilities = Net Worth
and
Liabilities + Equity = Total Assets

Profit & Loss (Income) Statement

Business Name:

For the Year: _____

	Jan	Feb	Mar	Apr	May	Jun	6-MONTH TOTALS	Jul	Aug	Sep	Oct	Nov	Dec	12-MONTH TOTALS
INCOME														
1. Net sales (Gr – R&A)														
2. Cost of goods to be sold														
a. Beginning inventory														
b. Purchases														
c. C.O.G. available for sale														
d. Less ending inventory														
3. Gross profit														
EXPENSES														
1. Variable (selling) expenses														
a.														
b.														
c.														
d.														
e.														
f.														
g. Misc. variable expense														
h. Depreciation														
Total variable expenses														
1. Fixed (admin) expenses														
a.														
b.														
c.														
d.														
e.														
f.														
g. Misc. fixed expense														
h. Depreciation														
Total fixed expenses														
Total operating expense														
Net Income From Operations														
Other Income (interest)														
Other Expense (interest)														
Net Profit (Loss) Before Taxes														
Taxes: a. Federal														
b. State														
c. Local														
NET PROFIT (LOSS) AFTER TAXES														

Profit & Loss (Income) Statement

Business Name: _____

Beginning: _____ ___, _____   **Ending:** _____ ___, _____

INCOME		
1. Sales revenues		$
2. Cost of goods sold (c – d)		
a. Beginning inventory (1/01)		
b. Purchases		
c. C.O.G. avail. sale (a + b)		
d. Less ending inventory (12/31)		
3. Gross profit on sales (1 – 2)		$
EXPENSES		
1. Variable (selling) (a thru h)		
a.		
b.		
c.		
d.		
e.		
f.		
g. Misc. variable (selling) expense		
h. Depreciation (prod/serv. assets)		
2. Fixed (administrative) (a thru h)		
a.		
b.		
c.		
d.		
e.		
f.		
g. Misc. fixed (administrative) expense		
h. Depreciation (office equipment)		
Total operating expenses (1 + 2)		
Net income from operations (GP – Exp)		$
Other income (interest income)		
Other expense (interest expense)		
Net profit (loss) before taxes		$
Taxes		
a. Federal		
b. State		
c. Local		
NET PROFIT (LOSS) AFTER TAXES		$

Cash to Be Paid Out Worksheet

Business Name: _____   **Time Period:** _____ **to** _____

---

1. START-UP COSTS   _____
  Business license   _____
  Accounting fees   _____
  Legal fees   _____
  Other start-up costs: _____
    a.   _____
    b.   _____
    c.   _____
    d.   _____

2. INVENTORY PURCHASES
  Cash out for goods intended for resale   _____

3. VARIABLE EXPENSES (SELLING)
    a.   _____
    b.   _____
    c.   _____
    d.   _____
    e.   _____
    f.   _____
  g. Miscellaneous variable expense   _____
  TOTAL SELLING EXPENSES   _____

4. FIXED EXPENSES (ADMINISTRATIVE)
    a.   _____
    b.   _____
    c.   _____
    d.   _____
    e.   _____
    f.   _____
  g. Miscellaneous fixed expense   _____
  TOTAL ADMINISTRATIVE EXPENSE   _____

5. ASSETS (LONG-TERM PURCHASES)   _____
  Cash to be paid out in current period

6. LIABILITIES
  Cash outlay for retiring debts, loans,   _____
  and/or accounts payable

7. OWNER EQUITY
  Cash to be withdrawn by owner   _____

  TOTAL CASH TO BE PAID OUT $ _____

Sources of Cash Worksheet

Business Name: _____

Time Period Covered: _____ ___, _____ to _____ ___, _____

---

1. CASH ON HAND _____

2. SALES (REVENUES)

Product sales income _____

Services income _____

Deposits on sales or services _____

Collections on accounts receivable _____

3. MISCELLANEOUS INCOME

Interest income

Payments to be received on loans _____

4. SALE OF LONG-TERM ASSETS _____

5. LIABILITIES _____

*Loan funds (to be received during current period; from banks,
through the SBA, or from other lending institutions)*

6. EQUITY

Owner investments (sole prop/partners) _____

Contributed capital (corporation) _____

Sale of stock (corporation) _____

Venture capital _____

A. Without sales = $ _____

TOTAL CASH AVAILABLE

B. With sales = $ _____

Pro Forma Cash Flow Statement

Business Name: _____

Year: _____

	Jan	Feb	Mar	Apr	May	Jun	6-MONTH TOTALS	Jul	Aug	Sep	Oct	Nov	Dec	12-MONTH TOTALS
BEGINNING CASH BALANCE														
CASH RECEIPTS														
A. Sales/revenues														
B. Receivables														
C. Interest income														
D. Sale of long-term assets														
TOTAL CASH AVAILABLE														
CASH PAYMENTS														
A. Cost of goods to be sold														
1. Purchases														
2. Material														
3. Labor														
Total cost of goods														
B. Variable expenses														
1.														
2.														
3.														
4.														
5.														
6.														
7. Misc. variable expense														
Total variable expenses														
C. Fixed expenses														
1.														
2.														
3.														
4.														
5.														
6.														
7. Misc. fixed expense														
Total fixed expenses														
D. Interest expense														
E. Federal income tax														
F. Other uses														
G. Long-term asset payments														
H. Loan payments														
I. Owner draws														
TOTAL CASH PAID OUT														
CASH BALANCE/DEFICIENCY														
LOANS TO BE RECEIVED														
EQUITY DEPOSITS														
ENDING CASH BALANCE														

Quarterly Budget Analysis

Business Name: _____   **For the Quarter Ending:** _____ __, _____

BUDGET ITEM	THIS QUARTER			YEAR-TO-DATE		
	Budget	Actual	Variation	Budget	Actual	Variation
SALES REVENUES						
Less cost of goods						
GROSS PROFITS						
VARIABLE EXPENSES						
1.						
2.						
3.						
4.						
5.						
6.						
7. Miscellaneous variable expense						
FIXED EXPENSES						
1.						
2.						
3.						
4.						
5.						
6.						
7. Miscellaneous fixed expense						
NET INCOME FROM OPERATIONS						
INTEREST INCOME						
INTEREST EXPENSE						
NET PROFIT (Pretax)						
TAXES						
NET PROFIT (After Tax)						

NON-INCOME STATEMENT ITEMS

1. Long-term asset repayments						
2. Loan repayments						
3. Owner draws						

BUDGET DEVIATIONS   This Quarter   Year-to-Date

	This Quarter	Year-to-Date
1. Income statement items:		
2. Non-income statement items:		
3. Total deviation		

Three-Year Income Projection

Business Name: Updated: _____ ___, _____

_____	YEAR 1 20___	YEAR 2 20___	YEAR 3 20___	TOTAL 3 YEARS
INCOME				
1. Sales revenues				
2. Cost of goods sold (c – d)				
a. Beginning inventory				
b. Purchases				
c. C.O.G. avail. sale (a + b)				
d. Less ending iventory (12/31)				
3. Gross profit on sales (1-2)				
EXPENSES				
1. Variable (selling) (a thru h)				
a.				
b.				
c.				
d.				
e.				
f.				
g. Miscellaneous selling expense				
h. Depreciation (prod/serv assets)				
2. Fixed (administrative) (a thru h)				
a.				
b.				
c.				
d.				
e.				
f.				
g. Miscellaneous fixed expense				
h. Depreciation (office equipment)				
TOTAL OPERATING EXPENSES (1 + 2)				
NET INCOME OPERATIONS (GPr – Exp)				
OTHER INCOME (interest income)				
OTHER EXPENSE (interest expense)				
NET PROFIT (LOSS) BEFORE TAXES				
TAXES 1. Federal, self-employment				
2. State				
3. Local				
NET PROFIT (LOSS) AFTER TAXES				

Breakeven Analysis Graph

Business Name: _____   **Analysis Date:** _____ __, _____

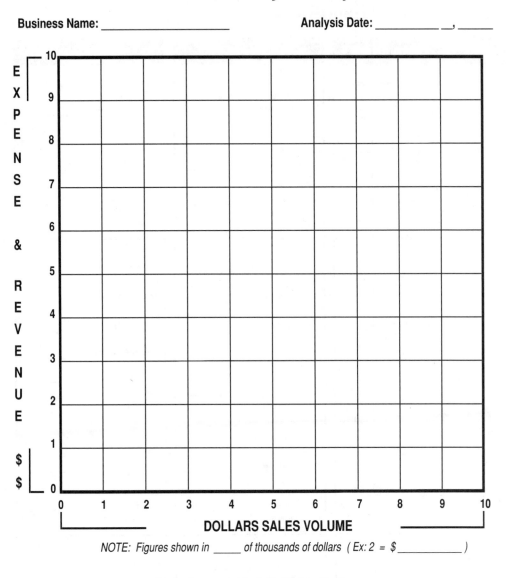

NOTE: *Figures shown in _____ of thousands of dollars (Ex: 2 = $_____)*

Breakeven Point Calculation

BE Point (Sales) = Fixed Costs + [(Variable Costs/Estimated Revenues) x Sales]

1. BE Point (Sales) = $_____ + [($_____ / $_____) x Sales]

2. BE Point (Sales) = $_____ + (_____ x Sales)

3. Sales = $_____ + _____Sales

4. Sales – _____Sales = $_____

5. _____Sales = $_____

6. Sales (S) = $_____ / _____

Breakeven Point

S = $_____

Financial Statement Analysis
Ratio Table

Business Name: _____   **For the Year:** _____

Type of Analysis	Formula	Projected: Year 1	Historical: Year 1
1. Liquidity analysis a. Net working capital	**Balance Sheet** Current Assets — Current Liabilities	Current Assets _____ Current Liabilities _____ **Net Working Capital** $ _____	Current Assets _____ Current Liabilities _____ **Net Working Capital** $ _____
b. Current ratio	**Balance Sheet** Current Assets Current Liabilities	Current Assets _____ Current Liabilities _____ **Current Ratio** . _____	Current Assets _____ Current Liabilities _____ **Current Ratio** . _____
c. Quick ratio	**Balance Sheet** Current Assets minus Inventory Current Liabilities	Current Assets _____ Inventory _____ Current Liabilities _____ **Quick Ratio** . _____	Current Assets _____ Inventory _____ Current Liabilities _____ **Quick Ratio** . _____
2. Profitability analysis a. Gross profit margin	**Income Statement** Gross Profits Sales	Gross Profits _____ Sales _____ **Gross Profit Margin** % _____	Gross Profits _____ Sales _____ **Gross Profit Margin** % _____
b. Operating profit margin	Income From Operations Sales	Income From Ops. _____ Sales _____ **Operating Profit Margin** % _____	Income From Ops. _____ Sales _____ **Operating Profit Margin** % _____
c. Net profit margin	Net Profits Sales	Net Profits _____ Sales _____ **Net Profit Margin** % _____	Net Profits _____ Sales _____ **Net Profit Margin** % _____
3. Debt ratios a. Debt to assets	**Balance Sheet** Total Liabilities Total Assets	Total Liabilities _____ Total Assets _____ **Debt to Assets Ratio** % _____	Total Liabilities _____ Total Assets _____ **Debt to Assets Ratio** % _____
b. Debt to equity	Total Liabilities Total Owners' Equity	Total Liabilities _____ Total Owners' Equity _____ **Debt to Equity Ratio** % _____	Total Liabilities _____ Total Owners' Equity _____ **Debt to Equity Ratio** % _____
4. Measures of investment a. ROI *(Return on Investment)*	**Balance Sheet** Net Profits Total Assets	Net Profits _____ Total Assets _____ **ROI (Return on Invest.)** % _____	Net Profits _____ Total Assets _____ **ROI (Return on Invest.)** % _____
5. Vertical financial statement analysis	**Balance Sheet** 1. Each asset % of Total Assets 2. Liability & Equity % of Total L&E **Income Statement** 3. All items % of Total Revenues	**NOTE:** *See Attached* **Balance Sheet &** **Income Statement**	**NOTE:** *See Attached* **Balance Sheet &** **Income Statement**
6. Horizontal financial statement analysis	**Balance Sheet** 1. Assets, Liab & Equity measured against 2nd year. Increases and decreases stated as amount & % **Income Statement** 2. Revenues & Expenses measured against 2nd year. Increases and decreases stated as amount & %	**NOTE:** *See Attached* **Balance Sheet** **&** **Income Statement**	**NOTE:** *See Attached* **Balance Sheet** **&** **Income Statement**

Form SS-4
Application for Employer Identification Number

Form **SS-4**	Application for Employer Identification Number	EIN	
(Rev. December 2001) Department of the Treasury Internal Revenue Service	(For use by employers, corporations, partnerships, trusts, estates, churches, government agencies, Indian tribal entities, certain individuals, and others.) ▶ See separate instructions for each line.　▶ Keep a copy for your records.	OMB No. 1545-0003	

Type or print clearly.

1 Legal name of entity (or individual) for whom the EIN is being requested

2 Trade name of business (if different from name on line 1)	**3** Executor, trustee, "care of" name

4a Mailing address (room, apt., suite no. and street, or P.O. box)	**5a** Street address (if different) (Do not enter a P.O. box.)
4b City, state, and ZIP code	**5b** City, state, and ZIP code

6 County and state where principal business is located

7a Name of principal officer, general partner, grantor, owner, or trustor	**7b** SSN, ITIN, or EIN

8a Type of entity (check only one box)

☐ Sole proprietor (SSN) _____

☐ Partnership

☐ Corporation (enter form number to be filed) ▶ _____

☐ Personal service corp.

☐ Church or church-controlled organization

☐ Other nonprofit organization (specify) ▶ _____

☐ Other (specify) ▶

☐ Estate (SSN of decedent) _____

☐ Plan administrator (SSN) _____

☐ Trust (SSN of grantor) _____

☐ National Guard　☐ State/local government

☐ Farmers' cooperative　☐ Federal government/military

☐ REMIC　☐ Indian tribal governments/enterprises

Group Exemption Number (GEN) ▶ _____

8b If a corporation, name the state or foreign country (if applicable) where incorporated

State	Foreign country

9 Reason for applying (check only one box)

☐ Started new business (specify type) ▶ _____

☐ Hired employees (Check the box and see line 12.)

☐ Compliance with IRS withholding regulations

☐ Other (specify) ▶

☐ Banking purpose (specify purpose) ▶ _____

☐ Changed type of organization (specify new type) ▶ _____

☐ Purchased going business

☐ Created a trust (specify type) ▶ _____

☐ Created a pension plan (specify type) ▶ _____

10 Date business started or acquired (month, day, year)	**11** Closing month of accounting year

12 First date wages or annuities were paid or will be paid (month, day, year). Note: If applicant is a withholding agent, enter date income will first be paid to nonresident alien. (month, day, year) . . . . ▶

13 Highest number of employees expected in the next 12 months. Note: If the applicant does not expect to have any employees during the period, enter "-0-." . . . . ▶

Agricultural	Household	Other

14 Check one box that best describes the principal activity of your business.

☐ Construction　☐ Rental & leasing　☐ Transportation & warehousing

☐ Real estate　☐ Manufacturing　☐ Finance & insurance

☐ Health care & social assistance　☐ Wholesale–agent/broker

☐ Accommodation & food service　☐ Wholesale–other　☐ Retail

☐ Other (specify)

15 Indicate principal line of merchandise sold; specific construction work done; products produced; or services provided.

16a Has the applicant ever applied for an employer identification number for this or any other business? . . . . ☐ Yes　☐ No

Note: If "Yes," please complete lines 16b and 16c.

16b If you checked "Yes" on line 16a, give applicant's legal name and trade name shown on prior application if different from line 1 o r 2 above.

Legal name ▶　　　　Trade name ▶

16c Approximate date when, and city and state where, the application was filed. Enter previous employer identification number if kn own.

Approximate date when filed (mo., day, year)	City and state where filed	Previous EIN

Third Party Designee	Complete this section **only** if you want to authorize the named individual to receive the entity's EIN and answer questions about the completion of this form.	
	Designee's name	Designee's telephone number (include area code) ( )
	Address and ZIP code	Designee's fax number (include area code) ( )

Under penalties of perjury, I declare that I have examined this application, and to the best of my knowledge and belief, it is true, correct, and complete.

Applicant's telephone number (include area code)
( )

Name and title (type or print clearly) ▶

Applicant's fax number (include area code)
( )

Signature ▶　　　　　　Date ▶

For Privacy Act and Paperwork Reduction Act Notice, see separate instructions.　　Cat. No. 16055N　　Form **SS-4** (Rev. 12-2001)

SMALL BUSINESS RESOURCES

The Small Business Administration. http://www.sbaonline.sba.gov/ The United States SBA is an independent federal agency that was created by Congress in 1953 to assist, council, and represent small business. Statistics show that most small business failures are due to poor management. For this reason, the SBA places special emphasis on individual counseling, courses, conferences, workshops, and publications to train the new and existing business owner in all facets of business development with special emphasis on improving the management ability of the owner.

Counseling is provided through Business Information Centers (BICs), the Service Corps of Retired Executives (SCORE), Small Business Development Centers (SBDCs), and numerous professional associations.

Business management training covers such topics as planning, finance, organization, and marketing and is held in cooperation with educational institutions, chambers of commerce, and trade associations. Pre-business workshops are held on a regular basis for prospective business owners. The following is a brief summary of what these programs include:

Business Information Centers (BICs). These are joint ventures between the U.S. Small Business Administration and private partners. They provide the latest in high-tech hardware, software, and telecommunications to help start-up and expanding businesses. BICs also offer a wide array of free on-site counseling services and training opportunities. Using BICs resources can result in a well-crafted comprehensive business plan, which can be used to guide you through product or service expansion.

SCORE. http://www.score.org SCORE is a 13,000-person volunteer program with over 350 chapters throughout the United States. SCORE helps small businesses solve their operating, marketing, and financial problems through one-on-one counseling and through a well-developed system of workshops and training sessions. SCORE counseling is available at no charge.

Small Business Development Centers (SBDCs). These centers draw their resources from local, state, and federal government programs, the private sector, and university facilities. They provide managerial and technical help, research studies, and other types of specialized assistance. These centers are generally located or headquartered in academic institutions and provide individual counseling and practical training for small business owners.

Federal agencies. Many federal agencies offer publications of interest to small businesses. There is a nominal fee for some, but most are free. Below is a partial list of government agencies that provide publications and other services targeted to small businesses. To get their publications, contact the regional offices listed in the telephone directory or write to the addresses below:

Consumer Information Center (CIC)
PO Box 100
Pueblo, CO 81002
http://www.pueblo.gsa.gov/
The CIC offers a consumer information catalog of federal publications.

Federal Trade Commission
6th Street & Pennsylvania Avenue, NW, Suite 700
Washington, DC 20580
http://www.ftc.gov/

U.S. Department of Commerce (DOC)
Office of Business Liaison
14th Street and Constitution Avenue, NW
Room 5898C
Washington, DC 20230
http://www.doc.gov/

U.S. Department of Labor (DOL)
200 Constitution Avenue, NW
Washington, DC 20210
http://www.dol.gov/

U.S. Department of Treasury
Internal Revenue Service (MS)
PO Box 25866
Richmond, VA 23260
800-829-1040
http://www.irs.ustreas.gov/

GLOSSARY

account A separate record showing the increases and decreases in each asset, liability, owner's equity, revenue, and expense item.

accounting The process by which financial information about a business is recorded, classified, summarized, and interpreted by a business.

accounting period The period of time covered by the income statement and other financial statements that report operating results.

accounts payable Amounts owed by a business to its creditors on open account for goods purchased or services rendered.

accounts receivable Amounts owed to the business on open account as a result of extending credit to a customer who purchases your products or services.

accrual basis of accounting The method of accounting in which all revenues and expenses are recognized on the income statement in the period when they are earned and incurred, regardless of when the cash related to the transactions is received or paid.

accrued expenses Expenses that have been incurred but not paid (such as employee salaries, commissions, taxes, interest, etc.).

accrued income Income that has been earned but not received.

aging accounts receivable The classification of accounts receivable according to how long they have been outstanding. An appropriate rate of loss can then be applied to each age group in order to estimate probable loss from uncollectible accounts.

assets Everything owned by or owed to a business that has cash value.

audit trail A chain of references that makes it possible to trace information about transactions through an accounting system.

balance sheet The financial statement that shows the financial position of a business as of a fixed date. It is usually done at the close of an accounting period by summarizing business assets, liabilities, and owners' equity.

bottom line A business's net profit or loss after taxes for a specific accounting period.

breakeven point That point at which a business no longer incurs a loss but has yet to make a profit. The breakeven point can be expressed in total dollars of revenue exactly offset by total expenses, or total units of production, the cost of which exactly equals the income derived from their sale.

budget The development of a set of financial goals. A business is then evaluated by measuring its performance in terms of these goals. The budget contains projections for cash inflow and outflow and other balance sheet items. Also known as cash flow statement.

business financial history A summary of financial information about a company from its start to the present.

capital See owner's equity.

capital expenditures An expenditure for a purchase of an item of property, plant, or equipment that has a useful life of more than one year (fixed assets).

cash flow statement See budget.

chart of accounts A list of the numbers and titles of a business's general ledger accounts.

closing entries Entries made at the end of an accounting period to reduce the balances of the revenue and expense accounts to zero. Most businesses close books at the end of each month and at the end of the year.

comparative financial statements Financial statements that include information for two or more periods or two or more companies.

corporation A business structure that is granted separate legal status under state law and whose owners are stockholders of the corporation.

cost of goods sold The cost of inventory sold during an accounting period. It is equal to the beginning inventory for the period, plus the cost of purchases made during the period, minus the ending inventory for the period.

credit An amount entered on the right side of an account in double entry accounting. A decrease in asset and expense accounts. An increase in liability, capital, and income accounts.

creditor A company or individual to whom a business owes money.

current assets Cash plus any assets that will be converted into cash within one year plus any assets that you plan to use up within one year.

current liabilities Debts that must be paid within one year.

current ratio A dependable indication of liquidity computed by dividing current assets by current liabilities. A ratio of 2.0 is acceptable for most businesses.

debit An amount entered on the left side of an account in double entry accounting. A decrease in liabilities, capital, and income accounts. An increase in asset and expense accounts.

debt measures The indication of the amount of other people's money that is being used to generate profits for a business. The more indebtedness, the greater the risk of failure.

debt ratio The key financial ratio used by creditors in determining how indebted a business is and how able it is to service the debts. The debt ratio is calculated by dividing total liabilities by total assets. The higher the ratio, the more risk of failure. The acceptable ratio is dependent upon the policies of your creditors and bankers.

declining-balance method An accelerated method of depreciation in which the book value of an asset at the beginning of the year is multiplied by an appropriate percentage to obtain the depreciation to be taken for that year.

depreciable base of an asset The cost of an asset used in the computation of yearly depreciation expense.

direct expenses Those expenses that relate directly to your product or service.

double entry accounting A system of accounting under which each transaction is recorded twice. This is based on the premise that every transaction has two sides. At least one account must be debited and one account must be credited and the debit and credit totals for each transaction must be equal.

expenses The costs of producing revenue through the sale of goods or services.

financial statements The periodic reports that summarize the financial affairs of a business.

first in, first out method (FIFO) A method of valuing inventory that assumes that the first items purchased are the first items to be sold. When ending inventory is computed, the costs of the latest purchases are used.

fiscal year Any 12-month accounting period used by a business.

fixed assets Items purchased for use in a business that are depreciable over a fixed period of time determined by the expected useful life of the purchase. Usually includes land, buildings, vehicles, and equipment not intended for resale. Land is not depreciable, but is listed as a fixed asset.

fixed asset log A record used to keep track of the fixed assets purchased by a business during the current financial year. This record can be used by an accountant to determine depreciation expense to be taken for tax purposes.

fixed costs Costs that do not vary in total during a period even though the volume of goods manufactured may be higher or lower than anticipated.

gross profit margin An indicator of the percentage of each sales dollar remaining after a business has paid for its goods. It is computed by dividing the gross profit by the sales.

gross profit on sales The difference between net sales and the cost of goods sold.

horizontal analysis A percentage analysis of the increases and decreases on the items on comparative financial statements. A horizontal financial statement analysis involves comparison of data for the current period with the same data of a company for previous periods. The percentage of increase or decrease is listed.

indirect expenses Operating expenses that are not directly related to the sale of your product or service.

interest The price charged or paid for the use of money or credit.

inventory The stock of goods that a business has on hand for sale to its customers.

investment measures Ratios used to measure an owner's earnings for his or her investment in the company. See return on investment (ROI).

invoice A bill for the sale of goods or services sent by the seller to the purchaser.

last in, first out method (LIFO) A method of valuing inventory that assumes that the last items purchased are the first items to be sold. The cost of the ending inventory is computed by using the cost of the earliest purchases.

liabilities Amounts owed by a business to its creditors. The debts of a business.

liquidity The ability of a company to meet its financial obligations. A liquidity analysis focuses on the balance sheet relationships for current assets and current liabilities.

long-term liabilities Liabilities that will not be due for more than a year in the future.

mileage log The recording of business miles travelled during an accounting period.

modified accelerated cost recovery system (MACRS) A method of depreciation or cost recovery used for federal income tax purposes for long-term assets purchased after January 1, 1987. Under MACRS, long-term assets fall automatically into certain classes, and the costs of all assets in a class are charged to expense through a standard formula.

net income The amount by which revenue is greater than expenses. On an income statement, this is usually expressed as both a pre-tax and after-tax figure.

net loss The amount by which expenses are greater than revenue. On an income statement, this figure is usually listed as both a pre-tax and after-tax figure.

net profit margin The measure of a business's success with respect to earnings on sales. It is derived by dividing the net profit by sales. A higher margin means the firm is more profitable.

net sales Gross sales less returns and allowances and sales discounts.

net worth See owners' equity.

note A written promise with terms for payment of a debt.

operating expenses Normal expenses incurred in the running of a business.

operating profit margin The ratio representing the pure operations profits, ignoring interest and taxes. It is derived by dividing the income from operations by the sales. The higher the percentage of operating profit margin the better.

other expenses Expenses that are not directly connected with the operation of a business. The most common is interest expense.

other income Income that is earned from nonoperating sources. The most common is interest income.

owner's equity The financial interest of the owner of a business. The total of all owner equity is equal to the business's assets minus its liabilities. The owner's equity represents total investments in the business plus or minus any profits or losses the business has accrued to date.

partnership The form of business legal structure that is owned by two or more persons.

personal financial history A summary of personal financial information about the owner of a business. The personal financial history is often required by a potential lender or investor.

petty cash fund A cash fund from which noncheck expenditures are reimbursed.

physical inventory The process of counting inventory on hand at the end of an accounting period. The number of units of each item is multiplied by the cost per item resulting in inventory value.

posting The process of transferring data from a journal to a ledger.

prepaid expenses Expense items that are paid for prior to their use. Some examples are insurance, rent, prepaid inventory purchases, etc.

principal The amount shown on the face of a note or a bond. Unpaid principal is the portion of the face amount remaining at any given time.

profit & loss statement See income statement.

property, plant, and equipment Assets such as land, buildings, vehicles, and equipment that will be used for a number of years in the operation of a business and (with the exception of land) are subject to depreciation.

quarterly budget analysis A method used to measure actual income and expenditures against projections for the current quarter of the financial year and for the total quarters completed. The difference is usually expressed as the amount and percentage over or under budget.

quick ratio A test of liquidity subtracting inventory from current assets and dividing the result by current liabilities. A quick ratio of 1.0 or greater is usually recommended.

ratio analysis An analysis involving the comparison of two individual items on financial statements. One item is divided by the other and the relationship is expressed as a ratio.

real property Land, land improvements, buildings, and other structures attached to the land.

reconciling the bank statement The process used to bring the bank's records, the accounts, and the business's checkbook into agreement at the end of a banking period.

retail business A business that sells goods and services directly to individual consumers.

retained earnings Earnings of a corporation that are kept in the business and not paid out in dividends. This amount represents the accumulated, undistributed profits of the corporation.

return on investment (ROI) The rate of profit an investment will earn. The ROI is equal to the annual net income divided by total assets. The higher the ROI, the better. Business owners should set a target for the ROI and decide what they want their investments to earn.

revenue The income that results from the sale of products or services or from the use of investments or property.

revenue & expense journal In single entry accounting, the record used to keep track of all checks written by a business and all income received for the sale of goods or services.

salvage value The amount that an asset can be sold for at the end of its useful life.

service business A business that provides services rather than products to its customers.

single entry accounting The term referring to a recordkeeping system that uses only income and expense accounts. Now generally used by many smaller businesses, this system is easier to maintain and understand, extremely effective, and 100 percent verifiable.

sole proprietorship A legal structure of a business having one person as the owner.

stockholders Owners of a corporation whose investment is represented by shares of stock.

stockholders' equity The stockholders' shares of stock in a corporation plus any retained earnings.

straight-line method of depreciation A method of depreciating assets by allocating an equal amount of depreciation for each year of its useful life.

sum-of-the-year's-digits method An accelerated method of depreciation in which a fractional part of the depreciable cost of an asset is charged to expense each year. The denominator of the fraction is the sum of the numbers representing the years of the asset's useful life. The numerator is the number of years remaining in the asset's useful life.

tangible personal property Machinery, equipment, furniture, and fixtures not attached to the land.

three-year income projection A pro forma (projected) income statement showing anticipated revenues and expenses for a business.

travel record The record used to keep track of expenses for a business-related trip away from the home business area.

trial balance A listing of all the accounts in the general ledger and their balances used to prove the equality of debits and credits in accounts.

unearned income Revenue that has been received, but not yet earned.

variable costs Expenses that vary in relationship to the volume of activity of a business.

vertical analysis A percentage analysis used to show the relationship of the components in a single financial statement. In vertical analysis of an income statement, each item on the statement is expressed as a percentage of net sales.

wholesale business A business that sells its products to other wholesalers, retailers, or volume customers at a discount.

work in progress Manufactured products that are only partially completed at the end of the accounting cycle.

working capital Current assets minus current liabilities. This is a basic measure of a company's ability to pay its current obligations.

INDEX

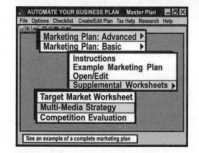

Share the message!

Bulk discounts
Discounts start at only 10 copies. Save up to 55% off retail price.

Custom publishing
Private label a cover with your organization's name and logo.
Or, tailor information to your needs with a custom pamphlet
that highlights specific chapters.

Ancillaries
Workshop outlines, videos, and other products are available on
select titles.

Dynamic speakers
Engaging authors are available to share their expertise and insight
at your event.

**Call Dearborn Trade Special Sales at
1-800-245-BOOK (2665)
or e-mail trade@dearborn.com**

Dearborn™
Trade Publishing
A **Kaplan Professional** Company